Patterns in Brand Monitoring

Patterns in Brand Monitoring

A Scientific Approach to Brand Protection Analysis

David N. Barnett

BEP

BUSINESS EXPERT PRESS

Leader in applied, concise business books

First published in 2025 by
Business Expert Press, LLC
222 East 46th Street, New York, NY 10017
www.businessexpertpress.com

ISBN-13: 978-1-63742-752-1 (paperback)
ISBN-13: 978-1-63742-753-8 (e-book)

Business Expert Press Marketing Collection

First edition: 2025

10 9 8 7 6 5 4 3 2 1

EU SAFETY REPRESENTATIVE
Mare Nostrum Group B.V.
Mauritskade 21D
1091 GC Amsterdam
The Netherlands
gpsr@mare-nostrum.co.uk

Description

Patterns in Brand Monitoring considers the ways in which a scientific approach can be applied to the analysis of brand protection data, essential for filtering and prioritizing the results and yielding insights into trends and patterns in infringement activity.

Throughout the book, technical definitions and formulations of key ideas are presented in information boxes and are illustrated by the use of real case studies.

The book is of relevance to stakeholders responsible for brand protection, intellectual property management, marketing or digital services in any organization, and to anyone with a general interest in the industry. It illustrates how an effective analysis approach can build efficiencies into a brand protection program, provide guidance on areas of focus, and demonstrate return on investment.

Contents

Testimonials

"Patterns in Brand Monitoring *looks at the challenges the internet poses to IP rights owners as well as the means to address them. A very popular topic these days, but David Barnett provides a level of detailed analysis that I have never seen before which elevates the conversation to a whole other level. Essential reading for anyone attempting to protect IP, or just interested in learning more about this fascinating subject—an outstanding piece of work."*—**Charlie Abrahams, Brand Protection Veteran and Market Commentator**

"David's unrivalled experience and knowledge provides a unique insight into brand monitoring. Using tried and tested methods, but also adapting to new challenges to find infringing or counterfeit content, this book is a must-read for anyone wanting to learn about how to find that key web page of interest."—**Mo Ali, Brand Protection Expert, Obviously**

"A must-read for professionals with an interest in, and responsibility for, the field of brand protection strategy, particularly in terms of rationalising the financial return on investment and impact on brand value from such activities."—**Bryn Anderson ACA, Valuation Director, Valuation Consulting**

"This book is absolutely packed with useful insights into the ways that brands are represented and misrepresented online, ranging from mild abuse to organised criminal fraud. The analysis, always clear and effectively presented, is evidently the result of years of work, and the author's extraordinary level of experience in the domain (no pun intended) shines through in every table, chart and paragraph. But it's not just data: the book is full of actionable guidance for brand owners and those responsible for protecting brands. An invaluable resource, really well written and nicely structured, with a huge amount of information and analysis – I love it!"—**Ben Coppin, Director, Google DeepMind**

"*Patterns in Brand Monitoring is a remarkable updated guide to safeguarding your online brand, whether you are an e-commerce retailer, a financial organisation, public sector, or any sort of enterprise with an online footprint. This book offers a wealth of knowledge on recognising various forms of domain abuse, infringements, phishing sites, and all sorts of nefarious activity geared to profit from, dilute or spoof your brand. David Barnett dives right into real-life case studies that shed light on the importance of proactive online brand protection with up-to-date information and practical insights needed to navigate the digital landscape effectively.*"—**Darcy Delich-Coull, IT Security & Compliance Officer, Footasylum Ltd**

"*Secure your digital frontier with confidence!* Patterns in Brand Monitoring *is an indispensable guide, empowering brand protection specialists to effectively safeguard their intellectual property in the rapidly evolving and increasingly challenging online landscape, including Web3 – this book is fabulous!*"—**Tess Diaz, Enterprise Domain Management Expert and Founder, DomainNation.com**

"*This book is brilliant – incredibly comprehensive and detailed; starts with the relative basics and builds on that. It should be a must-read for anyone involved with domain names and/or brand protection within an organisation.*"—**Stuart Fuller, Chief Commercial Officer, Com Laude Group**

"*Have you ever wondered how an IP infringer thinks? Have you ever considered that there is someone on this planet who is able to show you – and above all, to prove to you scientifically, through data – about unique IP infringement results? His name is David N. Barnett, and he has surprised me once more! He provides a deep but precise overview of the landscape of online brand protection, and uses visual illustrations allowing the reader to understand the extent of a complete monitoring service. This book is a brilliant gift, providing immersion into David B.'s brand protection galaxy, and is a unique piece of art that every IP practitioner must have! David reflects with professional humility and wisdom and is able to take you to all areas and depths of the internet—don't be scared; you are in the best of hands.*"—**María Alejandra López García, IP and Domain Name Attorney and UDRP Panelist; Director, IPRs On-line**

"*Patterns in Brand Monitoring is a valuable asset in the field of online brand protection, offering practical guidance on identifying patterns and proactively integrating them into brand protection strategies. It covers various aspects, including AI integration, web interconnection, open-source intelligence, and data analysis, making it a helpful resource for professionals navigating the challenges of brand protection. As someone dealing with the complexities of international intellectual property rights, I highly recommend and appreciate the book's focus on actionable patterns and real-world applications. It sheds light on crucial topics like deceptive URL creation, infringement trends, domain-name landscape analysis, and brand sentiment, providing invaluable insights for brand strategy and protection. Additionally, the emphasis on partnerships with law enforcement, clustering analysis, and continuous monitoring underscores the importance of staying ahead in the ever-evolving landscape of brand protection. Overall, the book offers practical strategies and insights that will undoubtedly benefit professionals in the field. Patterns that matter!*"—**Pia Mårtensson, Domain Administration and Brand Monitoring, Tetra Pak**

"*A practical and thoughtful guide to the intersection between new technologies and brand value.*"—**Rebecca Newman, IA Manager (Senior Solicitor) and AI Lead, Stobbs**

"*A remarkable and comprehensive overview of the brand protection landscape and the ways in which continually evolving threats can be detected and contained, David Barnett's book is required reading for anyone concerned about their brand presence online.*"—**David Price, Director of Insight and Analysis, IFPI**

"*I have known David for many years and have seen him presenting with great passion about brand monitoring and protection. Great to see that all the knowledge he has shared over the years for a broad audience is now documented in a book. For anyone who wants to get a basic understanding of brand monitoring it is easy to read, and for anyone looking for more in-depth technical insights, this book is definitely valuable as it provides informative topics.*"—**Robin Schouten, IT Security Expert, ABN AMRO Bank N.V.**

"The landscape for brands, and more specifically brand protection, has evolved dramatically over the last few years. Dr David Barnett's first book provided a snapshot of the industry at that time and was a must-read for anyone involved in protecting and developing brands. David's second iteration provides a modern view of the industry and encapsulates all that has changed over the last few years into one concise referenceable location. The book is exceptionally well written and not only provides a detailed and accurate view of a more scientific approach to brand protection, but also allows the reader to continue their education of this space in a very digestible form. I have no doubt I will be writing a further review in a few years' time of David's third brand protection book."—**Tom Smith, VP Account Management, Corsearch**

"I have known David for many years, having collaborated with him in the development of a brand protection product combining our respective internet technology and legal backgrounds. David is a leader in the field and has first-class knowledge of current and developing issues in brand protection, and I considered his first book, Brand Protection in the Online World, *to be a must-read for anyone involved in the industry.* Patterns in Brand Monitoring *provides a welcome update, highlighting the ever-changing facets of brand protection as consumers and brands have moved into different spaces, such as social media, and the use of newer technologies like AI and Web3. It will again be seminal reading for all brand protection professionals and I have no hesitation in giving it the strongest recommendation."*—**Dr Nishant Sood, IP Lawyer, Director, Trainer and Mentor, L-EV8.com**

"David has incredible expertise relating to the domain name system, brand protection and the technical underpinnings of the internet. This combination provides a unique perspective on how best to run brand protection programmes. If you have an interest in this area, do not proceed without reading this book!"—**Julius Stobbs, Founder and Director, Stobbs**

"This book is awesome! Sharing his 20-year experience without reservation, Dr. David Barnett has brought us a comprehensive guide covering every angle of brand protection in this encyclopedia, providing a novel approach showing that brand protection can be quantified with mathematical formulae. It is

a must-read for all practitioners and anyone looking to expand their knowledge."—**Paddy Tam, Brand Protection Expert and Domain Name Arbitrator**

"*Hear the word 'brand' in a conversation and the vast majority of people visualise immediately a company with revenue in the billions and a global following of millions. But there are over 300 million listed companies in the world, and all the household brands we take for granted today started off as relative unknowns. Given the power of a well-managed online presence to trigger exponential growth internationally, organisations of all shapes and sizes today need to take protection of their brand seriously from the get-go. With decades of experience in the world of brand protection, David Barnett is uniquely qualified to teach us all about how to approach brand protection analysis in a scientific way. You don't need a PhD to wrap your head around everything discussed in this gripping book; David has a way of drawing you in with real practical examples which easily hit home and I strongly recommend you give his latest publication a read. Learn from it and it could well end up saving you a lot of money in the long run…*"—**James Williams, VP Business Development, XConnect**

"*This book is essential reading for anyone working in brand protection, especially if they haven't had the privilege of working with David directly – a really comprehensive guide.*"—**J.W., Senior Brand Manager, FTSE 100 banking group**

"*This book is a great insight into the inner technical workings of brand protection and is a must-read for anyone with an interest in the subject, as it succinctly highlights key concepts and terminology. It could easily be part of any education curriculum where brand protection is included, as it is well researched and well explained. An expert empirical read with sound advice and insider tricks on how to approach a brand protection strategy.*"—**Sheena Yonker, Senior Brand Protection and IP Manager, Lipsy Group**

Foreword

Since the publication of *Brand Protection in the Online World* at the end of 2016, there have been enormous developments in the online landscape. It is striking that the book—written to provide an overview of the major areas of significance at the time—contains no mentions of what are now key areas of interest for many brand protection considerations. These include newer platforms and mobile-based technologies such as WhatsApp, TikTok, and Facebook Marketplace, other e-commerce sites and applications such as Shopee, Pinduoduo, Vinted, and a whole range of others, the growth of decentralized social media platforms including Mastodon and Bluesky, the development of artificial intelligence (AI) applications, and the whole ecosystem of Web3, blockchain, nonfungible tokens (NFTs), and the metaverse.

Nevertheless, many of the key underlying ideas and infringement types still apply, even if the landscapes across which they are manifested have evolved somewhat. An understanding of these principles will remain essential in the development of the next generation of monitoring and enforcement tools and technologies.

Patterns in Brand Monitoring considers the ways in which a scientific approach can be applied to the process of analysis in online brand monitoring, a crucial component in the filtering and prioritizing of results—necessary to identify key findings and exclude false positives—and in gaining insights from the findings.

This book also explores other specific areas of analysis of online data, including overviews of the methods used by infringers to create deceptive URLs, trends over time in infringement activity, methods for gaining insights into the domain-name landscape, assessment of brand prominence and sentiment, consideration of the return-on-investment of brand protection programs, methodologies for brand benchmarking, and information relating to Web3 technologies. It also considers how these areas may evolve in the near future.

The discussion is illustrated throughout by the use of case studies based on analysis of real data, covering many of the newer and emerging areas of internet content. Overall, the content shows how an analytical approach can yield insights into trends and patterns of infringement activity, and other factors relating to brand strategy, brand perception, and brand value.

Each of the main chapters begins with an *Overview* info-box, providing an outline of the main areas of content, and concludes with a *Key Points* section, providing a summary of the main takeaways.

The book is of relevance to stakeholders responsible for brand protection, intellectual property management, marketing, or digital services functions in any organization, to those involved in the provision of brand protection services, and to anyone with a general interest in the industry.

Throughout the book, portions of certain screenshots have been redacted, to avoid reproduction of protected intellectual property.

Acknowledgments

2024 marks the twentieth anniversary of the start of my career in brand protection, a journey that has taken me from the earliest days of the industry and offered a wide range of experiences.

I have been privileged to work with some amazing people and inspirational leaders along the way—those who truly understand that leadership is a series of behaviors, and not just a job title—and special mentions from my Envisional and NetNames days are due to Ben Coppin, David Franklin, and Edwina McDowall.

In 2023, I left CSC and was given a very exciting opportunity by Julius Stobbs and Richard Ferguson to join the exceptional team at Stobbs. It is an amazing company—due, not least, to Julius' vision to construct an environment where the primary consideration is the desire to provide a truly top-class service and create a setting where all members of the team are nurtured and supported—but also, in no small measure, to all of the amazing people with whom I am privileged to work. Specific appreciation goes to Chloe Long, for extensive support through my initial months at Stobbs, and Will Haig, for contractual advice and guidance.

Many of the case studies included in this book are based on previous work carried out in collaboration with a range of additional talented colleagues. Particular credit is due to Lan Huang, Alexandra Midgley, Agnes Czolnowska, Ernriel Bell, Quinn Taggart, Nipa Patel, Justin Hartland, Jason Hayden, David Riley, Rebecca Newman, Tom Ambridge, Martyna Sawicz, Bryn Anderson, Jessica Wolff, Tosshan Ramgolam, Claire Breheny, Mary White, Bryan Cheah, and Daniel Smith-Juggins.

Numerous other contacts, colleagues, and friends have kindly provided reviews and endorsements of the book, and their suggestions have greatly improved the final version. Thanks and appreciation go to Charlie Abrahams, Mo Ali, Ben Coppin, Darcy Delich-Coull, Tess Diaz, Stuart Fuller, Alex López G., Pia Mårtensson, Rebecca Newman, David Price, Robin Schouten, Tom Smith, Nishant Sood, Julius Stobbs, Paddy Tam, James Williams, J.W., and Sheena Yonker.

I am also indebted to Scott Isenberg, Naresh Malhotra, and the rest of the team at Business Expert Press, for believing in *Patterns in Brand Monitoring* and supporting me throughout the publication process.

Lastly, but by no means of least importance, special mentions must go to Vicky Adby and the rest of my family, for their continual love, encouragement, and support, throughout the production of the book and always.

David N. Barnett,
Cambridge (United Kingdom),
May 20, 2024

PART 1

Online Brand Protection Basics

CHAPTER 1

Overview of Online Brand Protection

Overview

This chapter will cover:

- The scale and evolution of internet use, and the meaning of Web 1.0 to 3.0.
- The types of brand infringement generally addressed by a brand protection program.
- The general philosophy of online brand protection, including consideration of the range of channels to be monitored, the potential relevance of nonenforceable results, and the interaction with domain name management.

1.1 Evolution of the Internet

More than 30 years from the start of the era of mainstream adoption of the internet, the online world has become a key area of operations for the vast majority of businesses. Corporations utilize websites to promote and sell their products and are reliant on internet technology for their email and other technical infrastructure; consumers go online to research and purchase items and services and to create and curate their own content; and bad actors take advantage of this ubiquitous usage by abusing trusted brand names and other protected intellectual property (IP) in order to carry out cybercrime, misdirect users to their own content, and generate

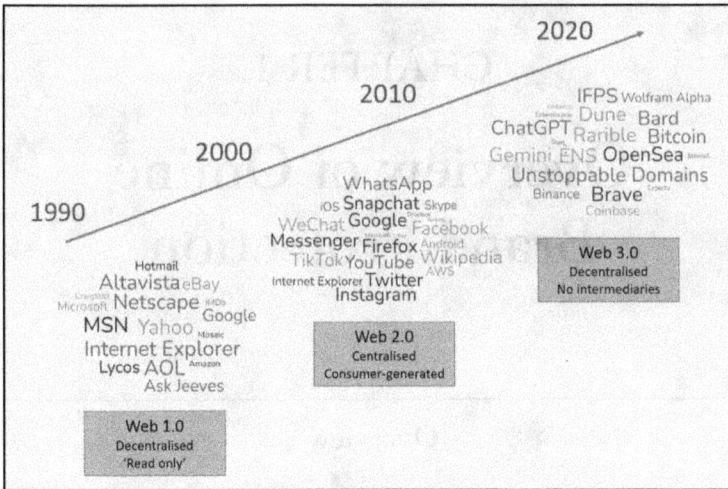

Figure 1.1 Representation of the evolution of the internet (after original versions by DEV Community, Developpez.com)

revenue. Overall, as of January 2024, there are estimated to be 5.4 billion internet users globally, or two-thirds of the total population.[1,2]

The evolution of the internet is often represented as a series of *phases* (Web 1.0 to 3.0) (Figure 1.1).[3] Whilst the distinction between these categorizations is somewhat arbitrary, and significant overlap exists between them, these types of schematics do highlight some of the major trends that have arisen since the early days of popular internet use. The internet of the 1990s (sometimes termed *Web 1.0*) was characterized by slow connections between individual servers on which the web content was hosted, but where the vast majority of users consumed material on only a 'read-only' basis. A major shift occurred in the 2000s, with the emergence of social media and user-generated content, across a range of platforms (*Web 2.0*).[4]

---

[1] https://www.statista.com/statistics/617136/digital-population-worldwide/

[2] https://www.itu.int/en/ITU-D/Statistics/Pages/stat/default.aspx

[3] https://dev.to/pragativerma18/evolution-of-web-42eh;
https://www.developpez.com/actu/329778/Le-concept-du-Web3-est-il-une-nou-velle-fumisterie-Ses-partisans-pensent-que-c-est-le-seul-moyen-de-retrouver-les-libertes-d-Internet-mais-les-critiques-estiment-qu-il-s-agit-juste-d-un-buzzword/;
https://brave.com/web3/versus-web1-and-web2/;
https://www.linkedin.com/pulse/evolution-internet-web-10-20-30-deepak-lyngdoh/

[4] https://hackernoon.com/from-web-10-to-web3-how-the-internet-grew-over-the-years-zac032g1

Web 3.0 (or *Web3*) is the general name given to many of the types of content and connectivity emerging from around 2020 onwards but is most usually taken to mean a growth in (actually a return to) decentralized content, with a specific focus on blockchain-related technologies[5] (Chapter 13).

1.2 Infringement Types

Regardless of the specific channels across which internet content is distributed, many of the primary areas of concern for brand owners have retained a series of common themes over time. The exact types of infringement that will be of greatest interest to any given organization will depend on a number of factors, not least the industry area in which they operate. However, three of the main areas continue to be:

1. The sale of **counterfeit goods** (or other e-commerce infringements), which is of particular interest to manufacturers of physical goods. The global annual spend on e-commerce is over six trillion dollars as of the end of 2023,[6] with the trade in counterfeits worth around $500 billion[7] (around 3 percent of the global economy).[8] Highly affected industries include pharmaceuticals, electronics, food, clothing, cosmetics, and toys.[9]

2. **Online fraud**, of greatest relevance to financial service providers and any organization holding customers' personal details. Recent studies consistently show over one million distinct phishing attacks recorded per quarter, typically with around 500 distinct brands targeted each month.[10]

3. **Digital piracy**, which can be damaging to any providers of content that can be distributed in digital form, such as music, movies, TV,

---

[5] https://www.quora.com/Has-Web-3-0-already-arrived

[6] https://artios.io/ecommerce-statistics/

[7] https://www.a-cg.org/newsdesk/latest-news/article/world-anticounterfeiting-day-highlighting-the-soaring-464-billion-global-trade-in-fake-products

[8] https://euipo.europa.eu/tunnel-web/secure/webdav/guest/document_library/observatory/documents/reports/2021_EUIPO_OECD_Report_Fakes/2021_EUIPO_OECD_Trate_Fakes_Study_FullR_en.pdf

[9] https://www.euipo.europa.eu/en/news/counterfeit-goods-cost-eu-industries-billions-of-euros-and-thousands-of-jobs-annually

[10] https://docs.apwg.org/reports/apwg_trends_report_q2_2023.pdf

software, and books. Between 130 and 190 billion visits to piracy websites per year were being made by 2020, with annual losses to just the movie industry estimated as between \$40 and \$97 billion in 2023. Numerous sources[11,12] state that around a quarter of all internet bandwidth is associated with the illegal sharing of content.[13]

Outside these 'core' areas, a number of other types of infringement can be damaging to brand owners, with some of the main types including:

- **Brand 'seeding'**, or **misdirection** of customers (i.e., web traffic), where a brand name is included in the content of a page that is unrelated to the brand in question, with the intention of manipulating search engines and causing the page to be listed in response to brand-related queries.
- **Negative brand association**, which is essentially a subset of the above type of abuse, but can be particularly detrimental to brand image or reputation if employed in conjunction with undesirable material, such as adult or gambling content, or malicious downloads.
- **Use and misuse of logos or other branded imagery**, which can be a means of falsely implying affiliation, monetizing protected IP, and/or can be associated with the construction of deceptive websites.

---

[11] https://www.go-globe.com/online-piracy-in-numbers-facts-and-statistics-infographic/

[12] https://dataprot.net/statistics/piracy-statistics/

[13] In fact, this figure was actually taken from a 2011 study (see https://www.screendaily.com/news/piracy-uses-24-of-all-bandwidth/5060528.article), in which most of the infringing bandwidth was associated with BitTorrent and cyberlocker traffic. With the more recent rise of licensed streaming services (e.g., Netflix, Spotify)—which, although not necessarily replacing piracy activity, will account for a significantly greater share of internet transmissions than at the time of the earlier study—this figure may be somewhat out-of-date. A recent report by Sandvine (https://www.sandvine.com/hubfs/Sandvine_Redesign_2019/Downloads/2023/reports/Sandvine%20GIPR%202023.pdf) now cites the largest users of internet bandwidth as providers such as Netflix, YouTube, Disney, and TikTok (D. Price, IFPI, pers. comm. 20-May-2024).

- **False or unauthorized claims of affiliation**, which can be used to build credibility for nonlegitimate websites, may incorporate sensitive or protected information, or may be citations made in a way that is noncompliant with brand guidelines.
- **Genericism**, where a brand name is used by third parties to be generally descriptive of the product type in question. Brand owners should be mindful to identify and enforce against such references as they arise, as this issue can lead to the loss of IP rights if the generic usage becomes sufficiently common. Examples of brands for which this has been an issue include Hoover, Band-Aid, Kleenex, Xerox, Google, Velcro, and Polaroid.[14],[15]
- **Negative comment and boycott activity**, which can have detrimental effects on brand value and reputation.

1.3 Philosophy of Online Brand Protection

The general aims of brand protection are the identification of content that infringes IP rights and/or is damaging to the brand (***monitoring***), and the execution of actions to remove or remediate the damaging content (***enforcement***). A key prerequisite of a successful enforcement program is a robust portfolio of protected IP rights (typically including at least trademark registrations covering—as far as possible—relevant brands and products, across appropriate product classes and geographical territories).[16]

The default option for a brand protection program should generally be for the monitoring to cover a *range* of channels (typically covering at least domain names (Box 1.1), general internet content, e-commerce marketplaces, social media, and mobile apps) on a *holistic* basis (though there will invariably be cases where certain specific areas are not relevant, or where additional coverage may be required). A more segmented approach

---

[14] https://en.wikipedia.org/wiki/Generic_trademark
[15] https://www.worldtrademarkreview.com/report/special-reports/q1-2024
[16] https://www.iamstobbs.com/opinion/brand-protection-clarifying-the-terminology

is generally not preferable, due to the fact that the same types of infringement can usually occur across multiple channel types, and (particularly as the internet has evolved) there is increasing overlap and interconnection between these areas (e.g., e-commerce can take place through standalone websites, marketplaces, social media channels, mobile apps, etc.).

Box 1.1 Technical definitions—domain names

A domain name (generally consisting of a *second-level domain* name, and a *top-level domain* (TLD), or domain name extension) is the basic piece of internet infrastructure on which a website can be built. Domain names are owned by an entity named the registrant and are purchased through an entity named a registrar. If a website is to be constructed, the domain name can be associated with one or more IP addresses (with which they are associated via the domain name system (DNS)), denoting the location where website content is hosted. The IP address corresponds to a physical machine (server) under the operation of a hosting provider. The infrastructure of the whole TLD is under the control of an organization known as a registry. The basic components of a uniform resource locator (URL), or web address—which defines a specific web page on the site in question—are shown in Figure 1.2.

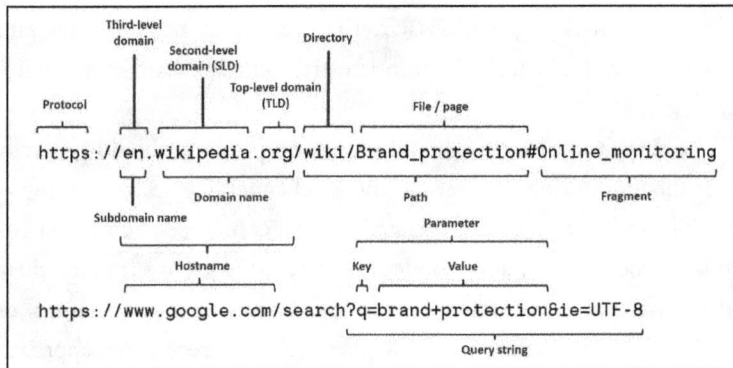

Figure 1.2 Components of a URL

(Continued)

In general, the owner of a domain name can set up whatever hierarchical structure of subdomains, directories, and so on, as they wish (via the configuration of records on the authoritative DNS server). In legitimate use, subdomains can serve a range of purposes, such as allowing the creation of individual microsites for sub-brands or campaigns, or the production of region- or subject-specific subsites. However, subdomains can also be abused, in the construction of infringements. Examples might include cases where a brand name is utilized in the production of a deceptive URL (see, e.g., Chapter 7) or in the construction of a site incorporating a brand infringement or a potentially unauthorized claim of affiliation. Some internet service providers, known as private subdomain registries, also offer the sale of specific commoditized subdomains of their site, allowing users to create their own sites (an analogous example is *blogspot.com*, which allows users to register URLs of the form *username.blogspot.com*).

Within this set of channels or content areas, branded domain names (i.e., those where the name of the brand being infringed is featured within the name of the infringing domain itself) constitute a key area of significance (such that domain name monitoring is very often the 'core' component of any brand protection program). Their significance arises from the fact that websites hosted on branded domain names are often ranked highly in search engine results in response to brand-specific queries (i.e., they have 'high visibility'), and they can additionally constitute some of the most explicit types of IP abuse (with consequently greater enforcement options available).[17] Furthermore, branded domains can be utilized by infringers in a range of different ways. For example, even where no live website content is present, domains can be used purely for their email functionality (e.g., as the 'from' addresses in deceptive emails). Determination of whether a domain is associated with an active mail exchange (MX) record (giving configuration information on any associated mail server

---

[17] https://www.worldtrademarkreview.com/global-guide/anti-counterfeiting-and-online-brand-enforcement/2022/article/creating-cost-effective-domain-name-watching-programme

and indicating that the domain has been configured to be able to send and receive emails) can be an indicator that a domain is being used in this way. This information can be identified by an automated monitoring tool via a technical look-up.

It is also important to note that some findings can be of interest to a brand owner even if enforcement (in the traditional sense) is not possible or appropriate. One familiar example is the identification of negative comment or boycott activity which, in many cases, may be protected by free-speech principles, such that it is not possible to have the content removed. However, knowledge of the content can still be valuable to the brand owner, providing them with informed input into their marketing and outreach activity and steering their product development strategies, for example. In other contexts, *enforcement* can take the form of internal or partner channel communications, or changes to management of distribution channels, rather than classic *takedowns*.

In general, online brand protection sits alongside domain name management as component parts of a holistic IP management program for brand owners. Domain names also hold a position of key importance for brand owners, with official domains often comprising key business assets, on which technical infrastructure (including the hosting of official websites and the management of email services) is dependent. Organizations will usually hold a portfolio of domains under ownership, including a *core* set of business-critical domains (e.g., those used to host official company websites and email infrastructure), accompanied by a series of additional *tactical* domain registrations, which may be *strategic* (e.g., relating to planned business expansions or future product launches) or *defensive* (i.e., held to prevent usage by third parties). It is, however, not scalable or appropriate to register every possible domain name variation that could be registered and utilized by a third-party infringer. For this reason, domain name management should be accompanied by a program of online brand protection, to monitor third-party activity on the internet generally ('*outside the firewall*'), and take enforcement actions where appropriate (Figure 1.3).

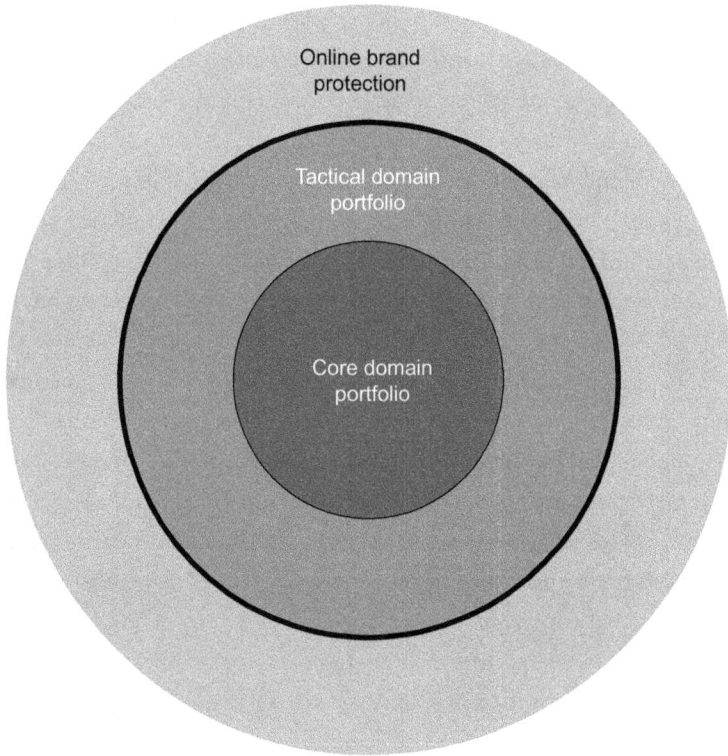

Figure 1.3 A schematic of how online brand protection works alongside domain name management

Programs of online brand protection can help brand owners manage a range of areas of risk, including protection of their IP, protection of their revenue and web traffic, defense of reputation, protection of customers (from harmful infringements) and official channels and partners (from damage to business), and overall making the brand a less attractive target to infringers. Proactive execution of brand protection can, in some cases, also be a regulatory requirement, and may be necessary in order for IP protection to be retained.

A key element of the online brand protection process is the analysis of results collected through monitoring, with a view to filtering and prioritizing the results, and gaining insights from the data. *Prioritization* of

findings is a key component of building efficiency into the analysis proce-
dure and is essential for identifying results requiring time-critical further
analysis or appropriate follow-up actions. *Filtering* approaches are necessary in order to remove false positives, which can arise particularly in cases
where the brand name under consideration is a common or generic term.

It is also important to note that the underlying regulatory landscape relevant to brand protection is continually evolving. One significant development is the approval by the Internet Corporation for
Assigned Names and Numbers (ICANN) of a global amendment to the
2013 Registrar Accreditation Agreement in January 2024,[18] incorporating major implications regarding the duty of registrars to investigate
reports of abuse,[19] and including explicit definitions for DNS abuse and
phishing.[20,21] Another key piece of legislation is the European Union
Digital Services Act (DSA), which is intended to put a greater responsibility onto online platforms to proactively enforce IP rights and protect
consumers, and which entered into force for all platforms as of February
2024.[22] The DSA requires platforms to collect comprehensive information from sellers targeting customers in the European Union (EU) and
to penalize repeat infringers, with large financial penalties for noncompliance. The act also provides a designation for *trusted flaggers*, to work
in conjunction with brand owners in order to build efficiencies into the
enforcement process.[23,24]

---

[18] https://www.icann.org/resources/pages/global-amendment-2024-en
[19] https://www.icann.org/en/system/files/files/registrar-accreditation-agreement-
redline-21jan24-en.pdf
[20] https://itp.cdn.icann.org/en/files/security-and-stability-advisory-committee-
ssac-reports/sac-115-en.pdf
[21] R. Iglesias Posse, Inditex (pers. comm., 17-Apr-2024).
[22] https://commission.europa.eu/strategy-and-policy/priorities-2019-2024/
europe-fit-digital-age/digital-services-act_en
[23] https://www.worldtrademarkreview.com/article/what-impact-will-the-eu-
digital-services-act-have-global-e-commerce-in-2024
[24] https://www.iamstobbs.com/opinion/what-is-the-digital-services-act-and-
how-will-it-protect-brands-and-support-online-enforcement

The key points from this chapter are as follows:

- The scale of use of the internet and the ease with which (potentially infringing) content can be produced highlight the requirement for brand owners to implement comprehensive brand protection programs. These programs should incorporate elements of both monitoring (for which the methodologies are discussed in Chapter 2) and enforcement, covering a range of relevant content channels on a holistic basis, and should generally exist alongside robust IP protection and domain name management initiatives.
- A key component of a brand protection program is the ability to filter and prioritize results, allowing enforcement and other follow-up actions to be focused in the most relevant areas. The techniques and methodologies for identifying the highest-priority findings are discussed in Chapters 3 to 6.

CHAPTER 2

Monitoring Techniques

Overview

This chapter will cover:

- The data sources and techniques used to identify relevant content on the internet, including zone-file analysis, parallel look-ups and exact-string searches (relevant for domain monitoring specifically), search-engine metasearching, direct site searches, and other techniques such as the use of spam traps.

2.1 Domain-Name Zone Files

A core source of data used in brand protection programs (for the identification of branded domain names) is domain name zone files. These are data files administered by the registry organizations responsible for the maintenance of individual TLDs (i.e., domain name extensions), containing technical configuration information (such as the location of nameservers from which DNS look-ups can be carried out) for every domain registered on the TLD in question (Figure 2.1).

The most fundamental feature making zone files useful from a brand monitoring point of view is the fact that they incorporate a comprehensive list of all registered domains.

For generic TLDs (the *gTLDs*; such as .com, .net, etc., and also including the group of over 1,000 new-gTLDs (such as .top, .xyz, .online, etc.), which have launched in the period since 2012), the registry organizations in question are required to 'publish' the zone files (i.e., make them available for download). Many brand protection service providers will

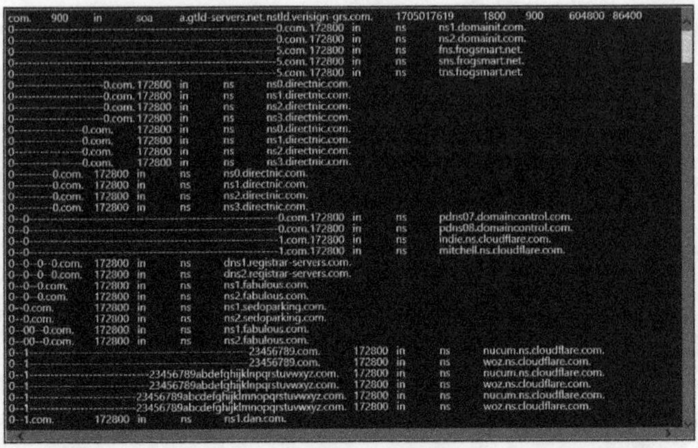

Figure 2.1 Content of part of the .com zone file, containing information relating to all registered domains (usually listed in alphabetical order)

make use of zone files as a data source by downloading the full set on a daily basis (thereby giving a comprehensive list of all registered domains on a particular day, across the TLDs in question). By comparing each day's downloads with those from the previous day, they can identify new domains (i.e., additions to the zone file) as they are registered, and dropped (de-registered, or lapsed) domains (i.e., removals from the zone files) (see e.g. Case Study 2.1).

Case Study 2.1: Patterns in Domain 'Tasting'[1,2]

Domain tasting is a long-established practice involving the short-lived existence of a domain, which is allowed to lapse a few days after its initial registration. The practice arose in response to an ICANN policy allowing a domain to be canceled—with all fees refunded—within a five-day grace period, intended to address the issue of accidental registrations.[3] However, the practice is open to abuse by infringers, and it is worth noting that many registrars no longer allow it.

---

[1] https://circleid.com/posts/20230215-patterns-and-trends-in-domain-tasting-of-the-top-10-global-brands

[2] https://www.linkedin.com/pulse/patterns-trends-domain-tasting-top-ten-global-brands-david-barnett/

[3] https://en.wikipedia.org/wiki/Domain_tasting

Domain tasting has been popularly used for determining the amount of web traffic received (e.g., through search engine queries or mistyped browser requests).[4] In many cases, domain prospectors would speculatively register large numbers of domains and, while live, monetize them through the placement of pay-per-click links. The domains could also, for example, be used for sending spam emails during this period. At the end of the grace period, those domains receiving significant amounts of web traffic could be retained for further use, or sold at a profit, with the others being allowed to drop.

This case study examines instances of short-lived (≤ 5 days) domains beginning with the names of any of the top ten most valuable brands in 2022,[5] based on an 18-month analysis period (between May 2021 and November 2022) using zone-file data. This will encompass both 'true' cases of domain tasting and other instances where a domain is dropped by its owner—potentially outside the grace period—after a period of use (say, for launching a phishing attack, noting that in many cases short-lived domains will be used as a means of evading detection and takedown—see, e.g., Case Study 9.2), or taken down by a brand owner or service provider following identification of an infringement.

Across the top ten brands, 9,284 domain tasting events were identified across the 18-month period, with the monthly numbers of tasting events shown in Figure 2.2.

Figures 2.3 and 2.4 show the total numbers of events, categorized by the delay between domain registration and drop. The statistics show that, for most domain tasting events, the domains are active only for a very short time—with lifespans of one or two days accounting for 62 percent of all cases—a trend that is consistent across all brands. Across the whole domain tasting dataset, the average domain lifetime was 2.35 days.

(Continued)

---

[4] https://www.techopedia.com/definition/15657/domain-tasting
[5] https://www.kantar.com/inspiration/brands/what-are-the-most-valuable-global-brands-in-2022

(Continued)

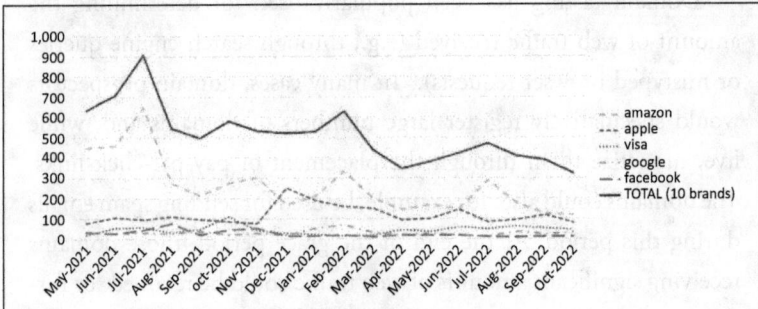

Figure 2.2 *Monthly total numbers of domain tasting events (categorized according to lapse date) per brand, for the top five most frequently targeted brands, and for all top ten brands in total*

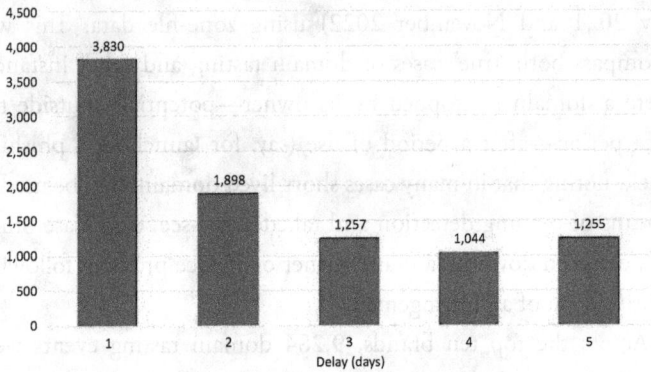

Figure 2.3 *Total numbers of domain tasting events, categorized by the delay between registration and drop*

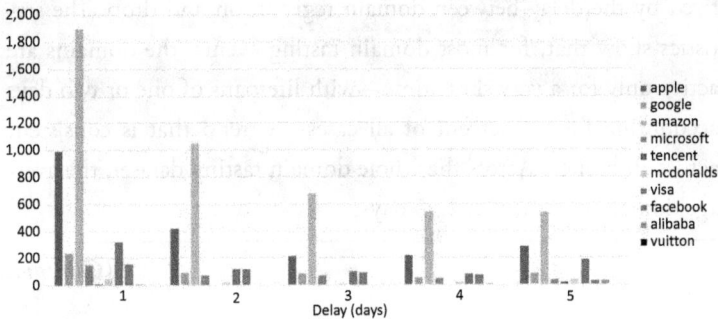

Figure 2.4 *Numbers of domain tasting events, categorized by the delay between registration and drop, for each brand*

Of particular additional concern is the fact that the dataset includes significant numbers of domains including keywords frequently associated with phishing activity, with examples including *verif** (for *verify* or *verification*, 182 domains), *secur** (for *secure* or *security*, 180), and *login* (99).

A number of specific additional trends and patterns were also identified within the dataset, of which some examples are given below.

1. 'Amazon Japan' domains

    Within the dataset, the most frequently targeted brand was Amazon, for which the number of domain tasting events was sufficiently large that it dominated the overall statistics for all ten brands. The activity for Amazon was itself dominated by what appears to be a single coordinated campaign of tasting events (1,091 instances) relating to domains containing the brand name *amazon* together with *japan* or *jp*, potentially associated with a high-volume phishing campaign. Specific domain-name patterns were consistently seen, including 562 domains with names of the form *amazon-jpAAAAAA.shop*, where *AAAAAA* is a six-character string, and 84 domains of the form *amazon-jpAAAA.pro* or *amazon-AAAAjp.pro*, where *AAAA* is a one to four character string.

2. Specific groups of probable phishing domains

    Among the dataset, specific groups of domains featuring consistent formats and keyword patterns, likely to be associated with phishing domains targeting particular brands, were also identified. These included:

    - Domains with names of the form *google-site-verification AAAAAAAA.com*, where *AAAAAAAA* is a long string of apparently random characters. These domains are likely to be spoofing the format of the configuration text used in Google's site verification process.[6]

(Continued)

---

[6] https://developers.google.com/site-verification/v1/getting_started

(*Continued*)

- A range of groups of Apple-related domains, including *apple-idXXXX-secure.com* (16 instances), *apple-supportidXXXX.com* (66), *apple-caseidXXXX.com* (295), and *apple-ticketidXXXX.com* (55), where *XXXX* is a four-digit string in each case.
- Numerous Amazon domains with names containing keywords such as *verify*, *billing*, *serv**, and *ticket* and ending with an apparently random alphanumeric string. By definition, all domains definitively determined as being associated with tasting events will be inactive at the point of identification. However, significant numbers of the above examples were found to display browser warnings indicating that deceptive content was formerly present. In general, by combining analysis of tasted domains with ongoing domain monitoring, it is possible to determine trends in the name structures of malicious domains, and thereby identify similar examples while still live (Figure 2.5), allowing for timely enforcement actions to be carried out.

3. 'Google SEO' domains

A spike of activity, comprising 51 similar domains all dropped on the same day, was identified within the dataset. All associated domains had names beginning *googleseo*, across the UK-centric extensions .uk, .co.uk, and .org.uk. This batch of domains may be associated with a search engine optimization project, possibly with the intention of determining which domains attract high volumes of traffic.

4. Facebook .top domains

The dataset was found to include 18 domains of the format *facebookcomXXXXXX.top*, where *XXXXXX* is a long numeric string (plus an additional 16 such domains active for longer periods, of between 7 and 22 days). Additionally, the start of what may be a new similar batch was also observed, with a single tasting event of a domain of the form *facebookdomainverificationYYYY.top*, where *YYYY* is an alphanumeric string, at the end of the analysis

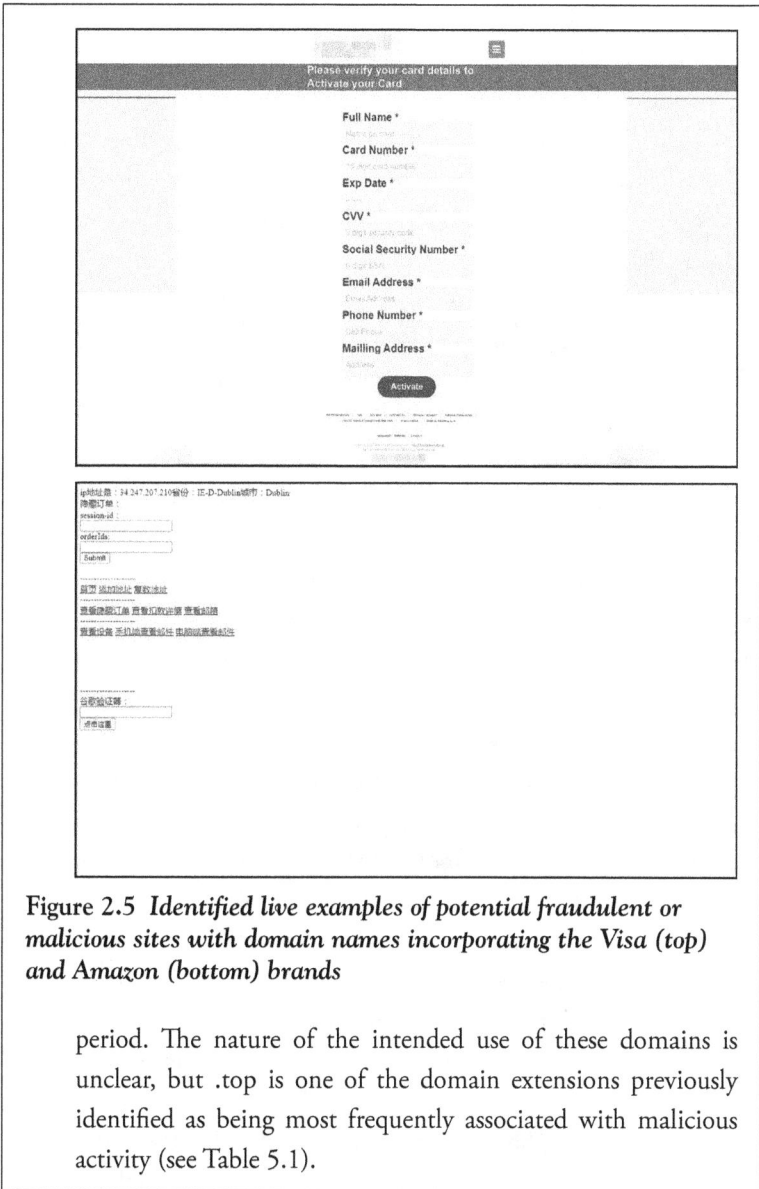

Figure 2.5 *Identified live examples of potential fraudulent or malicious sites with domain names incorporating the Visa (top) and Amazon (bottom) brands*

period. The nature of the intended use of these domains is unclear, but .top is one of the domain extensions previously identified as being most frequently associated with malicious activity (see Table 5.1).

For ccTLDs (country-specific extensions, such as .co.uk (United Kingdom), .fr (France), .de (Germany), etc.), the registry organizations are, in general, not obliged to publish zone files. For individual country extensions, therefore, zone files are often unavailable altogether or may contain only partial data.

Where zone files are available, providers will generally utilize technology that is able to search through these lists to identify domains containing a brand name of interest. It is also generally advisable to incorporate a component of monitoring for domains containing brand *variations* or misspellings, which may typically be used by infringers to create deceptive sites or in an effort to evade detection. Examples might include instances where a character in the domain name is replaced by another appearing visually similar, such as a zero ('0') for a letter *o*, a lower case *L* ('l') or a one ('1') for a letter *i*, a combination of an *r* and an *n* ('rn') for a letter *m*, or any of a range of non-Latin character substitutions (see Chapter 7 and Case Study 9.1).

2.2 Other Domain-Monitoring Techniques

The unavailability of ccTLD zone files generally means that additional techniques must be used to identify the registration of branded domains across country-specific extensions. The first such technique is the use of **parallel look-ups**, where—following the detection of a relevant gTLD domain via zone-file analysis—a series of checks are carried out to determine whether there exist registered domains with the same second-level domain (SLD) name (sometimes referred to as 'cousin' domains), across the range of ccTLDs of interest (potentially the full set). For example, if the registration of *website.com* is identified, parallel look-ups will check for the existence of *website.co.uk*, *website.fr*, *website.de*, and so on. This approach is most effective in cases where a registrant purchases domains across multiple extensions at the same time. However, parallel look-ups can, in general, also identify instances where the 'cousin' domains were registered at any time previously. The limitations of this approach are that—as mentioned above—there is no guarantee that the domains will be registered at the point of registration and, where the methodology is followed exactly as outlined, it will identify only domains where the SLD strings are identical (i.e., exact matches).

The second technique, which is appropriate if there are one or more high-relevance SLD strings of interest (such as may be the case if the brand owner's official site is (say) *brandX.com*, and the most concerning third-party registrations would be any of the form *brandX.TLD*), is to carry out regular checks for the existence of domain names featuring the SLD string in question (*'brandX'*) across the set of ccTLDs of interest. This approach, known as **exact-string searches**, can identify new domains at the time of registration, but will, of course, only identify exact matches. The technique works on the principle that, if a specific domain name of potential interest is known *in advance*, it is a relatively simple matter to carry out a lookup to check whether or not that domain is registered.

The limitations of these approaches mean that there may always be domain names of potential interest that are not guaranteed to be detectable. As such, these domain-monitoring techniques are often augmented by other search strategies, such as the use of search-engine metasearching.

2.3 Search-Engine Metasearching

Metasearching is a technique used to identify general internet content of interest, involving the submission of relevant queries to search engines and analysis of the pages returned. In many cases, monitoring tools will also identify relevant hyperlinks on the pages identified and can follow them to additional pages of potential interest (*crawling* or *spidering*). One of the main rationales behind this monitoring strategy is that it mimics the techniques employed by general internet users when searching for relevant content and can, therefore, identify those web pages that have the highest 'visibility', or potential level of exposure to users, which are therefore of greatest potential concern if infringing. It is often appropriate to 'tailor' the search terms used in this approach, in order to focus the findings on the most relevant content, through the use of, for example, language-, industry-, or issue-specific keywords (see Chapter 4).

2.4 Direct Site Searches

In cases where there are specific sites of interest known at the outset of monitoring (such as specific e-commerce marketplaces, social media sites, or app stores), it may be appropriate to monitor these sites directly on a regular basis, using their own in-built search functionality. This approach is known as site *monitoring*, as distinct from the *discovery* techniques outlined above.

Where the content of such sites is presented in a consistent format from page to page (e.g., the listing pages on e-commerce marketplaces), it is often possible within automated monitoring tools to construct website **scrapers** to extract key pieces of information (such as listing title, seller name, price, quantity, etc.) from their known location on the page and use this data as a basis for summarizing and prioritizing results.

Some sites may also permit data to be extracted via an application programming interface (API), in which information is provided in a structured, predefined format.

2.5 Other Techniques

There will, however, always be categories of content that are not visible via the aforementioned monitoring techniques, such as websites hosted on non-brand-specific domain names (or on ccTLDs where there is no available zone-file coverage), and which are not linked-to from any other known sites (and are therefore potentially not indexed by search engines). This can be problematic in cases where the sites feature high-risk content (such as deceptive phishing sites impersonating trusted brands). It is often the case that the operators of such sites deliberately set up sites in this way (specifically to evade detection), relying instead on other techniques (such as the sending of fraudulent spam emails with embedded links) to drive users to the content in question. Accordingly, in cases where this type of content is of concern, the above techniques may need to be augmented with the use of spam traps and/or related technology.

Spam traps are tools specifically designed to attract a cross-section of as much general spam traffic as possible and analyze the content of the intercepted mails to identify references to the brand(s) of interest. These tools often make use of a number of components, such as honeypot email accounts (for which the addresses are deliberately 'seeded' online in the hope that they will be harvested by bad actors in the construction of spam mailing lists), and may be augmented by the use of components such as open relays (deliberately compromised servers through which spammers will sometimes redirect their email traffic so as to disguise its original source). However, these approaches really only achieve a 'sampling' of spam emails and will be ineffective for certain types of campaigns (such as where emails are targeted to known lists of recipients). Tools to detect fraudulent sites can also incorporate data feeds from abuse mailboxes, and information from brand owners' web server logs (working on the principle that deceptive sites may sometimes 'call' content from, or redirect users (after use) to, official sites), but none of these techniques will give complete comprehensive coverage.

Furthermore, monitoring may be further complicated by the fact that—particularly on certain websites or platforms—the content (such as advertisements or search results) presented to a user may be specifically customized according to factors such as their location or search history. This difficulty can be mediated to some degree through the use of features such as geographical proxies (i.e., servers in appropriate locations, through which search queries can be routed), specifically 'tuned' accounts (with relevant sets of 'likes', 'follows', and search histories), or other tools (such as Meta's Brand Rights Protection Manager tool,[7] to which brand owners can sign up, in order to review potentially infringing content across the group's platforms), but it is often the case that fully comprehensive detection is not possible.

Key Points

The key points from this chapter are as follows:

- Domain name zone files are data files administered by the registry organizations responsible for overseeing the infrastructure of individual TLDs (top-level domains, or domain extensions), which contain comprehensive lists of all registered domains across the extension in question.
- Analysis of zone files makes it possible to identify new registrations and lapsed domains. However, comprehensive zone files are generally only available

(Continued)

(*Continued*)

> for gTLDs, and the data are usually less complete or
> unavailable for many ccTLDs.
>
> - Where comprehensive coverage is not possible,
>   detection of additional domains can be achieved (to a
>   degree) through the use of other techniques, such as
>   parallel look-ups, exact-string searches, and internet
>   metasearching.
> - For other types of internet content, metasearching and
>   other techniques (such as direct site searches) can be
>   used to identify relevant findings, but it is generally
>   not possible to achieve comprehensive detection of all
>   potentially relevant results.

PART 2

Filtering and Prioritizing

CHAPTER 3

Brand Content Scoring

Overview

This chapter will cover:

- The concept of brand content scoring, as a way of
  quantifying the degree of brand-related content on a page
  (i.e., the extent to which the page 'is about' the brand), as
  a key parameter for identifying the most significant pages
  within a dataset of results identified through monitoring.

Following the collection of sets of pages of potential interest by a
brand-monitoring tool, there generally follows a process of analysis of
the content (frequently comprising inspection of the full HTML source
code of the page) before decisions are made on appropriate actions (such
as enforcement) on the pages in question.

A key part of this analysis process is the ability to automatically prioritize
results according to the likelihood of the content being of interest or relevance. This process has a number of purposes, including the identification of:

- Priority targets for further analysis.
- Candidates for content tracking (i.e., regular reinspection of
  content or configuration, and the generation of an alert if high-
  concern findings are identified)—this may be most appropriate
  in cases where (say) a domain name presents a high level of risk
  but is not currently associated with any live site content.
- Priority targets for enforcement actions.
- Frequently used keyword patterns, TLDs, and so on,
  commonly used by infringers, which can help inform policies
  on appropriate defensive domain registrations.

In its broadest sense, prioritization of results often involves the iden-tification of the presence of keywords on the pages (specifically brand names or other relevant terms), and may also take account of factors such as the number and prominence of such mentions, and their proximity to other relevant terms. Identification of *negator* keywords (i.e., keywords implying that the brand name is being mentioned in a *non*-relevant con-text) can also be an element of the process of filtering out false positives. This concept is particularly relevant when the brand name under con-sideration is a generic term (e.g., if monitoring for the Apple brand, a suitable negator keyword may be *fruit*).

One of the simplest concepts applicable to the formulation of web page prioritization techniques is the calculation of a **brand content score**. Essentially, given a brand name (or other term) of interest, it allows a score to be calculated for any given web page, based on the number of mentions of the term on the page, and the relative prominence of each mention. This gives a metric providing a measure of the extent to which the content of the page pertains to (i.e., 'is about') the brand in question and is also key to the calculation of general online brand prominence (Chapter 10).

The formulation involves counting each mention of the brand on the web page (generally by inspecting the HTML directly), and weighting each one according to its prominence—for example, a mention in the URL may be deemed to 'score' more highly than a mention in the page title, which scores more highly than a mention in a level-1 heading, and so on. The relative weightings can be selected and 'tuned' as necessary, and it may also be appropriate to *cap* the contribution to the total score from each specific area, to avoid the results being 'skewed' by the presence of 'junk' pages which may be 'stuffed' with large numbers of mentions of particular terms. The range of scores obtained will thereby be dependent on the relative weightings and caps used (in addition to the types of search queries used to identify the results and the keywords being matched).

An example of how this calculation can be carried out in practice is shown below, for a particular (arbitrary) combination of score weightings and caps (Table 3.1) (considering the brand name '*Google*' on a page of Google's official site—*https://about.google/belonging/at-work/* (as of Janu-ary 2024) (Tables 3.2 and 3.3, and Figure 3.1)).

Table 3.1 Relative weightings and caps for mentions of the brand term in each location of the page, in the calculation of brand content score

Location (HTML tag)	Weighting	Cap (Max Total no. of Contributions to Score)
URL	50	—
Page title (title)	25	—
Level-1 heading (h1)	20	—
Level-2 heading (h2)	5	—
Any	1	50

Table 3.2 Snippets of web page source code and contributions to total score

HTML Snippet	Score Contribution
<title>Building a More Inclusive Workplace—Google</title>	25
<h1 id="module-modal-self-id-heading" class="glue-headline glue-headline--headline-3">Supporting the intersectional communities at Google with Self-ID </h1>	20
<h2 class="glue-headline module-card-collage__heading glue-spacer-4-bottom glue-text-center glue-headline-headline-3"> We are making sure every Googler feels seen, connected, supported, and empowered to participate fully: </h2>	5

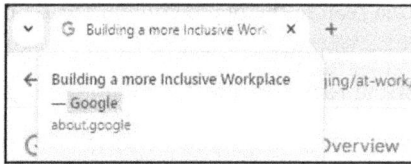

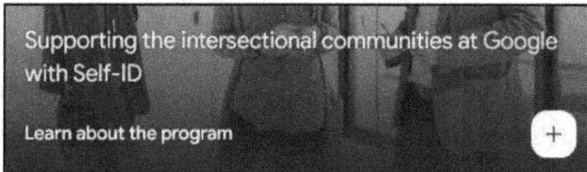

Figure 3.1 Visible appearance of the brand references corresponding to the HTML snippets shown in Table 3.2

Table 3.3 Calculation of overall brand content score for the page

Location (HTML tag)	Weighting	Cap	No. Identified Mentions	Score Contribution
URL	50	—	1	50
Page title (*title*)	25	—	1	25
Level-1 heading (*h1*)	20	—	8	160
Level-2 heading (*h2*)	5	—	1	5
Any	1	50	153	50 (capped)
Total score				290

Case Study 3.1: An Analysis of the Brand Content Score of Top-Ranked Google Results

This case study presents the findings from a very simple investigation into the extent to which brand content score is relevant to the ranking (order) of results returned by Google. The analysis considers the first page of results returned in response to searches on google.com in the United Kingdom (as of January 2024) for each of the top five most valuable global brand names in 2023. For each web page returned by each search, the brand content score for the brand name (i.e., search term) in question was calculated, and compared with the ranking of the result (Figure 3.2). For the purposes of the analysis, only *organic* search results were considered, and any embedded YouTube video results, and web pages that could not be accessed by the automated analysis script, were excluded (though with the original search ranking positions retained).

A simple-minded assumption would be that the higher ranked results (i.e., those to the left of the graph in Figure 3.2) should be those with the highest brand content scores, but the analysis shows that this is not the case (and that there is no meaningful correlation between the two parameters). This suggests—perhaps unsurprisingly—that

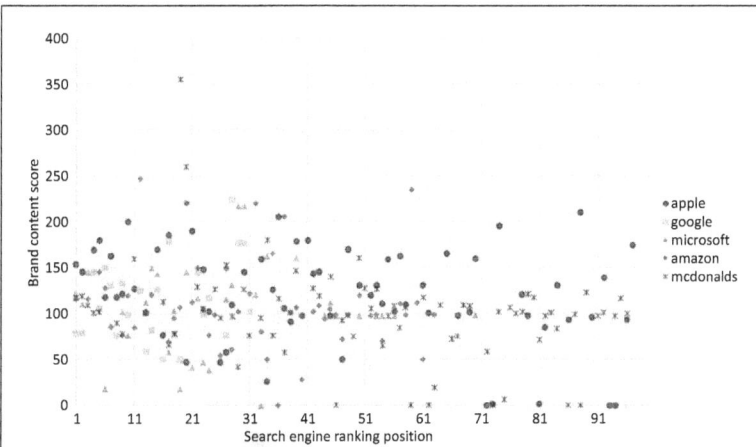

Figure 3.2 Comparison of brand content score with search engine ranking, for results returned on the first page of Google in response to searches for each of the top five most valuable global brand names

the Google algorithm for ranking results is much more complicated than considering just the number and prominence of the mentions of the search term on the pages in question, and takes account of a number of additional factors. These are likely to include characteristics such as levels of trust and relevance, numbers of incoming links, and web traffic, among others.[1,2,3] The effectiveness of Google's algorithm is reflected in the fact that the top-ranked result for each search query is, in each case, the homepage of the official website of the brand in question. In the case of google.com, the brand content score (for the term *google*) for this page is rather low (a value of 78), largely a reflection of the 'minimalist' design of the Google website.

The application of the brand content scoring approach does, however, make it generally possible to sort (potentially large) sets of web pages, in order to identify priority candidates for analysis and potential enforcement, by determining which examples contain

(Continued)

[1] https://www.google.com/intl/en_uk/search/howsearchworks/how-search-works/ranking-results/
[2] https://en.wikipedia.org/wiki/PageRank
[3] https://backlinko.com/google-ranking-factors

(*Continued*)

the greatest degree of brand-related references (and may constitute potential infringements). This is shown by the high brand-relevance of the most highly scored examples in each of the sets of results returned by the individual brand queries:

- **Apple**: *https://www.apple.com/careers/us/work-at-apple. html*; page title: "*Work at Apple - Careers at Apple*" (score: 210; Google rank 88)
- **Google**: *https://books.google.co.uk/ books?id=8r9gEAAAQBAJ*; page title: "*Google Workspace User Guide: A practical guide to using ...*" (score: 224; Google rank 28)
- **Microsoft**: *https://www.amazon.co.uk/Software-Microsoft/ s?srs=3881972031*; page title: "*Amazon.co.uk: Microsoft: Software*" (score: 217; Google rank 29) and *https://www.theverge.com/2024/1/15/24038726/microsoft-copilot-microsoft-365-business-launch-availability*; page title: "*Microsoft unlocks Copilot AI inside Office apps for all ...*" (score: 217; Google rank 30)
- **Amazon**: *https://www.independent.co.uk/topic/amazon*; page title: "*Amazon—latest news, breaking stories and comment*" (score: 247; Google rank 12)
- **McDonald's**: *https://www.independent.co.uk/topic/ mcdonalds*; page title: "*Mcdonald's—latest news, breaking stories and comment*" (score: 355; Google rank 19)

Key Points

The key points from this chapter are as follows:

- The ability to prioritize results identified through brand monitoring is a key element of brand protection programs, allowing the identification of the most significant targets for further analysis or enforcement.
- The brand page score parameter is a metric that can be calculated for any brand or keyword on any web page and provides a measure of the extent to which the page relates to that particular brand (or other relevant term), based on the number of mentions and the prominence on the page of the individual mentions.
- Extensions of this concept can be applied to the analysis of additional keywords, as discussed in Chapter 4.

CHAPTER 4

Use of Relevance Keywords

Overview

This chapter will cover:

- Ways in which analysis of relevance keywords can be used to expand on the ideas presented in Chapter 3, as part of the process of filtering out nonrelevant results identified through monitoring, and carrying out prioritization of the remainder.
- Analysis of web pages based <u>just</u> on the appearance of relevance keywords, and analysis techniques where the <u>proximity</u> of relevance keywords to brand terms is considered.

Consideration of keywords appearing in conjunction with brand mentions can be a key component of methodologies to prioritize sets of web pages and filter out nonrelevant 'false positives' and is particularly important in cases where the name of the brand being monitored is a generic word or term in its own right.

In general, keyword-based filtering falls into two main categories:

- **Inclusional** (or *positive*) filtering, based on **relevance** keywords (i.e., keywords whose presence indicates that a mention of a brand term is pertaining to the brand itself, rather than a nonrelevant reference to the brand name in a different context)—examples might be keywords relating to the industry area of the organization in question.
- **Exclusional** (or *negative*) filtering, based on **nonrelevance** keywords (i.e. keywords pertaining to the subject area in which the brand name might be referenced in a context unrelated to the brand itself).

Note that the terms *positive* and *negative* in this context are used in a sense which is distinctive from their utilization in the description of sentiment analysis (Chapter 10).

The simplest implementation of this approach in the filtering out of false positives would be to assign each web page as either relevant or nonrelevant purely on the basis of the identification on the page of *any* keyword of the appropriate type. However, this method is unsatisfactory because of the possibility of the appearance of a nonrelevance keyword on a page that is otherwise relevant (or vice versa). Instead, more sophisticated methods will take account of *all* mentions on the page of keywords under consideration. Consideration of (only) relevance keywords allows a potential relevance *score* for the page to be calculated, which can serve as a useful basis for ranking (prioritizing) web pages of potential interest. In order to take the analysis one stage further, it is possible to also calculate a *nonrelevance* score for each page (based on the identification of nonrelevance keywords) and calculate an *overall* potential relevance score for the page by considering the balance between the two (i.e., taking the difference between them). One implementation of this approach, where *content scores* (Chapter 3) are calculated for each of the keywords, based on the number *and* prominence of their mentions, rather than relying just on simple word counting, is illustrated by Case Study 4.1.

Case Study 4.1: Monitoring for References to Google Gemini—An Application of Keyword-Based Relevance Filtering[1]

The announcement of Google's AI model *Gemini* in December 2023[2] was one of the highest-profile brand launches of the year. As such, it was followed by a spike in infringements targeting the brand, highlighting the need for a brand protection program. However, the generic nature of the brand name (which also occurs frequently in the context of astrology or astronomy) presents difficulties in the

---

[1] https://www.iamstobbs.com/google-gemini-ebook
[2] https://deepmind.google/technologies/gemini/

separation of relevant content from other findings, making it a good example of an instance where keyword-based relevance filtering can be applied.

As a proof-of-concept, it is reasonable to consider the first page of results returned by Google.com in response to a search for the term '*gemini*' (as of December 2023). This yields a mixture of results, including web pages relating to Google Gemini, content relating to astrology, and other material (such as third-party usage of the same brand name in a way that may or may not be infringing).

The case study involves the use of two sets of keywords, as follows:

- **Inclusional** (relevance) keywords—implying that the content relates to Google Gemini specifically or AI generally
  - DeepMind
  - Google
  - AI/A.I.
  - Large Language Model (*LLM*)
  - Massive Multitask Language Understanding (*MMLU*)
  - GPT/ChatGPT
- **Exclusional** (nonrelevance) keywords—implying that the content relates to astrology or astronomy
  - Capricorn
  - Aquarius
  - Pisces
  - Taurus
  - Scorpio
  - Sagittarius
  - astrolog* (covers wildcard variants such as '*astrology*' and '*astrologer*')
  - zodiac
  - Castor
  - Pollux (Castor and Pollux are the 'twin' stars in the Gemini constellation)

(*Continued*)

(*Continued*)

> **Notes:**
>
> - In general, the analysis uses wildcard matching, so that a mention of the keyword is considered to have been identified even if it appears as an element of a longer string (i.e., as a substring), as may be the case if the term appears in the URL of the page, for example. The exception to this principle is for short or highly generic terms (denoted previously as terms in italics), in which case it is required that the strings must be prefixed or suffixed by characters *other* than letters (so that— for example—words containing the string '*ai*' (such as '*traits*') are not counted as a mention of AI).
> - For the above reason, certain additional keywords were excluded from the list to be used in the analysis (such as '*aries*', which appears frequently as a substring within longer words).

The analysis then involves the calculation of the keyword *content score* for each keyword on each page, in a way identical to that used for a brand term in the calculation of brand content score (Chapter 3). The total *relevance* score for the page is then the sum of the scores for the inclusional keywords, and the *nonrelevance* score is the sum of the scores for the exclusional keywords. An overall measure of the potential relevance of the page is then the difference between these two scores (the overall *potential relevance score*).

Note that a score of zero does not necessarily constitute a satisfactory threshold below which a page should be deemed altogether nonrelevant and unworthy of further analysis and potential enforcement. There are a number of reasons for this, including the facts that the numbers of inclusional and exclusional keywords may differ from each other, and the fact that some of the most significant pages from the point of view of brand protection considerations may be those where a third party is making use of the same brand name in an industry area which may be only tangentially relevant.

It is also worth noting that this approach provides a measure of the potential level of relevance of the page *overall*, based on an assessment of the subject area of the content, and also does not take into account the *proximity* between references to the brand name and the keywords (cf. Case Study 4.2).

Overall, this approach does provide a meaningful separation of relevant pages from nonrelevant pages, with the pages with the highest potential relevance scores confirmed to feature content relating to the Google Gemini brand, and those with the lowest (i.e., most highly negative) scores found to relate to astrology (Tables 4.1 and 4.2).

In order to present a more visual summary of the data, it is also possible to manually categorize each of the pages within the dataset as either definitively relevant (i.e., relating to Google Gemini), definitively nonrelevant (relating to a false positive—i.e., astrology), or *neutral* (potential third party or other references to the Gemini name). By so doing, it is possible to see that the relevant pages and the nonrelevant pages are indeed 'clustered' on the basis of their potential relevant scores, which therefore constitutes a useful diagnostic metric (Figure 4.1).

Table 4.1 *Top five pages by potential relevance score*

Page Title	Web page Host Domain	Potential Relevance Score
Google launches Gemini, the AI model it hopes will take ...	theverge.com	444
Google Gemini vs OpenAI ChatGPT: What's Better?	businessinsider.com	359
Google I/O 2023: Making AI more helpful for everyone	blog.google	358
Google Says New AI model Gemini Outperforms ChatGPT in ...	theguardian.com	322
Google's New AI, Gemini, Beats ChatGPT in 30 of 32 Test ...	forbes.com	319

(*Continued*)

(Continued)

Table 4.2 Bottom five pages by potential relevance score

Page Title	Web page Host Domain	Potential Relevance Score
Gemini Zodiac Sign: Characteristics, Dates, & More	astrology.com	−248
Gemini Zodiac Sign: Horoscope, Dates & Personality Traits	zodiacsign.com	−232
The Gemini—Zodiac Sign Dates and Personality	thoughtcatalog.com	−200
Gemini Personality Traits—The Times of India	indiatimes.com	−186
All About Gemini	tarot.com	−174

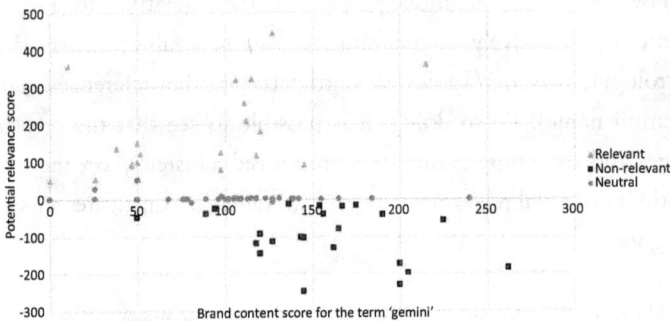

Figure 4.1 Relationship between potential relevance score and manual categorization of actual relevance (triangles = relevant; squares = nonrelevant; circles = neutral), for each of the pages in the dataset

Please note: The horizontal axis shows the brand content score (Chapter 3) of each page for the term *gemini*, which the data shows is not, in itself, a helpful basis for categorization, since the term can appear in *either* relevant or nonrelevant contexts.

Furthermore, this categorization—using an overall potential relevance score based on the *balance* between individual relevance and nonrelevance scores—provides a better separation between those results that are actually relevant and those that are nonrelevant than just using either of the individual score types in isolation.

It is also possible to make a further 'clean' separation of relevant from nonrelevant results by actually incorporating relevant (inclusional) keywords in the search queries used to bring back candidate pages in the first place (i.e., the use of 'focused' search queries). However, caution must be exercised if *neutral* (or 'borderline') web pages are also of interest (as will be the case when considering the usage of the same brand name by third parties in industry areas that are not exactly identical (and where relevance keywords may not appear), since the use of queries which are overly focused may result in pages of this type not being returned).

More sophisticated approaches of keyword-based filtering techniques may take account of keyword mentions only where they appear *in close proximity* to the brand name. One such approach is to *weight* these mentions, based on the absolute measured proximity between each keyword and a brand mention (in terms of the number of words' separation on the page) (see an example of such a formulation in Box 4.1).

Box 4.1: Formulation Definition—Proximity Score

For keyword-based analysis, it can be beneficial to define a *proximity score*, to determine the score component assigned when a keyword-brand pair is identified on a page, according to the proximity of the two terms to each other (i.e., the separation between the two, measured in terms of the number of words, such that a proximity of 1 indicates that the two terms appear consecutively on the page). The score function should decrease as the proximity between the words decreases (i.e., as their separation increases), indicating a decreased likelihood that the keyword reference appears in relation to the brand reference.

One such formulation uses an exponentially decaying function, defined in terms of a maximum proximity score (i.e., the score assigned for a proximity of 1) and a proximity *'half life'* (i.e., the separation over which the proximity score drops to half its maximum

(*Continued*)

(Continued)

value). It may also be more elegant to round down the score for each proximity value to the next whole number below the calculated value; this has the added benefit of introducing a maximum separation for which the keyword pairs are considered to relate to each other (i.e., a proximity at which the score drops to 0).

Formally, this can be formulated as follows:

$$S_p = \left\lfloor S_{max} \times (\tfrac{1}{2})^{(p/P_{0.5})} \right\rfloor$$

where:

S_p is the proximity score

S_{max} is the maximum proximity score (i.e., the score for a proximity of 1 word)

p is the proximity (in words)

$P_{0.5}$ is the proximity *half life* (i.e., the increase in separation for which the proximity score drops to half of its value)

$\lfloor\ \rfloor$ denotes the *floor function*—that is, rounding the value down to the greatest integer below the value in question Figure 4.2 shows the variation of this function for four different combinations of maximum score and proximity half life (denoted in the key as "$S_p \mid P_{0.5}$").

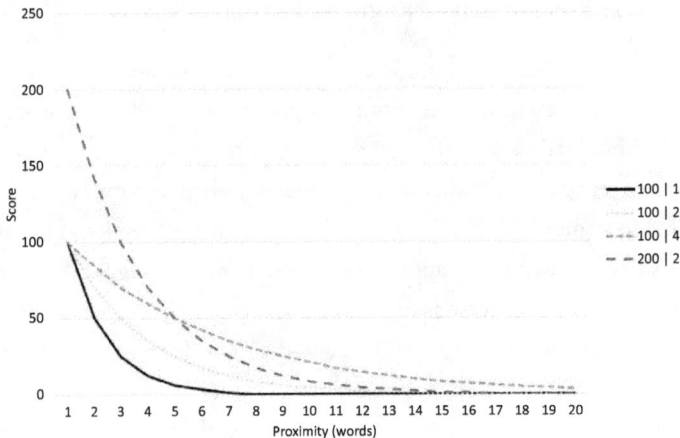

Figure 4.2 Proximity score as a function of proximity (separation), for four combinations of maximum proximity score and proximity half life

Table 4.3 *Proximity score values for the parameters* $S_p = 100$ *and* $P_{0.5} = 1$

Proximity (words)	Proximity Score
1	100
2	50
3	25
4	12
5	6
6	3
7	1
8	0

Table 4.3 shows the actual values of the proximity score for the case where the maximum score is 100, and the proximity half life is 1 word (i.e., "100 | 1" in Figure 4.1).

Keyword-based approaches using proximity scoring can be used to calculate a potential relevance score for mentions of a brand on a page, without needing to make any determination of the subject area of the content of the page *as a whole*. In general, this approach is applicable to an area of brand protection referred to as *'issue monitoring'*, where content relating to a brand (or brand name) is of interest only if it relates to a particular subject area. Examples might include content pertaining to a specific sub-brand or product, a news story, or an association with a particular individual, other company, or category of content and require the use of relevance keywords relating to the subject area in question.[3] The approach can augment the use of focused search queries (see Case Study 4.1) to identify and prioritize specific types of content. An illustration of how this approach can be applied in practice, involving the use of 'high-risk' e-commerce keywords to identify websites most likely to be involved in the sale of counterfeit products, is shown in Case Study 4.2.

---

[3] https://www.iamstobbs.com/utilisation-of-relevance-keywords-ebook

Case Study 4.2: Use of Proximity Scoring With 'High-Risk' E-Commerce Keywords to Identify Potential Counterfeits[4]

Previous analysis of e-commerce content has established that there are particular product descriptors that can be considered 'high risk', due to their frequency of association with listings for products determined (via more in-depth analysis) to be counterfeit or otherwise potentially infringing (e.g., involving the use of brand names to sell own-brand lookalikes). Examples of such keywords include terms such as *dupe*, *mirror-quality*, *A-grade*, and so on.

This case study concerns the prioritization of a set of web pages featuring e-commerce content (identified through search engine queries), in terms of the likelihood of their association with the sale of infringing goods, based on the identification of references to 'high-risk' keywords in close conjunction with brand-name mentions. This focus on *standalone* e-commerce—as opposed to listings on known marketplaces—is partly so as to demonstrate an approach that is effective on general internet content (on which there is no limitation on the ways in which the product information can be presented), but is also because some marketplaces explicitly prohibit the posting of listings with branded product references (meaning many sellers will resort to the use of brand misspellings and variations). However, similar approaches can be tailored to content from other online channels.

The analysis considers the sale of luxury goods, using Gucci and Chanel as representative brand examples. The set of 'candidate' pages for analysis is obtained through search engine queries featuring the brand name combined with product-related keywords (*handbag*, *shoes*, etc.) and e-commerce keywords (including those which are particularly likely to result in 'high risk' results being returned, such as *buy*, *shop*, *cheap*, *discount*, *replica*, etc.).

---

[4] https://www.iamstobbs.com/opinion/finding-the-fakes-another-application-of-keyword-based-filtering

The searches generated a dataset of around 2,000 candidate pages (as of January 2024), of which (for proximity matching using a maximum score of 100 and a proximity 'half life' of 1 word) around 200 were found to yield nonzero potential relevance scores for each of the two brands considered (indicating the presence of 'high-risk' keywords near to the brand names and thereby possible content pertaining to the sale of infringing goods). In a 'live' brand protection service, these most highly scored pages would constitute the priority targets for further analysis and potential enforcement.

Manual inspection of the results suggests that this is indeed the case, and almost all of the non-zero-scored pages featured content that would be considered to be of potential concern (Table 4.4 and Figure 4.3, and Table 4.5 and Figure 4.4).

Table 4.4 *The web page titles of the top 12 pages in the dataset, based on potential relevance score (pertaining to the use of high-risk keywords in close conjunction to brand references), for Gucci (examples marked with an asterisk are shown in Figure 4.3)*

Web page Title	Potential Relevance Score
Replica Gucci Handbags Wallets Gucci Replica Purses ...	4652
GUCCI REPLICA HANDBAG—SomaliNet Forums	4307
Gucci Replicas Expert—Buy the Best Quality Fake Gucci*	3966
Gucci First Copy Shoes	3485
A 1:1 Quality Gucci Replicas Online Sale Store*	2829
Gucci Shoes Discount	ShopStyle UK	2515
Discount Gucci Belt	2400
Gucci Replica—RoyalPurse	2113
75% OFF Gucci Discount Code: (3 ACTIVE) Jan 2024	1912
Replica Gucci Women Shoes Collection	1829
Best Replica Gucci Accessories on Topbiz.md	1688
Gucci Handbags Discount	1686

(Continued)

(Continued)

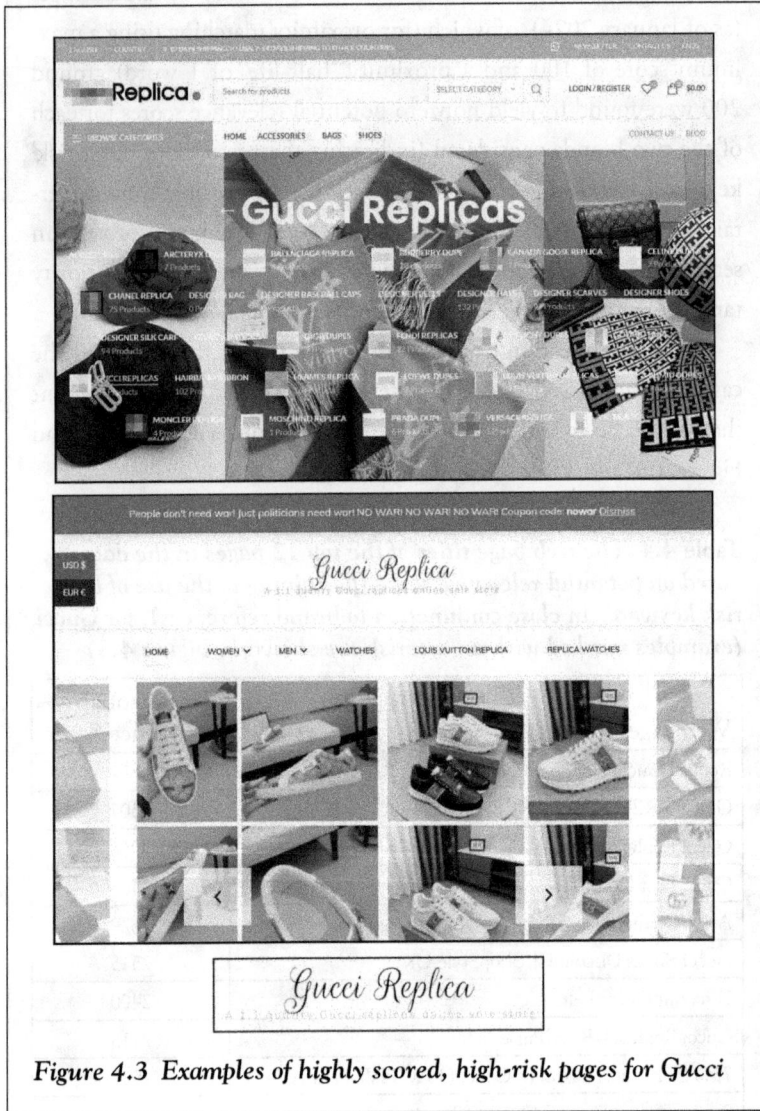

Figure 4.3 Examples of highly scored, high-risk pages for Gucci

Table 4.5 *The web page titles of the top 12 pages in the dataset,*
based on potential relevance score (pertaining to the use of high-
risk keywords in close conjunction to brand references), for Chanel
(examples marked with an asterisk are shown in Figure 4.4)

Web page Title	Potential Relevance Score
Best 25+ Deals for Copy Chanel Bags	4092
Best 25+ Deals for Copies of Chanel Bags	3631
Chanel Double Flap Medium Replica Bag Review (Caviar ...	2055
Top Chanel replicas—Affordable Luxury Inspired Handbags*	2038
How to Pick Chanel Replica Jewelry for Love	1956
Replica Chanel Classic Flap Bag Full Review	1483
Chanel Replica Jewelry	1450
Best 25+ Deals for Copy Chanel Bags—Poshmark	1399
Replica Chanel Sandals	1375
Authentic vs. Replica Chanel Flap Bag: A Detailed Comparison	1177
Wholesale and retail best Chanel Jewelry Replica*	1173
Best Chanel Replica Bag—Full Review	1104

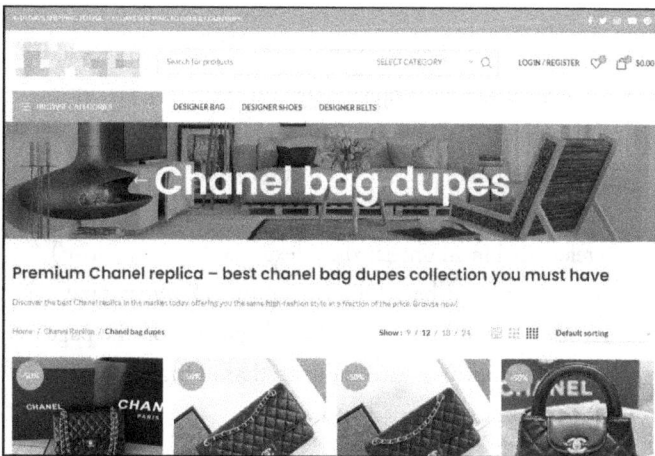

Figure 4.4 *Examples of highly scored, high-risk pages for Chanel*

(Continued)

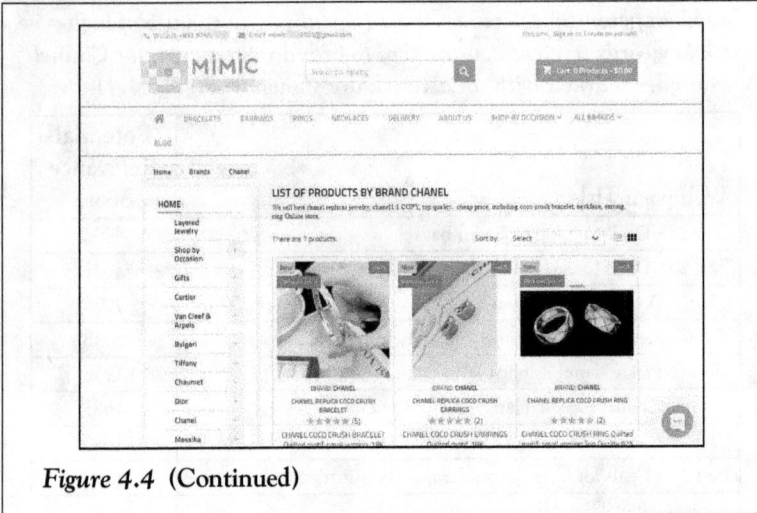

Figure 4.4 (Continued)

Key Points

The key points from this chapter are as follows:

- Keyword-based filtering can make use of relevance keywords (*inclusional* filtering, implying that the content is relevant to the subject area of interest) or nonrelevance keywords (*exclusional* filtering, implying that the content is not of interest, such as may be identified in cases where a brand name is referenced in an unrelated context—i.e., a 'false positive').
- Simple keyword-based filtering approaches may take account only of mentions of the keywords on the page (using an approach analogous to that of brand content scoring, discussed in Chapter 3).
- More sophisticated analysis methods take account of the proximity of keywords to the brand name under consideration (and can involve the assignment of scores which are weighted based on the proximity on the page of the brand name and keyword to each other). This approach can be applied to the area of *issue monitoring*, for cases where content is of interest only if it relates to a particular subject area (to which the keywords pertain).

CHAPTER 5

Prioritization Criteria for Specific Types of Content

Overview

This chapter will cover:

- Criteria that can be used for prioritizing (i.e., quantifying the potential level of threat posed by) web content, based on general characteristics of the findings in question.
- General features of domain names that can provide insight into potential risk, even in cases where no associated live website is present.
- Features of e-commerce marketplace listings that may be associated with higher-threat content, including price point and quantity information, which can be used as the basis of analyses used to benchmark marketplaces against each other (and thereby identify focuses for priority monitoring).

5.1 Introduction

As noted previously (Chapter 3), the ability to rank results according to the level of threat they pose (based on, e.g., the extent to which a web page relates to a brand of interest) is a key component of many brand protection services. This allows the most significant targets to be prioritized for initial action and builds efficiency in the analysis process. Chapter 4 discussed how a more detailed, keyword-based analysis of website page content can also be a key component of this prioritization process.

For certain other general internet content types, there are also general characteristics that can be used as a basis for result prioritization. The specific cases of domains, and features of e-commerce marketplace listings, are discussed in this section.

5.2 Domains

5.2.1 Overview

Domains constitute a special area of analysis, as there are a range of features of the domain *itself*—in many cases, even in the absence of any associated live website[1,*]—which can provide insights into the inherent level of potential risk posed by the domain and by any website content that may subsequently be added. Some of these characteristics are outlined below.

- **Domain name characteristics**—relevant features include the structure of the second-level domain (SLD) name—that is, the part of the domain name to the left of the dot—considering factors such as the inclusion of a **brand name or variant**; the **TLD** or domain extension; and the **domain name entropy**. These are discussed in detail in Section 5.2.2.
- **Registrant characteristics**—where contact information is available in the whois (ownership) record for a domain (as is often *not* the case following the introduction of GDPR and other similar privacy-driven legislations), certain features may be indicative of intentions of nonlegitimate use. These might include:
  - o **The host domain of the registrant email address**, with the use of services such as webmail providers (gmail.com,

---

[1] These ideas are also relevant to the concept of the *passive holding doctrine*, which is a principle in the UDRP dispute process asserting that a domain name registrant can be acting in bad faith even if the domain is not being actively used. The doctrine was initially set forth in the 2000 UDRP decision from the *Telstra v. Nuclear Marshmallows* case regarding the domain *telstra.org*; see https://giga.law/blog/2020/11/4/udrp-case-study-telstra-v-nuclear-marshmallows-passive-holding-doctrine

yahoo.com, qq.com, 163.com, etc.) often an indicator of nonlegitimacy and/or a desire for anonymity (as opposed to the more usual use of corporate domains for official sites).

o **Registrant country**, which may be an indicator of risk if associated with a 'high-risk' region (where, e.g., there are high rates of infringement and/or enforcement is notoriously difficult, such as Russia or China).

o The explicit use of a **privacy-protection service** to anonymize or redact the contact details; while this is not an uncommon practice, it is often more unusual for official websites.

o Indicators of nonlegitimacy associated with **registrant telephone numbers**, such as categorization as a premium-rate number, a record that the number is unassigned or has recently been ported to an alternative provider, or is making use of a call-forwarding service (as would be available from an authoritative number information provider).[†]

• **Registrar characteristics**—some registrars (particularly lower-cost *retail-grade* registrars, as opposed to the *enterprise-class* providers more frequently used by official corporations) are more popular with infringers and are accordingly more often associated with infringing domains,[2] and their association with domain registration can be an indicator of the potential level of risk. Brand protection service providers will often have information on the average level of compliance (to takedown requests) of individual registrars, based on previous enforcement experience.

• **Hosting provider (ISP, or internet service provider) characteristics**—similarly, website hosting providers may be associated with differing levels of potential risk, depending on their levels of compliance or other relevant factors, such as having server locations in 'high-risk' geographical regions. Some

---

providers actually promote their noncompliance to takedown requests as an explicit benefit, in some cases making use of factors such as 'offshore' servers and/or multiple domain address records (A records) (to provide redundancy in hosting and thereby increase website up-time), with the most extreme examples billing themselves as *'bulletproof'* hosts.[3]

- **MX records**—as discussed in Section 1.3, the presence of an MX record implies that a domain has been configured to be able to send and receive emails, and could therefore potentially be associated with (say) phishing activity.
- **Secure Sockets Layer (SSL) certificate provider**— An SSL certificate is a feature associated with a website, which authenticates its identity and enables an encrypted connection between a web server and browser (reflected in the use of *https* in the URL). However, in many cases, the owner of an infringing website will purchase a certificate from a budget or free provider, which may not carry out appropriate legitimacy checks, as a means of adding credibility to the site (cf. a 2021 study by APWG, finding that over 80 percent of phishing sites had active SSL certificates).[4] Accordingly, prioritization of websites by the level of trust of the provider of the SSL certificate (if present) can be a key feature.
- **Web traffic**—for live sites, measures of the amount of traffic (i.e., number of visitors) received by a website are available through a number of online tools and services (such as Similarweb and Comscore) and can provide a useful input into prioritization metrics, working on the principle that a more popular website is accessed by a greater number of potential customers/internet users, and thereby presents a greater potential risk.

In addition, other clear indicators of risk, such as previous reports of abuse associated with the domain (as in public databases such as those

---

[3] https://hostings.info/hostings/rating/bulletproof-hosting
[4] https://docs.apwg.org/reports/apwg_trends_report_q2_2021.pdf

provided by Lumen[5] and WIPO), website hosting on a blacklisted IP address, or the use of wildcard DNS (allowing the use of any arbitrary subdomain name to constitute a valid, resolving URL), may also be significant.

It is possible to construct algorithms taking account of some or all of the aforementioned characteristics to generate a metric (or score) quantifying the overall level of potential threat posed by a domain. In general, the individual components may also be given appropriate relative weightings, depending on their importance and/or their reliability as an indicator of potential risk. For example, the fact that a domain is hosted on an IP address shared by a large number of other sites determined to be high threat may be a stronger indicator of risk than, a case where a smaller proportion of the cohosted sites are high threat, or an instance where high-threat sites are hosted on a *similar* (but nonidentical) IP address.

5.2.2 Specific Domain Name Characteristics

5.2.2.1 Presence of a Brand Name or Variant

Inclusion of a brand name in a third-party domain registration is a very common type of infringement and can be utilized by bad actors in a variety of ways, including brand impersonation, claim of affiliation, and misdirection of users. Accordingly, where a reference to a brand name is identified in a third-party domain, this is a clear indicator that the registration is of interest and may be infringing (sometimes described as an instance of *cybersquatting*, in cases where a protected mark is being abused).

The context in which a brand name is referenced can also be relevant when considering the potential level of risk—where the SLD name is an identical match to that of the brand owner's official website (i.e., a 'cousin' domain), the domain has the highest potential for deceptive use and/or misdirection, and may be of greatest concern. Similar comments are true of domains featuring common misspellings (e.g., 'goolge' for 'google') or visually similar character replacements, such as the use of non-Latin or accented characters (e.g., 'góogle' for 'google') (see Case Studies 7.1 and 9.1).

---

[5] https://lumendatabase.org/

Following on from this point, domain names where the SLD consists of the brand name with only a *small number* of additional characters (such as (say) *'wwwgoogle'* or *'google24'*) may be of more concern than those featuring longer additional strings (and which are less likely, in general, to be confused with official sites, and more likely to constitute other types of affiliation claim), *unless* the additional strings feature high-risk keywords, such as those commonly associated with common scam types (*login, verify, jobs,* etc.) or relevant industry areas.

5.2.2.2 TLD

Certain TLDs, or domain name extensions, are associated with much greater frequencies of infringing websites (covering areas such as phishing sites, association with spam emails, and distribution of malicious content) than others. There are a number of reasons why this may be the case, including factors such as the cost of domain registrations and the associated security policies of the providers, and even the degree of wealth of the country with which a ccTLD is associated (which can affect the level of technical expertise of ISPs, and therefore the likelihood of website compromise).[6]

Accordingly, some TLDs are much more popular with infringers, and domains registered on these TLDs can, in general, therefore be assigned higher potential risk scores when prioritizing results. Many new-gTLDs are disproportionately associated with infringements, as are many ccTLDs in regions such as Africa, Asia, and the Caribbean (Table 5.1).

5.2.2.3 Domain Name (SLD) Entropy

The concept of domain name (SLD) entropy (*Shannon entropy*) is a mathematical construct for quantifying the amount of information stored in a string of characters (in this case, a domain SLD name)—or, equivalently, the smallest number of bits (binary digits) needed to optimally encode the string. Broadly, this means that domain names that are short and/ or have large numbers of repeated characters will have low entropy, and

---

[6] https://circleid.com/posts/20230112-the-highest-threat-tlds-part-1

Table 5.1 The 30 highest-risk TLDs, from a study[7] combining data relating to phishing, spam, and malware activity

TLD [country/type]	Normalized threat score	TLD [country/type] (cont.)	Normalized threat score (cont.)
.ci [Ivory Coast]	1.000	.dev [new-gTLD]	0.222
.zw [Zimbabwe]	1.000	.quest [new-gTLD]	0.209
.sx [Sint Maarten]	0.945	.top [new-gTLD]	0.196
.mw [Malawi]	0.862	.page [new-gTLD]	0.195
.am [Armenia]	0.608	.gq [Eq. Guinea]	0.192
.date [new-gTLD]	0.506	.cf [Cent. Afr. Rep.]	0.168
.cd [Dem. Rep. Congo]	0.391	.ga [Gabon]	0.164
.ke [Kenya]	0.381	.ml [Mali]	0.157
.app [new-gTLD]	0.377	.buzz [new-gTLD]	0.149
.bid [new-gTLD]	0.361	.cyou [new-gTLD]	0.141
.ly [Libya]	0.356	.cn [China]	0.130
.bd [Bangladesh]	0.351	.monster [new-gTLD]	0.106
.surf [new-gTLD]	0.325	.bar [new-gTLD]	0.104
.sbs [new-gTLD]	0.250	.host [new-gTLD]	0.101
.pw [Palau]	0.240	.io [Brit. Ind. Oc. Terr.]	0.085

domain names that are longer and/or contain large numbers of distinct characters will have high entropy. The mathematical definition, and a discussion of how it can be applied in practice, is shown in Box 5.1.

Box 5.1 Technical Definition—Domain Name (SLD) Entropy

Mathematically, Shannon entropy (**H**) is defined[‡] as:

$$H = - \sum_i [\, p_i \times \log_2(p_i) \,]$$

where p_i is the proportion of the string made of the ith character, with the summation is carried out over the pool of possible characters.

(Continued)

7 https://circleid.com/posts/20230117-the-highest-threat-tlds-part-2

(Continued)

As an example, the following table can be used to calculate the Shannon entropy of the string *google* (i.e., the SLD of google.com):

Character	No. of Instances	Proportion of String
g	2	2/6
o	2	2/6
l	1	1/6
e	1	1/6
Total (i.e., length of string)	6	

$\therefore H = -\{ [\frac{2}{6} \times \log_2(\frac{2}{6})] + [\frac{2}{6} \times \log_2(\frac{2}{6})] + [\frac{1}{6} \times \log_2(\frac{1}{6})] + [\frac{1}{6} \times \log_2(\frac{1}{6})] \}$

$= 1.918$

Note that this definition implies a special case for SLDs consisting just of a single repeated character, where the calculated entropy will be zero, regardless of the length of the SLD name (mathematically, the string contains no information).

The main application of this concept in domain name analysis relates to the fact that large coordinated infringement or attack campaigns (such as those utilizing domains for spamming activity, malware distribution, or botnet creation) will often make use of bulk registrations of domain whose names are long, nonsensical strings generated using automated algorithms.[8,9]

Accordingly, scam domains of this type often have high SLD entropy values and, furthermore, domains generated using a particular algorithm may have similar or identical entropy values, which can serve as a basis for *clustering* together related domains, for bulk takedown actions (Chapter 6).[10]

The converse is also true to some extent; legitimate domains may (in general) be more likely to have lower entropy values, particularly

---

[8] https://interisle.net/sub/CriminalDomainAbuse.pdf

[9] https://www.splunk.com/en_us/blog/security/random-words-on-entropy-and-dns.html

[10] https://www.linkedin.com/pulse/investigating-use-domain-name-entropy-clustering-results-barnett/

where there is a desire for businesses to utilize strongly branded, short, memorable web addresses—as can be seen in many of the globally most popular websites.[11]

These assertions are borne out by previous research; an analysis outlined in a blog posting by Tiberium,[12] for example, states that the use of an entropy threshold of >3.1 (as an indicator of potential concern) correctly categorizes 80 percent of malicious domains classified by the National Cyber Security Center, and incorrectly classifies only 8 percent of the top 1,000 most popular (legitimate) domains overall.

Case Study 5.1: Investigating the Link Between TLD Threat Level and Mean SLD Entropy

As discussed in Section 5.2.2.2, different TLDs have varying levels of frequencies of association with infringing domains (i.e., popularity with infringers), and thereby present differing levels of indication of potential domain risk. It is therefore informative to analyze whether the independently estimated level of threat for each TLD shows any correlation with the mean SLD entropy of the set of domains registered across that extension (as might be expected if the majority of the malicious domains had long, pseudo-random names generated using automated algorithms).

.zip domains

As an initial example of a related study,[13] it is instructive to consider domains on the .zip domain extension, a new-gTLD that entered its

(Continued)

---

[11] https://circleid.com/posts/20230703-an-overview-of-the-concept-and-use-of-domain-name-entropy

[12] https://www.tiberium.io/blog/chapter-2-classifying-domains-through-string-entropy/

[13] https://www.iamstobbs.com/opinion/un-.zip-ping-and-un-.box-ing-the-risks-associated-with-new-tlds

(Continued)

General Availability phase (in which the option to register domains is open to all) in May 2023.

Even around the time of launch, there were concerns that the extension may be associated with potential security threats, due to the potential for confusion with the filename suffix commonly used for compressed or archived data files (*zip files*), and the risk that this confusion may be exploited by bad actors to misdirect internet users to their own content, collect sensitive information, distribute malware, and/or create brand infringements. Similar comments also applied to other extensions launched around the same time, such as .mov and .box (presenting the potential for confusion with hosting and file-sharing services). Within two months of launch, there were around 30,000 .zip domains registered, including significant numbers with names featuring high-risk terms and keywords. Multiple instances of domain names targeting trusted brands were identified, in addition to several examples of live websites downloading potentially malicious content.

Among the wider .zip dataset, large numbers of long, apparently random domain names had also been registered by July 2023, consistent with patterns of those seen previously for automated registrations intended for malicious use, and another indication that the TLD was proving popular with bad actors.

It is possible to use the concept of domain name entropy to demonstrate on a quantitative basis that the .zip TLD was (as of the time of analysis) indeed disproportionately highly populated with long, pseudo-random (i.e., high entropy) domains, compared with the general domain population. A visualization of this analysis is shown in Figure 5.1, showing a peak of .zip domains with much higher entropy values than is present in a sample of all registered domain names (across all extensions) on a particular day.

Overall, the .zip domains had a mean entropy of 3.39, compared with 2.86 for the domains in the general dataset. As an illustration of the types of .zip registrations identified, Table 5.2 shows the top 12 domains with the highest entropy values.

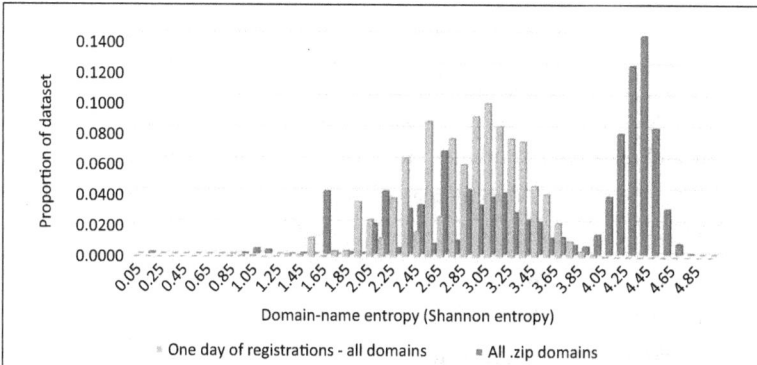

Figure 5.1 Distribution of domain name entropy values for the dataset of .zip domains, compared with a general set of all domain registrations from a specific single day

Table 5.2 Top 12 .zip domains by entropy values

Domain Name	Entropy Value
g0kfctpdb18t7vkidqj2me5ls9rjo46g.zip	4.6875
r5s0mo4tl315achnpvrkie76j84unba2.zip	4.6875
abcdefghijklmnopqrstuvwxy.zip	4.6439
98lgdq7c064nmbs1olvuejsnvhbt82ri.zip	4.6250
cph1ukfm2n1bvd8jsaqetc3o47a7lfq6.zip	4.6250
cr9qpcoiaklt1f53m6bj0u07r3eud2k4.zip	4.6250
g4umroti85bj0vfes01d3oqau2n74fpj.zip	4.6250
hj23qhtvgcsd4pqcs765r8meuf014dba.zip	4.6250
ke6h76jnpefh2s2aivau98mc453ogtb7.zip	4.6250
l5eujm8vksnetqd1714fm2o3a3hgrpkd.zip	4.6250
mlf7v0nmbhia9rgil68jsp15qk2s0ech.zip	4.6250
piuvk9qg4indoljemab245fks3cn075b.zip	4.6250

Comparing TLD Mean Domain Entropy Across the Set of gTLDs

The next stage of analysis[14] considers the full set of publicly available gTLD and new-gTLD zone files published by ICANN,[15] from which

(Continued)

---

[14] https://www.iamstobbs.com/opinion/the-randomest-domain-names-entropy-as-an-indicator-of-tld-threat-level

[15] https://czds.icann.org/home

(Continued)

datasets for around 1,050 domain name extensions were obtained (as of August 2023). For each TLD (excluding those containing fewer than 100 registered domains), the mean SLD entropy of all domains on that extension can be calculated, with the extensions featuring the highest-entropy domains shown in Table 5.3.

Figure 5.2 shows the relationship between the mean entropy of the domains within each TLD, and the independent estimate of TLD *risk level* (Table 5.1), for all TLDs which were present across both studies.

Table 5.3 Top ten TLDs with greatest mean domain name entropy (N = no. of domains in dataset)

TLD	Mean Entropy	N
.bayern	3.5788	60,318
.crs	3.5561	1,144
.man	3.5482	361
.nrw	3.5431	36,313
ابوظبي. (.xn--mgbca7dzdo) (Arabic for *Abu Dhabi*)	3.5334	117
.gov	3.5249	19,542
.goog	3.4705	543
.med	3.4619	69,735
.page	3.4618	102,978
.eus	3.4448	27,950

Although there is no strong correlation between the two data-sets (correlation coefficient = +0.07), there is a suggestion that the highest-entropy TLDs (those with a mean entropy value greater than 3.2) do tend to sit at the higher end of the risk spectrum (with threat scores above approximately 0.2). This is at least suggestive of some self-consistency in the assertion that higher-entropy domain names (and the TLDs with which they are more frequently associated) tend to be more likely to be linked to a range of classes of fraudulent and malicious activity.

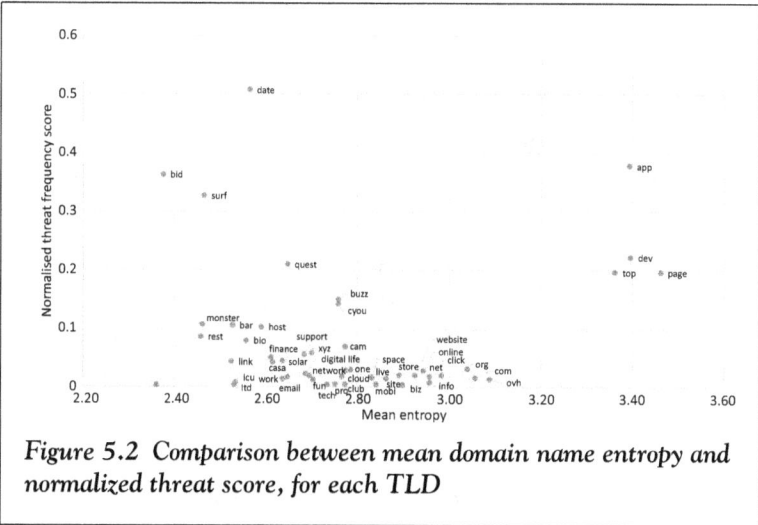

Figure 5.2 *Comparison between mean domain name entropy and normalized threat score, for each TLD*

5.3 E-Commerce Marketplaces

When considering listings of branded products on e-commerce marketplaces, there are a number of factors determining which listings pose the greatest level of potential threat to the brand owner. In part, this depends on the type of infringement that may be present, with some of the most common categories including the sale of counterfeit goods, unauthorized use of copyrighted imagery, breaches of patents or design rights, and other kinds of trademark infringement (such as the use of a brand name in a listing for a third-party or generic product—i.e., misdirection or brand 'seeding'; see Section 1.2). Additionally, there are other types of listings of concern, such as parallel or grey-market imports (i.e., where the goods on offer are legitimate, but are being sold 'out-of-region' for which the sales are authorized). In this latter case, many marketplaces will not accept this issue as legitimate grounds for a takedown, and it may instead be necessary for the brand owner to address the matter via tighter controls in their supply or distribution chains or partner networks.

In general, the type of infringement will determine the specific characteristics that will serve as the most appropriate basis for prioritization of the listing(s) in question. However, frequent factors such as the **price point** (e.g. goods being sold significantly below the official recommended retail price (RRP) for the official item—though care must be taken to separate infringing goods from second-hand sales of legitimate items) and **quantity** (either large volumes being sold in a single listing or high volumes of sale across multiple listings by the same seller—which can be established through 'clustering' analysis (Chapter 6)) can be useful indicators. Box 5.2 gives an example of how a methodology can be constructed to calculate a metric making it possible to '*benchmark*' the sales in one marketplace against those in an alternative marketplace (or for an alternative product in the same marketplace), based on the average price point (compared to the RRP) of a highly-ranked sample of the listings.

Box 5.2 Formulation Definition—Marketplace Product Price-Point Benchmarking[16]

The formulation presented in this section is constructed to be applicable to the first page of results returned on a marketplace and is appropriate in cases where relevant search terms and product-type filters can be used in order to return only listings relating to the product in question (rather than also associated accessories, etc.), and where the product is available only in a single variant (such that there is a single, well-defined official price point).

The illustration presented here considers the sales of the iPhone 14 Pro (RRP $999) and compares the findings against those for the Samsung Galaxy S23 Ultra (RRP = $1199.99)—both relatively new, high-desirability products of a type typically prone to counterfeits and other infringement issues—on a specific marketplace, as of March 2023.

The formulation makes use of a measure that can be referred to as **relative price**; that is, the listing item price as a proportion of RRP.

For illustration, Table 5.4 shows key features of the top five listings for iPhone 14 Pro on the marketplace in question (as of the date of analysis).

---

[16] https://www.linkedin.com/pulse/developing-methodology-benchmarking-marketplace-brand-david-barnett/

It is worth noting that many of the listings identified in this specific case are not likely to constitute *counterfeits* as such, and instead comprise a variety of other trademark infringements, specifically the fourth and fifth examples listed earlier, in which the *14 Pro* name is referenced in conjunction with a product for which third-party brand names are explicitly cited. Some of the listings also appear unrelated to the iPhone 14 Pro altogether, having apparently been

Table 5.4 *Details of top five listings returned in response to a search for iPhone 14 Pro, with the product filter set to mobile phones*

Listing Title	Price Per Item ($) (Min. Listed)	Min. Order Quantity	Quantity (Max. Listed)	Brand Name as Stated	Relative Price
Wholesale mobile phone Original Smart 5G Mobile Cell Phones for iPhone 11 128GB	50.00	2	300	For Apple	0.050
New Arrival Original Brand Phone 11pro max 12 mini Waterproof Face Recognition 256gb 512gb 1TB Game Mobile Phone for iPhone 13	399.00	2	50	Original	0.399
Smartphone mobile iPhone 11ProMax 256gb 5g usa spec original no scratches body low price for wholesale 6.5inch screen game phone	497.00	1	1	Other	0.497
Hot Selling PHONE 14 PRO MAX 12GB+ 512GB 6.7 Inch full Display Android 10.0 Mobile Phone I13 PRO MAX Cell Phone Smartphone	27.72	1	99,999	Android	0.028
Low price wholesale smartphone 14 Pro Max 8GB+256GB 7.3in 8core 4G LET global Edition smartphone	72.00	1	1,000	W&O	0.072

(*Continued*)

(Continued)

presented by the marketplace in response to only a *subset* of the terms
included in the full search query. In practice, it will generally be necessary to separate out these listing types when carrying out a rigorous
benchmarking analysis.

Figure 5.3 shows the distribution of relative price (per item)
across all listings from the first page of results (48 in total). Note that,
for simplicity, the data are categorized into 'bins' of equal width.

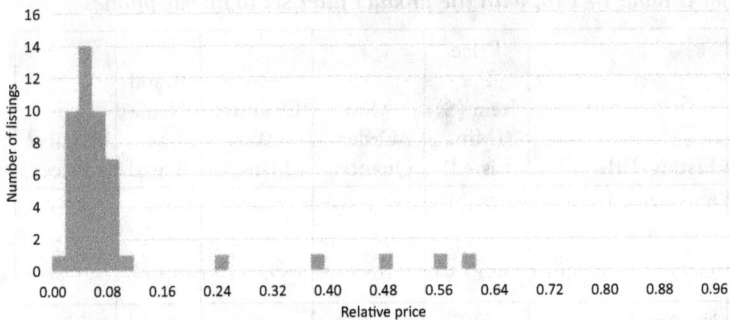

**Figure 5.3 Distribution of relative price per item, for the full set of
48 listings (iPhone 14 Pro)**

However, it is instead preferable to express the number of listings in each bin as a proportion of the total number of listings considered; this removes any reliance on absolute numbers, making it
more straightforward to compare data across marketplaces (where
the number of results returned by page may differ) and allowing
for the exclusion of results from the analysis (e.g., if categorizing
by infringement type) without needing to 'renormalize' the data.
Accordingly, the distribution accordingly becomes as shown in Figure 5.4, in which nonrelevant/noninfringing listings have also been
removed from the analysis.

The next stage is to construct a single metric providing a measure
of the distribution of relative price points across the set of listings.
The objective is for this number to represent the proportion of the

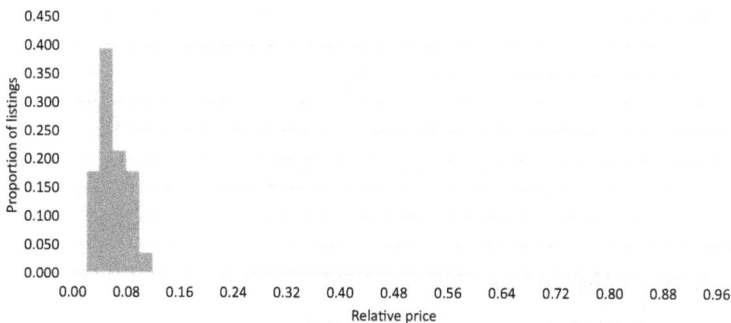

Figure 5.4 Normalized distribution of relative price per item, for the relevant/infringing listings only (iPhone 14 Pro)

'area under the graph' at the low-price-point end of the normalized relative price distribution chart.

This can be achieved by summing up the heights of the individual columns, but weighting more heavily (i.e., applying a larger multiplying factor to) the columns at the low-price end. The weightings can be selected in a number of different ways; one possible methodology is to calculate a weighting that is inversely proportional to the relative price value at the mid-point of the bin in question, such that, for example, the height of the column for the bin associated with a price-point range of 0.00 to 0.02—that is. with a mid-point of 0.01—is weighted by a factor of (1/0.01), or 100.

It is thereby possible to calculate a *price-point metric*, **P**, for which the value increases for distributions where there are a greater proportion of listings at lower price points. Formally (as defined):

$$\mathbf{P} = \sum_i [(1 / \mathbf{m}_i) \times \boldsymbol{\ell}_i]$$

where $\mathbf{m}_i$ is the relative price at the mid-point of the ith bin; $\boldsymbol{\ell}_i$ is the proportion of listings in the ith bin.

In the case where all listings have a relative price of 1.00 (as may be the case for a series of legitimate product listings through an

(Continued)

(Continued)

official channel), the value of **P** will be 1 (approximately—depending on exactly where the bin boundaries are set).

Higher values of **P** will indicate a greater proportion of listings at lower price points (and thereby potentially a greater proportion of infringements). For the distribution shown in Figure 5.4, **P** = 19.180.

For comparison, the distribution for Samsung Galaxy S23 Ultra (relevant) listings on the same marketplace is shown in Figure 5.5. The value of **P**, in this case, is 21.643, consistent with the visually larger skew of the distribution toward the lowest price-point end of the scale, compared to that for the iPhone listings.

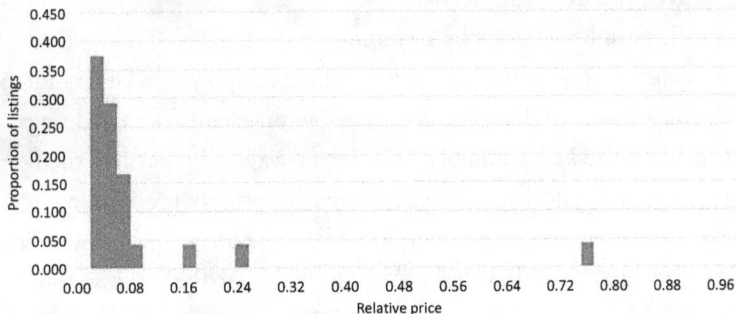

Figure 5.5 *Normalized distribution of relative price per item, for the relevant/infringing listings only (Samsung Galaxy S23 Ultra)*

5.4 Other Areas

For other types of internet content, it may be appropriate to use the same (where available and appropriate), or analogous, web page characteristics as a basis for prioritizing results. In some instances, this may involve the use of data *proxies* (i.e., the use of a distinct, but analogous, metric)—for example, on social media, website traffic (which gives information on the popularity of the social media platform *as a whole*) will not be an appropriate metric to use, but more meaningful insights may be gained by considering (say) the numbers of '*likes*' for a posting, or the number of followers for a profile. Consideration of data proxies is also discussed in Section 11.2.4, in the context of brand protection return on investment calculations. Furthermore, other general web page characteristics, such as the inclusion of a brand logo or branded imagery, can affect the overall potential relevance or level of concern of a piece of content.

In addition, the overall degree of similarity of an identified web page to other examples which have previously been established as being infringing (or otherwise of concern) can be a useful basis for prioritization. This type of approach can be particularly applicable in cases where infringers make use of specific web page templates to construct their sites and/or reuse content from previous cases.

Key Points

The key points from this chapter are as follows:

- Criteria used for prioritizing (or quantifying potential threat level of) findings from brand monitoring can include consideration of a range of characteristics, some of which can be applied even in cases where no live site content is present.
- For domain names, 'high-risk' factors may include registrant, registrar, or hosting provider characteristics (including redacted contact details, use of webmail email addresses, locations in high-threat geographical regions, and use of 'retail-grade' registrars or '*bulletproof*' hosting providers), use of brand name variants (such as typos or character replacements, hosting on high-threat TLDs, high domain name entropy (as may be associated with high-volume, automated registrations), presence of MX records (implying that the domain has been configured to be able to send and receive emails), use of SSL

(Continued)

(Continued)

certificates from 'low-trust' providers, and high levels of web traffic.

- For listings on e-commerce marketplaces, low price point and high item quantity might typically be indicators that the items for sale may be nonlegitimate. Analysis of these parameters can be used as a basis for *benchmarking* marketplaces against each other (in terms of the level of concern, for any given brand or product) as a means of identifying platforms for high-priority monitoring and enforcement.

CHAPTER 6

Result Clustering

Overview

This chapter will cover:

- Techniques for *'clustering'* results—that is, establishing connections between associated findings, on the basis of shared characteristics, with a view to identifying high-priority targets for enforcement and allowing bulk takedowns.

'Clustering' in brand monitoring is the process of establishing connections between findings (such as domain names or websites, social media accounts, etc.), on the basis of shared characteristics, with the aim of determining that they are linked to each other, and potentially associated with a specific individual or entity. In general, this analysis can be carried out manually (using open-source investigation (*OSINT*) techniques, and/or via the use of automated tools to extract relevant pieces of information from online content. The characteristics on which clustering are based can comprise a variety of types, from highly distinctive pieces of information (such as email addresses and telephone numbers), which are most diagnostic of a definitive connection, through to less distinctive details, such as generic company or personal names (which may, in general, be shared by multiple entities), similarities in features such as domain names or their structure, or shared use of particular service providers (domain registrars or hosting providers), which may provide only much more tenuous indications that the underlying entities may have an association.

There are a number of benefits to being able to cluster together associated results:

- It can identify high-volume or serial infringers, who will often be priority targets for enforcement action.
- In cases where multiple infringements can be determined to be linked (e.g., domains registered via a specific registrar), clustering provides the potential to allow the infringements to be taken down in bulk via a single notice, thereby building efficiency into the enforcement process.
- Demonstration of an infringer's involvement in multiple attacks, or targeting a range of different brands, can bring a stronger case for *bad faith* intentions, which can help to build a stronger case for enforcement.
- It can allow a fuller picture of an entity (such as the individual behind a network of connected infringements) to be constructed, as part of an OSINT investigation to determine the extent of activity, and links to 'real-world' contact details, which can form part of the basis of the research for on-the-ground actions (such as raids and seizures) or litigation.

It is worth noting that, since the introduction of the General Data Protection Regulation (GDPR) (and, specifically, the resulting lack of registrant contact information typically available in a domain name whois records),[1] efforts to cluster together related findings are in many cases much more difficult. However, the introduction of ICANN's new Registration Data Request Service (RDRS)[2] for gTLD domains, intended to allow relevant data to be more easily requested by entities with a legitimate interest (say, for the protection of intellectual property), may mediate this situation to some degree.[3]

Presented in the remainder of this section are two case studies illustrating how analysis techniques can be applied to cluster together related infringements.

---

[1] https://www.international.eco.de/topics/names-numbers/gdpr-domain-industry-playbook/

[2] https://www.icann.org/rdrs-en

[3] https://www.linkedin.com/pulse/rdrs-slight-un-darkening-domain-name-whois-landscape-david-barnett-5xuyf/

Furthermore, even in the emerging Web3 ecosystem (see Chapter 13), where content is often not explicitly associated with any 'real-world' contact details, it may still be possible to make use of unique identifiers to cluster together related findings and build links between infringers and entities. This point is discussed in more detail in Case Study 14.3.

Case Study 6.1: Domain Clustering: 1 —Chinese Gambling Sites[4]

The first illustration of domain clustering concerns the analysis of the full set of all domains registered on a particular day (in December 2022), comprising a dataset of around 205,000 domains. The analysis serves to explore whether features of the domains which are readily available through standard look-ups can be used as a basis for identifying clusters of related registrations from within this large dataset.

The case study begins by considering the top 1,000 highest-entropy domains within the dataset (which, as discussed in Section 5.2.2.3, can be a helpful indicator of potential use by high-volume infringers or scammers). These top 1,000 have entropy values of 3.823 and above, and the SLD names of majority of these examples consist of visually apparently random strings (Table 6.1).

It is also noteworthy that significant proportions of the top 1,000 also feature other indicators that are frequently associated with active and/or suspicious use, as outlined below.

- In all, 847 (84.7 percent) have active A records (i.e., are associated with a specific IP address, and potentially live website content).
- Overall, 275 (27.5 percent) have active MX records (i.e. are configured to be able to send and receive emails and may therefore be associated with phishing activity).
- In all, 777 (77.7 percent) use domain privacy services or have redacted registration, potentially demonstrating

(Continued)

---

4 https://www.linkedin.com/pulse/investigating-use-domain-name-entropy-clustering-results-barnett/

(Continued)

Table 6.1 Top ten domains in the dataset by SLD entropy value

SLD Name	TLD	SLD length (chars.)	Entropy value
abcdefghijklmnopqrstuvwxyz	.space	26	4.700
viqxacb7wo6l3hfujw3agf3stcce6een-l4kovfza3rzri4gwyxg6auid	.com	56	4.642
b4su4qo65fkefg3cpd5muxwekbn4vx6fr7i-eroavxqwco2xrqmrrwlad	.com	56	4.591
oz5winfavnvbmgdspa633wdnpmbjjrp-6crwutyt4uxgxkvytbjdmdc	.com	54	4.569
hydraclubbioknikokex7njhwuahc2l67l-fiz7z36md2jvopda7nchidshop	.com	60	4.550
q374uuwdlgtkveh2acqi6ubhic4m3bnwb-32kc2yqmxf2ilv36leujnid	.com	56	4.539
mekck2mf2uju3ssjl2woyddfrunwc-nevfql3imp4tfr3z6wmjmo4jvid	.com	56	4.497
facebook-domain-verificationyx7q3w-storn4idf9xqtzdz842q0b6x	.com	58	4.475
vh6bjre5lw9iuegs1b9fspitswrdnbtsm1emu-nvlulbo6uc0	.top	48	4.470
skjcd-98729871cnf5bnb8ewr2e-vq438vn-jy0mtg1mdcumty2n	.xyz	51	4.464

intention by the domain owners to mask their identity and could indicate nefarious intentions.

The dataset is also dominated by domains registered via retail-grade registrars, also often popular choices with infringers.

The most significant cluster within the overall dataset is a group of 125 domains with a range of shared characteristics:

- All have apparently random 15-character SLD names with identical entropy values (3.907). (Note that this value arises because all domains in the cluster have SLD names consisting of 15 *distinct* characters.)
- All are hosted on the .buzz TLD (one of the thirty highest-threat TLDs, as listed in Table 5.1).
- All are registered through the registrar Dynadot LLC and have redacted whois records.

- All 114 of the domains with active A records resolve to one of five similar IP addresses (mostly in similar netblocks).

It therefore appears highly likely that all domains within the cluster comprise part of a coordinated registration event by a single entity. Indeed, for the cases where live website content was available as of the time of analysis, all domains resolved to one of a range of similar Chinese-language gambling sites (Figure 6.1). Based on

Figure 6.1 Examples of visible web page content for domains within the cluster

(Continued)

(*Continued*)

> trends observed with similar websites previously, it is highly likely that these sites are in some way infringing, either comprising scams in their own right, set up as part of an affiliate revenue-generating scheme, or acting as 'placeholder' content for other material which may be *geolocked* or intended for subsequent upload.

Case Study 6.2: Domain Clustering: 2 —Health Scam Domains[5]

A second case study concerns a report[6] of a scam involving the use of large numbers of domain registrations to promote bogus health products such as '*keto*'-related dietary supplements, using a particular style of web page featuring spoof news articles. The campaign made use of TLDs offering relatively low-cost registrations, such as .sbs and .cloud, with one detailed analysis[7] finding the utilization of multiple domain names beginning with *keto*, followed by a string of (typically six or seven) random alphabetical characters, followed by three random digits, mostly registered between March and June 2023.

The analysis below explores whether clustering techniques can be used to identify a comprehensive set of the domains in question, from those registrations present in the .cloud zone file (as of January 2024). If so, the determination of their shared characteristics could potentially be used in the construction of an algorithm to determine new, potentially related registrations as they appear, going forward.

As of the time of analysis, over 364,000 .cloud domains were registered, of which over 3,400 had names beginning with *keto*. Only around 1 percent were found to resolve to live website content (none of which were relevant to the specific style of scam in question),

---

[5] https://www.iamstobbs.com/opinion/health-scam-websites-identifying-related-domains-using-clustering-techniques
[6] https://www.techradar.com/pro/security/scammers-are-buying-up-cheap-domain-names-to-host-sites-that-sell-dodgy-health-products
[7] https://www.netcraft.com/blog/health-product-scam-campaigns-abusing-cheap-tlds/

meaning that other domain characteristics would need to be used as a basis for the clustering.

Within the set of *keto* websites, a cluster of 1,611 domains was identified, which featured the following characteristics:

- All were between 11 and 15 characters in (SLD) length and ended with a string of three digits.
- All had SLD entropy values within a narrow range (between 2.6 and 3.9), significantly less broad than the distributions seen for the full set of *keto* domains and for the full set of .cloud domains generally (Figure 6.2).
- In all, 98.3 percent of the domains were registered in a 10-day period between 19 and 28 May 2023 (Figure 6.3).
- Overall, 99.7 percent of the domains were registered through the same registrar (a retail-grade provider previously noted as being popular with infringers) and using the same privacy-protection service provider.

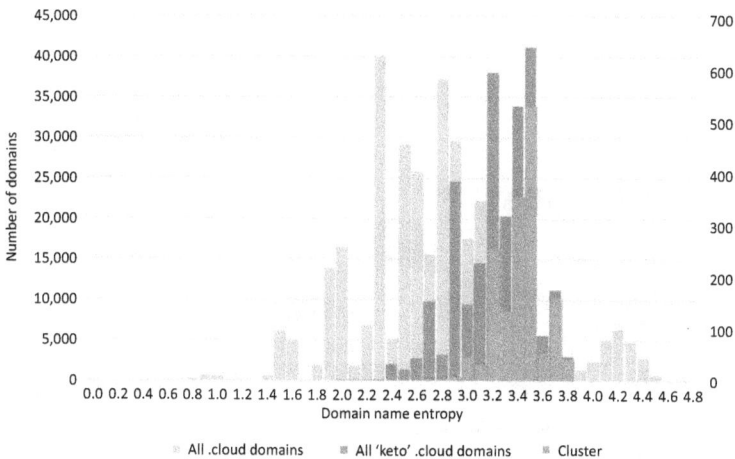

Figure 6.2 Distributions of SLD entropy values for the 1,611 domains in the cluster, compared with the set of all keto .cloud domain names (right-hand axis) and the total set of all .cloud domains (left-hand axis)

(*Continued*)

(Continued)

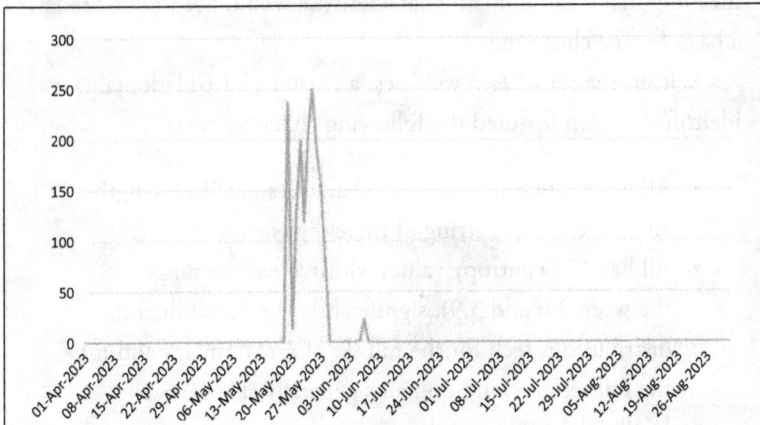

Figure 6.3 Daily numbers of registrations for the domains in the cluster

Figure 6.4 Cached screenshot of content from an example of one of the sites in the cluster (ketoekezat333.cloud) (source: DomainTools)[8]

---

[8] https://research.domaintools.com/research/screenshot-history/ketoekezat333.cloud/#1

For certain examples of domains within the cluster for which historical (cached) copies of the former website content are available, it is possible to verify that these sites were indeed previously associated with the 'fake news' health scams (Figure 6.4).

The large number of domains associated with this campaign also provides a suggestion that the scam sites are likely to have been short-lived (borne out by the fact that none of the domains in the cluster currently resolve to live sites), presumably with the intention of generating revenue quickly and then being deactivated before they could be found and shut down through enforcement actions.

Key Points

The key points from this chapter are as follows:

- Clustering, or the identification of links between findings, can be based on a number of characteristics, including contact details, company or personal names, similarities in website or URL structure, or use of associated service providers. In general, details that are more distinctive or unusual provide the basis for stronger or more definitive connections.
- The ability to group together associated infringements has a number of benefits, including the identification of serial infringers for priority enforcement, building stronger cases for bad-faith activity, providing options for efficient bulk takedowns, and providing a fuller picture of the activity associated with a particular entity.

PART 3

Gaining Insights in Other Areas

CHAPTER 7

Creation of Deceptive URLs

Overview

This chapter will cover:

- Techniques utilized in the construction of infringing websites by bad actors, involving the use of deceptive URLs that appear confusingly similar to those of official branded content.
- Ways in which specially registered domain names can be used to create deceptive URLs.
- Ways in which non-brand-specific domain names can be used in conjunction with branded subdomains to create deceptive URLs and other categories of subdomain infringements.
- The use of a specific class of subdomain/domain name combinations (i.e., hostnames) appearing similar to the official domain name of a targeted brand.

7.1 Introduction

For bad actors looking to configure an effective scam or infringement, one of the key elements is the production of the appearance of authenticity. This often involves creating confusion between the fake content and that of the brand owner being impersonated, as part of the process of driving user traffic to the scam site. Deception can involve components such as the creation of look-alike URLs, websites, products, or all of the above. In addition, tactics where the true URL is 'masked'—such as through utilization of QR codes or URL shorteners—can also be employed in conjunction with other such techniques.

7.2 Domain Name Abuse

In many cases, attempts to create a convincing URL involve the registration of a domain name containing the name of the brand in question, or a variant such as a typo[§] or homoglyph[¶] (i.e., where one or more characters have been replaced with another appearing visibly similar) (see Case Studies 7.1 and 9.1). Depending on a range of factors, many brand protection monitoring technologies will be able to identify these sorts of registrations (to a degree; see Chapter 2) and, in some cases, trends in infringement activity can be drawn out of the data (see, e.g., Case Study 7.2).

Case Study 7.1: Domains Featuring Brand Variants[1,2]

This case study considers instances of registrations of domains where the second-level domain (SLD) is an exact or very close match to the name of any of the top ten most valuable brands in 2022 (according to the Kantar study used in Case Study 2.1), based on a one-year analysis period (August 2021 to 2022). In this context, the analysis covers exact matches (where the SLD is identical to the brand term, but with a different TLD to the official brand website—i.e., a 'cousin' domain), and homoglyph and other 'fuzzy' matches (comprising replaced, missing, additional, and transposed characters). Each of these categories therefore appears extremely similar to the brand's official domain name and raises significant potential for customer deception (particularly given the ability of the human brain to automatically 'correct' misspellings in written text[2]). Additionally, the use of brand *variants* may represent a specific attempt by the registrants to circumvent detection efforts by brand owners who may be monitoring only for exact matches to the brand string.

In total, 8,552 unique relevant domain names were identified in the dataset, of which only 72 (<1 percent) explicitly appear to have been registered by the official brand owner. The remaining analysis focuses on the 8,480 third-party domains. In total, just over 3

---

[1] https://www.cscdbs.com/en/resources-news/threatening-domains-targeting-top-brands/

[2] https://en.wikipedia.org/wiki/Transposed_letter_effect

percent of the dataset comprised internationalized domain names (IDN) homoglyph domains (considered in Case Study 9.1).

Overall, 253 of the domains were found to incorporate transposed characters. Analysis of this dataset can provide insights into common or popular typo-variants and can help to inform a domain registration policy (Section 9.5). The most common transposed variants are shown in Table 7.1.

Table 7.1 *Most common transposed brand variant SLDs identified within the dataset*

Brand Variant	No. Domains
googel	29
appel	25
goolge	23
micorsoft	17
faecbook	15
amzaon	14
mircosoft	13
amazno	13
gogole	13
amaozn	11

Tables 7.2 and 7.3 show the most commonly used character replacements, in cases where Latin (alphabetic) and non-Latin characters were used.

In many of these cases, the characters have been replaced with visually similar alternatives, to create a convincing lookalike domain name. There are instances, however—notably in the Latin alphabet character replacements—where characters have been replaced with others, which are adjacent to them on a standard QWERTY keyboard (e.g., n → m, o → i, g → b, etc.), presumably with the intention of catching misdirected traffic from browser requests containing common typing errors. It is also worth noting that some of the most frequently occurring character replacements in the dataset may relate to true third-party brand use or unrelated terms (e.g., all the observed g → m replacements in the dataset appear as the term *moogle*, which can refer to a creature in the Final Fantasy gaming series).

(*Continued*)

(Continued)

Table 7.2 Top ten most common character replacements using Latin (alphabetic) characters

Character Replacement	No. Instances
l → i	93
n → m	59
o → i	52
a → o	47
c → k	47
o → a	45
a → e	42
o → g	40
g → d	38
g → b	37

Table 7.3 Top ten most common character replacements using non-Latin characters

Character Replacement	No. Instances
o → 0	78
l → 1	24
o → õ	20
o → ó	17
o → ö	15
l → ł	15
e → 3	13
e → é	12
z → ·	10
o → o	10

Of the 8,480 unique domains in the dataset, 4,552 (54 percent) were still registered at the time of analysis, and 56 percent of these produced a live website response. Furthermore, 1,590 domains (19 percent of the dataset or 35 percent of the registered domains) were configured with active MX records, indicating possible use for their email functionality (e.g., in phishing attacks). Among the live sites, a range of classes of content of potential concern were identified, including instances of lookalike sites, potential unauthorized use of branding, third-party sites using similar branding, instances of misdirection (e.g., sites featuring third-party content in a related business area) (Figure 7.1), gambling-related or adult material. Additionally, many displayed pay-per-click links (as a means of monetizing the web traffic) or pages offering the domain name for sale (i.e., potential cybersquatting). Many displayed browser warnings indicating that threatening content is or was formerly present.

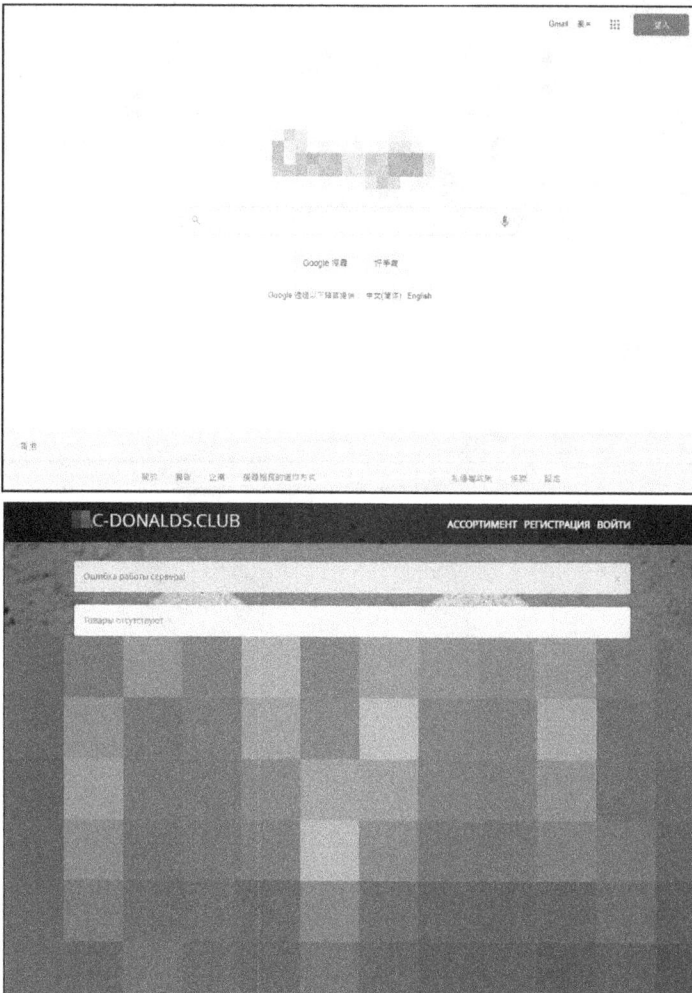

Figure 7.1 Examples of potential brand infringements within the dataset (top to bottom): lookalike site; potential phishing; potential unauthorized use of similar branding; third-party content in related business area (SLD names: googe, mc-donalds, armazon, fgoogle)

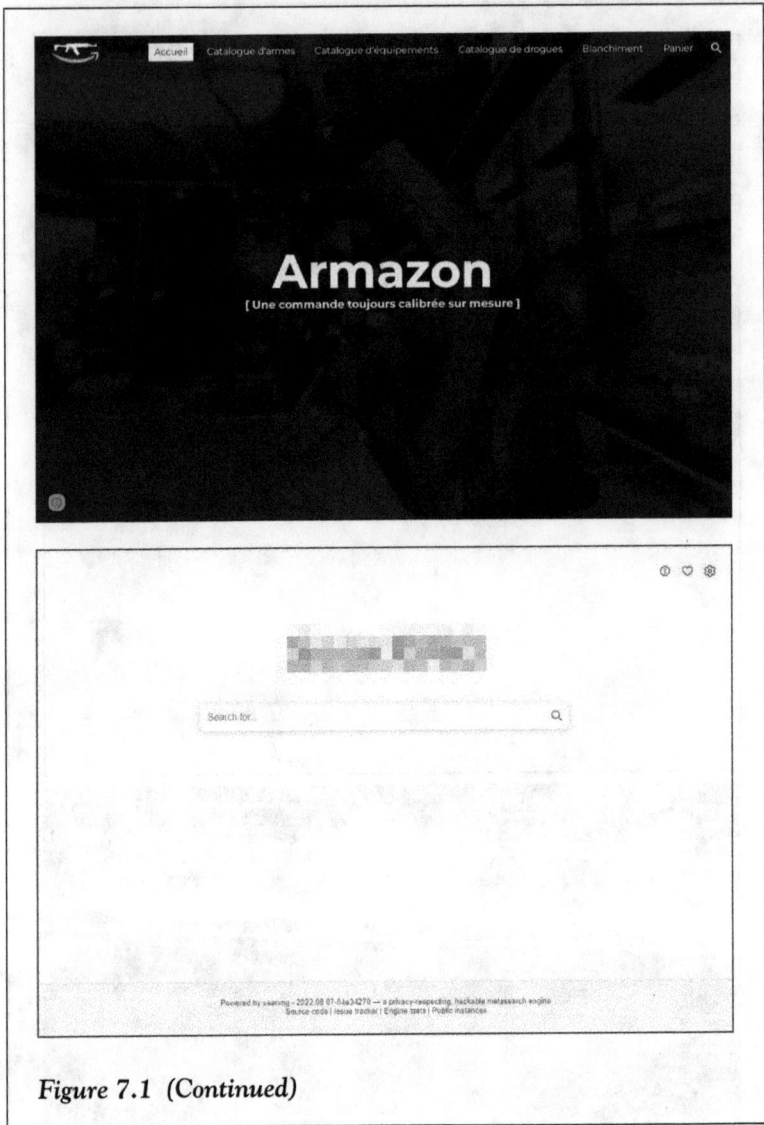

Figure 7.1 (Continued)

Case Study 7.2: Analysis of a High-Volume, Domain-Based Phishing Campaign

Across Q4 2020 and Q1 2021, a large, coordinated, coordinated phishing campaign delivered via SMS (Short Message Service, i.e., text message), using brand-specific domain names to target a FTSE-100 multibrand banking group, was identified. The domains (resolving to fake branded websites soliciting customer log-in credentials) were determined to be part of a large-scale attack by a single entity (or group of connected entities), on the basis of similarities in registration dates, keyword permutations, and URL structure, plus common use of privacy protection services. At the time of analysis, the domains resolved to a mixture of live and inactive sites, suggesting each phishing site may only have been active for a short period. The use of large volumes of short-lived sites is a common technique for circumventing the efforts of a program of takedowns to disrupt the campaign.

The campaign moved from one brand (Brand A), being targeted primarily in October and November 2020, to a second brand (Brand B), with a smaller peak in activity around February 2021. The numbers of domains used in these attacks were sufficiently large that the campaign dominated the overall pattern of the *total* set of third-party domain registrations for the brands across the period in question, manifesting as overall peaks in activity for each of the two brands, in turn (Figure 7.2).

(Continued)

(Continued)

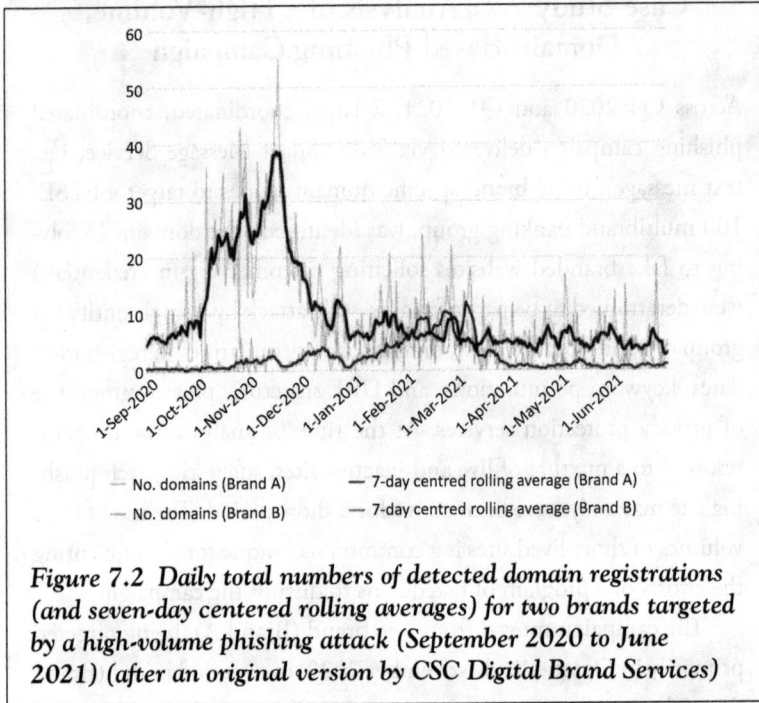

Figure 7.2 *Daily total numbers of detected domain registrations (and seven-day centered rolling averages) for two brands targeted by a high-volume phishing attack (September 2020 to June 2021) (after an original version by CSC Digital Brand Services)*

Case Study 7.3: Other Patterns in Deceptive Domain Names: 1—*www* and *http* Domains[3]

One well-established threat vector employed by bad actors is the use of domains with names beginning *www* or *http* (also encompassing examples beginning with *https*), intended to produce confusion with the appearance of a full URL. This case study focuses on registration (or drop) events for such domains, based on a monitoring period of one year (August 2021 to August 2022), during which 230,000 cases of *www* domains and 12,000 cases of *http* domains were identified.

Within the dataset, numerous SLD strings were identified multiple times (reflecting registrations of the same SLD across alternative TLDs and/or repeated registrations of the same domain name), giving insight into some of the brands most commonly targeted in this way (Tables 7.4 and 7.5).

---

[3] https://circleid.com/posts/20220913-registration-patterns-of-deceptive-domains

Table 7.4 Most frequently occurring, brand-specific 'www' SLD names

SLD String	No. Instances
www-roblox	21
www-lcloud	16
www-apple	15
wwwgoogle	13
www-avito	12
www-citizens	11
www-yandex	10
www-torproject	10
www-icloud	10
www-blablacar	10
www-bitstamp	10
www1royalbank	10

Table 7.5 Most frequently occurring, brand-specific 'http' SLD names

SLD String	No. Instances
https-skinbaron	9
https-www-ruraivla-com-lsum-main	8
httpsgoogle	7
https-csmoney	7
httpgoogle	7
http18comic	7
httpsstreamlabs	6
https-googlecom	6
https-httpsgoogle	6
httpsgoogledotcom	6
httpsgoogleplay	6
https--google	6
httpsgoogle-com	6
httpsgooglecom	6
httpsecuregoogle	6
httpsdealersvwcredit	6

(Continued)

(*Continued*)

SLD String	No. Instances
https-anydesk	6
httpqgoogle	6
httpagoogle	6
httpcredito-app-nubank	6
http2google	6

Table 7.6 *Number of registration events for 'www' and 'http' domains with names containing the names of the top ten most valuable company brands*

Brand String	No. Instances	
	www Domains	*http* Domains
apple	212	43
google	143	120
amazon	114	19
microsoft	14	6
tencent	0	0
mcdonalds	8	2
visa	58	10
facebook	38	31
alibaba	7	4
vuitton	1	0

Considering specifically the most valuable company brands in 2022 (on the assumption that these are likely to be attractive targets for infringers), the numbers of registration events are shown in Table 7.6.

Several of these also feature additional keywords indicative of intended use for phishing—for example, within the set of *apple* instances, associated terms include *login* (13 instances), *support* (47), and *activate* (17). Furthermore, 16 percent of the unique domain names were found to have active MX records.

Case Study 7.4: Other Patterns in Deceptive Domain Names: 2—Hyphenated Domain Infringements[4]

This case study considers a special subset of domains featuring 'fuzzy' matches to trusted brand names (cf. Case Study 7.1); specifically, cases where the SLD name differs only from the brand string by the addition of a hyphen. Hyphenated domain infringements are of particular concern from the point of view of their capability to generate deceptive URLs, as illustrated by the scam shown in Figure 7.3 (an anonymized mock-up of a real SMS phishing scam detected in November 2022, using the fictitious brand *FinanceBrand* (*financebrand.com*) as an illustration).

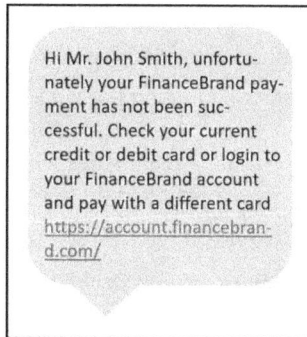

> Hi Mr. John Smith, unfortunately your FinanceBrand payment has not been successful. Check your current credit or debit card or login to your FinanceBrand account and pay with a different card https://account.financebran-d.com/

Figure 7.3 Mock-up of an SMS phishing message targeting the fictitious brand FinanceBrand (financebrand.com) utilizing a hyphenated domain infringement

The scam—which utilizes the infringing domain name *financebran-d.com* (containing a hyphen)—is effective as it takes advantage of the tendency of SMS readers to split URLs after a hyphen, thereby creating the appearance of the official domain name (*financebrand.com*), but split across a line-break with a breaking hyphen (as is seen in the other text at the start of the message).

(Continued)

---

[4] https://www.linkedin.com/pulse/hyphenated-domain-infringements-david-barnett/

(Continued)

The analysis—to determine the extent of these types of infringement—considers registration activity events for domains where the SLD is an exact match to the name of any of the top ten most valuable brands in 2022 (according to Interbrand[5]), but with the inclusion of a hyphen between any pair of adjacent characters (e.g., for Google, the following variants are considered: *googl-e, goog-le, goo-gle, go-ogle,* and *g-oogle*). The case study is based on a monitoring period covering approximately 18 months to November 2022.

On this basis, 140 distinct domain names featuring hyphenated variants of any of the top ten brands were identified, of which only 14 (10 percent) were found explicitly to be registered to the brand owner in question. In all, 11 of the 14 officially owned domains have been configured to redirect to the main brand website (in accordance with recommended practice for defensive domain registrations).

Of the 126 third-party infringing domains:

- Overall, 27 (21 percent) are configured with active MX records.
- One (no longer live) displays a browser warning indicating that dangerous content was formerly present.
- Two are configured to redirect to the corresponding official brand website (which can be a possible indicator of risk for domains under third-party ownership, as it may imply that the domain is intended to deceptively appear as if it is affiliated with the official brand owner).

The remaining sites display a range of content, including one log-in page, eight instances of third-party content, and numerous instances of domains monetized through the inclusion of pay-per-click (PPC) links or displaying pages explicitly offering the domain name for sale.

Of the 73 possible permutations of .com domains (i.e., those with the greatest potential for confusion with the primary official .com site for the respective brand in question), 30 are present in the dataset, of which only nine are registered to the brand owner, and nine are configured with active MX records (of which only one is officially owned).

---

[5] https://interbrand.com/best-global-brands-2022-download-form/

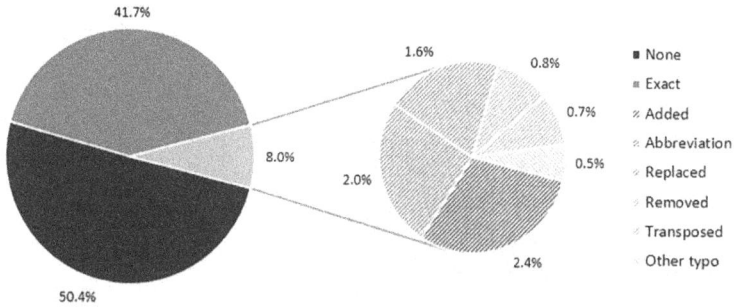

Figure 7.4 Proportion of phishing-site domain names (2021 data) featuring each type of match to the name of the brand being targeted (after an original version by CSC Digital Brand Services)

However, there are a number of other ways customer confusion can be generated (beyond the use of branded domain names). A study of phishing campaigns (based on data from 2021),[6] for example, showed that the scam sites made use of a mix of styles of phishing-site URLs, with only around half utilizing brand-specific domain names (comprising instances of exact matches and variations). Of these, brand variants—which incorporate instances of added, removed, replaced, and transposed characters—were used in around 8 percent of the cases (Figure 7.4). The other half of the cases did not utilize brand-specific domains at all, comprising a mix of cases where, in some instances, brand terms were used elsewhere in the URL (and others where the URL featured no reference to the brand at all).

The following sections present an overview of a selection of other techniques that can be used by infringers, specifically to construct URLs appearing superficially similar to those of a brand owner's official website.

7.3 Subdomain Abuse

Figure 7.5 shows an example (from 2021) of an SMS-based phishing scam targeting customers of HSBC.[7]

---

[6] https://www.cscdbs.com/blog/branded-domains-are-the-focal-point-of-many-phishing-attacks/

[7] https://www.circleid.com/posts/20210615-phishing-scams-how-to-spot-them-and-stop-them/

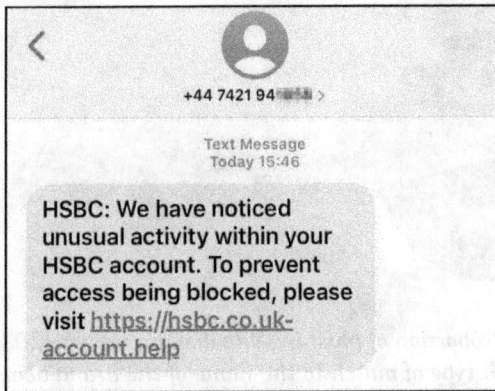

Figure 7.5 *Example of an SMS-based phishing scam targeting HSBC customers*

In this case, the phishing site URL has been cleverly constructed to resemble *hsbc.co.uk/account-help*, a plausible URL for a page hosted on HSBC's official UK site (*hsbc.co.uk*). However, the actual domain name registered by the infringer is *uk-account.help*, upon which they have created an HSBC-specific subdomain name (see Box 1.1) to create the illusion of a legitimate URL. In this case, the attempt is made more effective through the tendency of SMS message readers to split URLs across line breaks at the position of a hyphen. Another effective component is the use of a new-gTLD extension (.help), which may not be familiar to a wide cross-section of users.

Zone-file analysis showed that, at the time the scam was live, there were at least several hundred other (UK-centric) new-gTLD domains with names of a similar format, which had the potential to be used fraudulently. Identified examples included *uk-authorization-online.support*, *uk-gov.tax*, *uk-insurance.claims*, *uk-border.agency*, and *uk-lottery.win*. Other subdomain-based phishing scams reported in the same study also included examples utilizing the URLs *hermes.online-parcel-reschedule.com* (for logistics company Hermes) and *o2.billing9k7j.com* (for telecommunications organization O2).[8]

With this type of infringement, the avoidance of the use by an infringer of a brand-specific domain registration means that the brand owner would not be able to identify the existence of the scam site through

---

[8] https://circleid.com/posts/20220504-the-world-of-the-subdomain

zone-file analysis and would be reliant on other monitoring techniques. Partial coverage with the identification of relevant subdomains can be achieved through methods such as analysis of domain name zone configuration information (e.g., passive DNS analysis), certificate transparency analysis, or via the use of explicit queries on particular domains for the existence of specific subdomain names, but these techniques are not comprehensive.

In other cases, subdomains of *official* company websites can be abused in order to misdirect users to fraudulent content. This can be carried out in a variety of ways, including hijacking of official subdomains that are no longer used (i.e., exploitation of '*dangling*' DNS records—which can commonly arise through the use of cloud-based services, for example)[9] and the creation of new subdomains through the use of DNS compromise (i.e., domain '*shadowing*'). These approaches can be particularly effective, because the URLs used are—by definition—hosted on official trusted sites, meaning their deceptive nature is not detectable through simple inspection of the web address, and the use of an official site will often mean inclusion in site blacklists is circumvented.

7.4 Hostname-Based Infringements

An alternative way of constructing a deceptive URL is through the use of a subdomain/domain name combination (known as a hostname) identical to the name of the brand site being targeted (though with the addition of a dot between the sections of the hostname). For example, the hostname *goo.gle.com* could be used to impersonate *google.com*, requiring the infringer to register a truncated version of the official domain name (in this case, *gle.com*) and then create an appropriate subdomain name (in this case '*goo*') (see Box 1.1). An investigation of the extent of use of this technique is presented in Case Study 7.5.

---

[9] https://cyberint.com/blog/research/subdomain-hijacking-the-domains-silent-danger/

Case Study 7.5: Hostname-Based Infringements Targeting the 50 Most Popular Websites[10]

This case study involves checking for the existence of hostname-based variations of each of the top 50 most popular brand websites on the internet according to Similarweb (October 2022),[11] based on the analysis carried out in November 2022, and considering all possible permutations in each case (e.g., for *google.com*, checking for *g.oogle.com*, *go.ogle.com*, *goo.gle.com*, *goog.le.com*, and *googl.e.com*). The approach of checking the subdomain *specifically* is more robust than simply checking whether the truncated versions of the domain names (e.g., *oogle.com*, *ogle.com*, etc.) have been registered, since some of these—particularly the shortest domain names—are likely to be in unrelated use by third parties.

Of the 262 possible variants of the top 50 most popular website domain names, 89 (34 percent) have active A records (indicating that they are associated with a live IP address) and 37 (14 percent) have active MX records. The live sites were found to feature a range of content, including third-party material, PPC pages, pages offering the domain name for sale, and a range of holding pages and error pages.

Significantly (where whois information is available), only six (2.6 percent) of the 233 (excluding duplicates) potential truncated domain name variants were found to be registered to the brand owner, who could be targeted using an associated hostname infringement.

It is worth noting that some of the instances of URLs found to resolve to live content may arise through the use of wildcard DNS records[12] (i.e., where the domain has been configured such that *any* arbitrary subdomain will resolve, rather than the specific subdomain having been explicitly configured). However, any URL pointing to a live IP address does raise the potential for fraudulent or infringing use.

At the time of analysis, none of the 262 URLs resolved to live phishing sites targeting the brand in question, but it has been

---

[10] https://www.linkedin.com/pulse/exploring-domain-hostname-based-infringements-david-barnett/

[11] https://www.similarweb.com/top-websites/

[12] https://en.wikipedia.org/wiki/Wildcard_DNS_record

previously noted that, in many cases, attack sites are left in a '*dormant*' state—in some cases, for an extended period of time—before being activated, highlighting the importance of ongoing monitoring.[13]

Furthermore, some of the identified instances of hostname-based variant URLs resolving to third-party content may be of particular concern to the brand owner, if they misdirect web users to competitor content or provide an undesirable brand association. Some examples include:

- *g.oogle.com* → resolves to a page promoting a VPN product.
- *y.andex.ru* → redirects to a flight sales website.
- *x.videos.com* (a hostname variant of *xvideos.com*) → resolves to a third-party adult website.
- *p.ornhub.com* → redirects to a third-party adult website.
- *l.inkedin.com* → resolves to a gambling site portal page.
- *e.bay.com* → redirects to the Google website.

Additionally, the frequency of PPC pages within the dataset (observed in 52 of the 89 cases with active A records) indicates the popularity by infringers of monetizing domains while in an otherwise dormant state. Furthermore, the fact that many of the examples were found to display content unrelated to the brand in question may also suggest that they have been configured simply to attract web traffic arising from mistyped browser requests, rather than being intended as explicitly deceptive variants of the brand domain name in question.

It is also informative to compare the date of registration of the (truncated) domain names with their SLD length (where registered and information is available), as shown in Figure 7.6.

The dataset shows that the domains in question have been registered over an extended period, between 1986 and 2022. The shorter domain names—that is, those that are more likely to have been used

(Continued)

(Continued)

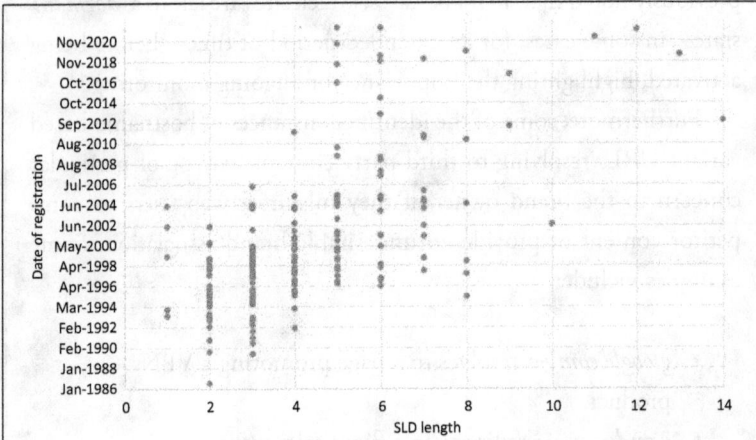

Figure 7.6 Comparison of date of registration with SLD length, for the domains comprising truncated versions of the top 50 most popular domain names

for unrelated third-party or generic use—tend to comprise the oldest registrations. However, many of the domains with longer SLD string lengths (those less likely to be associated with 'accidental' brand collisions, and more likely to have been registered specifically to create hostname-based infringements) tend to have been registered over more recent years, highlighting a potential growth in popularity over time of this particular attack vector.

Key Points

The key points from this chapter are as follows:

- The creation of a URL appearing deceptively similar to that of a brand owner's official website can be a key component in the construction of a convincing infringement.
- A range of categories of specially registered domain names can be utilized to create deceptive URLs, including instances featuring brand variants (typos or

replaced characters, and hyphenated variants) and use of other terms intended to produce confusion with other elements of URLs (e.g., domains including strings such as www or http).

- Branded subdomain names can also be utilized in conjunction with nonbrand-specific domain names (which would not be identified through zone-file monitoring for domains containing the brand name), to create deceptive URLs.
- Subdomain/domain name combinations (hostnames) that together form a string identical to the second-level domain name of a brand owner's official site can also be an effective way of constructing a confusingly similar URL.

CHAPTER 8

Trends in Infringement Activity

Overview

This chapter will cover:

- A series of case studies showing how real-world events can trigger spikes in associated infringement activity, with a particular focus on trends in numbers of domain registrations.
- An analysis of trends over time in levels of activity associated with one specific fraudulent campaign.

A simple examination of trends over time in online activity can provide valuable insights into which issues, brands, and products are high-profile and generating online 'buzz' at a particular point. The converse is also true, and brands in the public eye often find themselves correspondingly targeted by infringements (which may 'spike' following a particular news story or significant event), as infringers take advantage of increased public interest and volumes of search queries to drive users to their own content. Accordingly, there is often a requirement for an increased focus on brand protection activities by a brand owner following a high-profile event.

One obvious example is the 2020/2021 COVID pandemic, which drove a massive increase in scams and infringements of a variety of types, across a wide range of channels. Aside from the more obvious areas of technology-related scams associated with an increase in home-working, and a spike in counterfeit versions of in-demand products such as health care supplies in the e-commerce arena, there were also increases in egregious content of a range of other types. These included areas as diverse as malware disguised as virus tracking apps or advisory attachments in emails, fake websites impersonating high-profile brands such as pharmaceutical companies and health organizations (e.g., the WHO and CDC), phishing sites purporting to be collecting donations or offering financial support schemes, and advance-fee frauds associated with the sale of purported vaccines.[1]

One area that lends itself particularly to tracking these types of trends is the analysis of infringing domain names, both because of the availability of comprehensive data through zone-file analysis, but also because the exact registration dates of the domains in question are usually available through their whois records. In the case of COVID, it was even possible to link individual spikes in registration activity of COVID-related domain names to specific related events in the pandemic (Figure 8.1).

In this section, a selection of case studies illustrating the link between real-world events and associated spikes in related infringements are presented. The case studies focus particularly on trends in numbers of domain name registrations, but more generally, spikes in infringements may typically be observed across a wide range of online channels.

---

[1] https://www.circleid.com/posts/20200409-coronavirus-online-threats-going-viral-part-1-domain-names/;
https://www.circleid.com/posts/20200416-coronavirus-online-threats-going-viral-part-2-marketplaces/;
https://www.circleid.com/posts/20200419-coronavirus-online-threats-going-viral-part-3-mobile-apps/;
https://www.circleid.com/posts/20200423-coronavirus-online-threats-going-viral-part-4-phishing/;
https://www.circleid.com/posts/20200427-coronavirus-online-threats-going-viral-part-5-social-media/

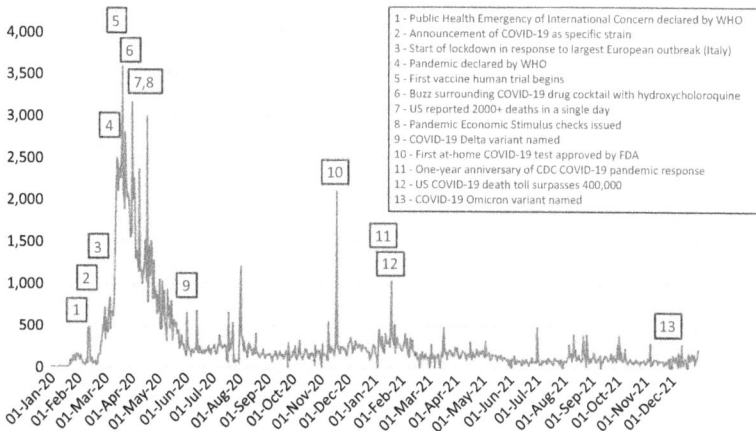

Figure 8.1 *Daily total numbers of registration of COVID-related domain names (2020/2021) (after an original version by CSC Digital Brand Services[2])*

Case Study 8.1: The GameStop Saga

In January 2021, U.S.-based retailer GameStop rose to prominence following an online campaign on Reddit, following an earlier phase of 'short selling' (i.e., predicting a drop in share price) by a number of hedge-fund organizations. In an effort to take a stand against the finance industry, users of Reddit's *WallStreetBets* group tipped the company for success, and purchased shares, leading instead to a sharp (temporary) rise in GameStop's value[3]—a situation that was accentuated when Elon Musk tweeted about the issue.[4]

In response to the spike in 'buzz' surrounding GameStop, a sudden rise in online infringements targeting the brand was observed,

(Continued)

(Continued)

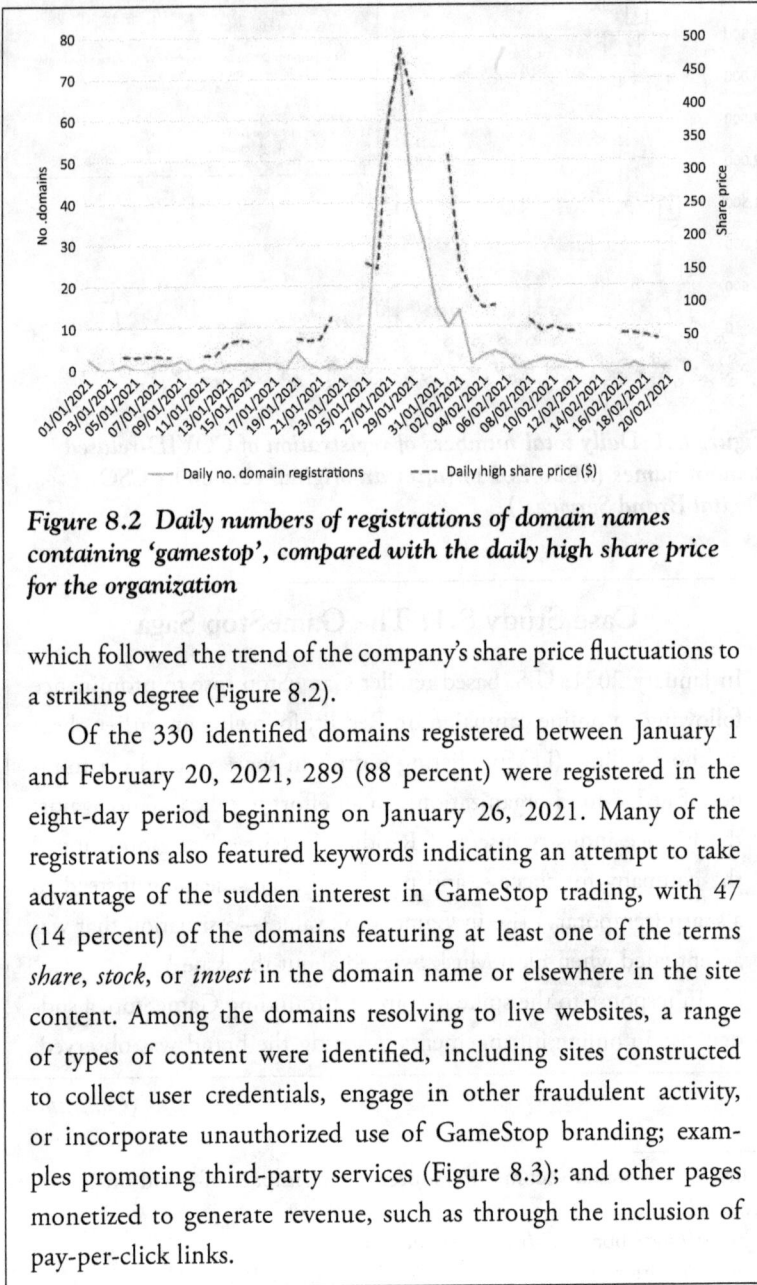

Figure 8.2 *Daily numbers of registrations of domain names containing 'gamestop', compared with the daily high share price for the organization*

which followed the trend of the company's share price fluctuations to a striking degree (Figure 8.2).

Of the 330 identified domains registered between January 1 and February 20, 2021, 289 (88 percent) were registered in the eight-day period beginning on January 26, 2021. Many of the registrations also featured keywords indicating an attempt to take advantage of the sudden interest in GameStop trading, with 47 (14 percent) of the domains featuring at least one of the terms *share*, *stock*, or *invest* in the domain name or elsewhere in the site content. Among the domains resolving to live websites, a range of types of content were identified, including sites constructed to collect user credentials, engage in other fraudulent activity, or incorporate unauthorized use of GameStop branding; examples promoting third-party services (Figure 8.3); and other pages monetized to generate revenue, such as through the inclusion of pay-per-click links.

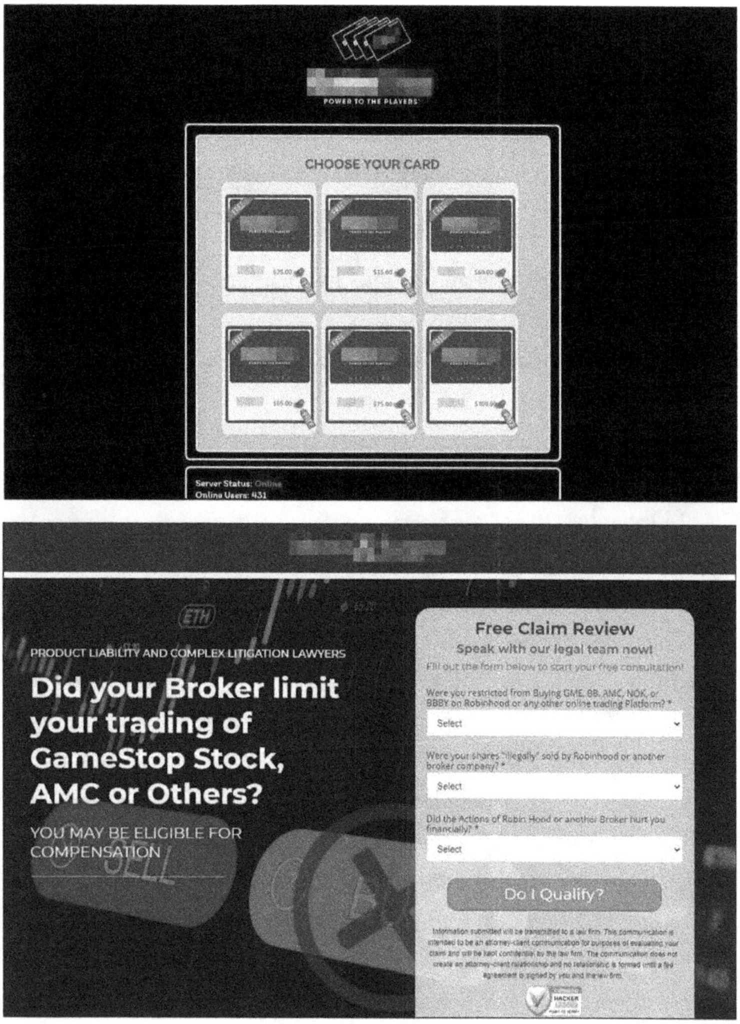

Figure 8.3 Examples of live websites hosted on GameStop-related domains registered during the monitoring period

Case Study 8.2: FIFA World Cup Qatar 2022[5]

The 2022 football World Cup took place in Qatar between November 20 and December 18, 2022. This case study analyzes registration activity for domains specifically relating to the event, by considering those containing:

- *world(-)cup* (with an optional hyphen) and *qatar*
  or
- [*world(-)cup* or *qatar*] and [*football* or *futbol* or *soccer* or *2022* or *fi(-)fa*]

based on those domains still registered (i.e., present in the zone files) as of December 2022.

The analysis yielded a dataset of 977 domain names, for which the registration profile over time is shown in Figure 8.4.

The daily data are rather noisy, but the aggregated monthly statistics do show (unsurprisingly) a ramp-up in new registrations toward the date of the event itself, as a broad trend. However, the activity profile over time is relatively complex, with an earlier spike in activity in April 2022. A detailed analysis of the data shows that this peak relates to what appears to be two specific short-lived, coordinated registration campaigns of domains with names of the form *qatar-2022-iX.xyz* and *worldcup2022-jYYX.buzz* (where *X* is any digit and *Y* is any character). Although none of these domains was found to resolve to any live site at the time of analysis, the .xyz and .buzz TLDs have previously been noted as frequently being associated with malicious or infringing content.

Of the 977 high-relevance domains, 633 (65 percent) were found to resolve to active websites at the time of analysis. Inspection of the

---

[5] https://www.linkedin.com/pulse/four-new-case-studies-domain-registration-activity-spikes-barnett/

sites in detail revealed a significant number of nonofficial sites featuring potentially infringing or high-threat content, including instances of potential phishing, TV piracy, nonofficial sites purporting to offer gambling services or ticket sales, e-commerce (of potential counterfeits), and cryptocurrency and NFT-related scams (Figure 8.5).

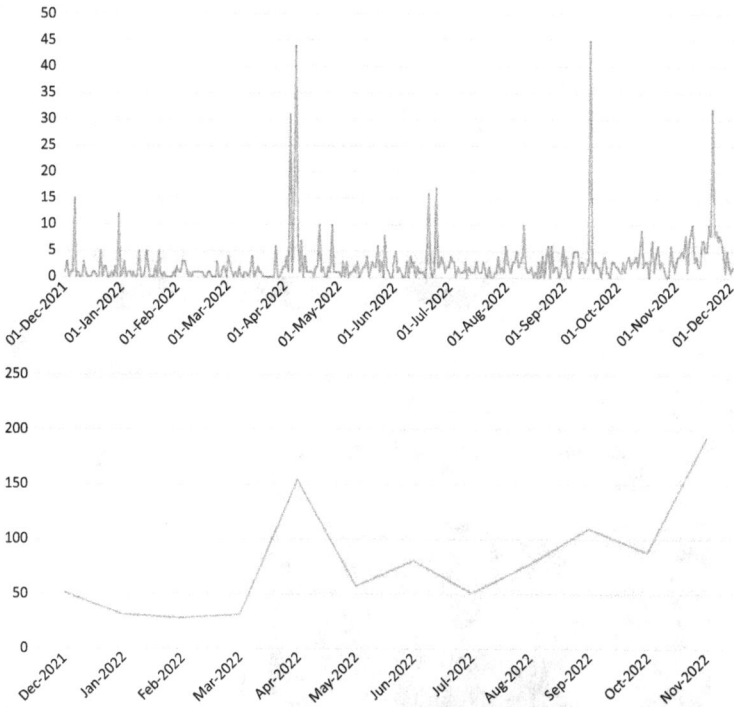

Figure 8.4 Daily (top) and aggregated monthly (bottom) numbers of registrations of domains with names highly relevant to the 2022 World Cup (December 2021 to November 2022)

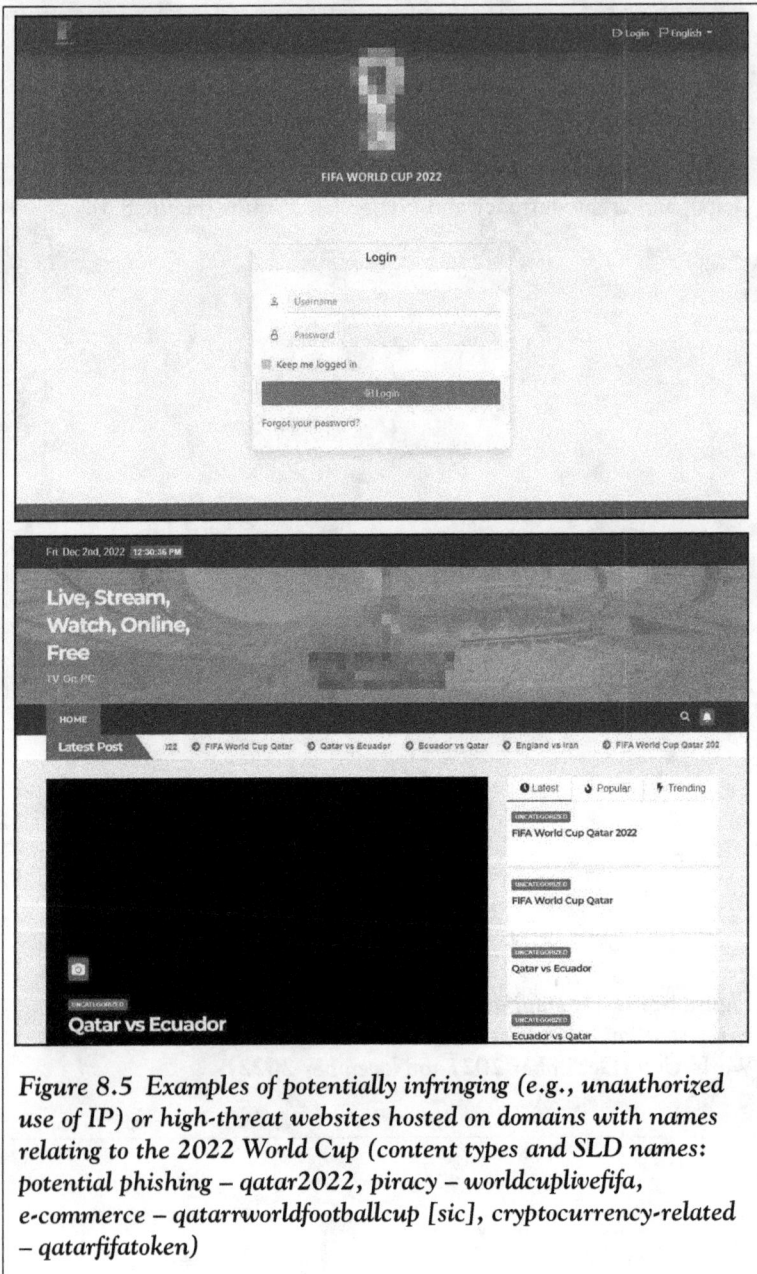

Figure 8.5 Examples of potentially infringing (e.g., unauthorized use of IP) or high-threat websites hosted on domains with names relating to the 2022 World Cup (content types and SLD names: potential phishing – qatar2022, piracy – worldcuplivefifa, e-commerce – qatarrworldfootballcup [sic], cryptocurrency-related – qatarfifatoken)

Figure 8.5 (Continued)

Case Study 8.3: Barbenheimer

The simultaneous launch of the *Barbie* and *Oppenheimer* movies on July 21, 2023 was associated with a significant amount of online excitement and—following a reported marketing spend of $150 million on *Barbie* alone[6]—the *Barbenheimer* phenomenon emerged, a 'mash-up' of both titles, associated with a popular campaign encouraging audience-goers to view both films.

Domain registration activity for all three terms (*barbie, oppenheimer,* and *barbenheimer* (and misspellings)) was observed in the run-up to the releases, with levels peaking around the date of launch, in response to the 'buzz' (Figure 8.6).

It is worth noting that numbers of *barbie* domains were much greater than for the other two terms, and with activity consistently observed throughout the year (in addition to starting from a much higher 'baseline')—presumably a reflection of the general level of popularity of,

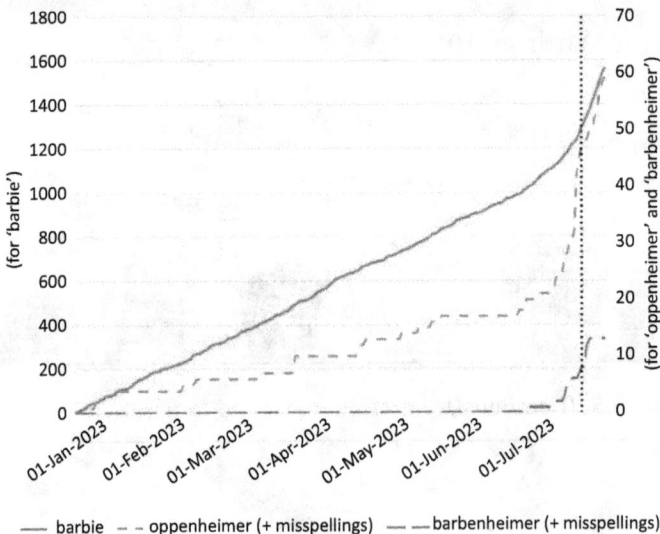

Figure 8.6 Growth during 2023 of numbers of registered domains with names containing 'barbie' (left-hand axis) and 'oppenheimer' and 'barbenheimer' (right-hand axis), relative to 'baseline' numbers at the start of 2023 (with movie launch date shown as a dotted line)

---

[6] https://www.insider.com/barbie-had-150-million-marketing-budget-2023-7

and awareness in, the Barbie brand, even where unrelated to the new movie. The ramp-up in activity around the time of launch was most pronounced for the *oppenheimer* domains, suggesting that the majority of the activity for this term was indeed related to the film itself.

Again, the live sites to which these domains were found to resolve incorporated a range of infringement types, including e-commerce, brand association with adult content and gambling, promotion of cryptocurrency schemes and investments, and scam ticket offers. It is significant that *Barbenheimer* was not an official term used by the movie producers and, accordingly, it is likely that the vast majority of the domains using this term were nonofficial (Figure 8.7).

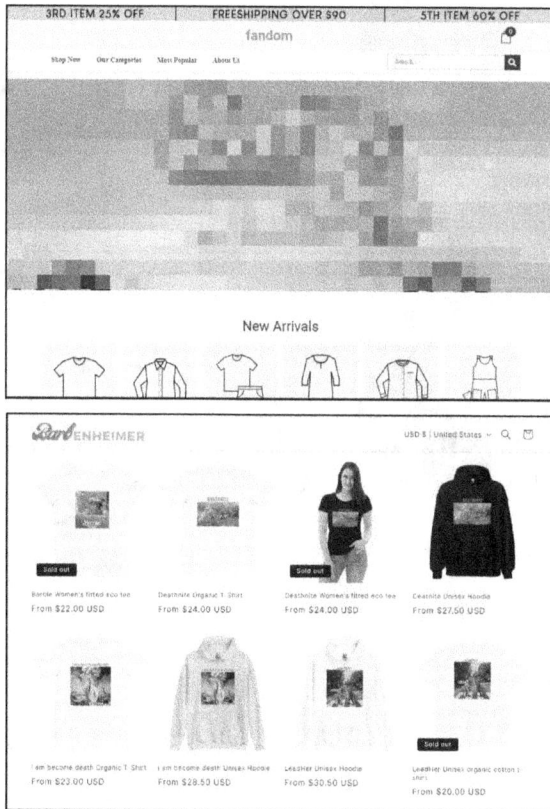

Figure 8.7 *Examples of live e-commerce websites hosted on barbenheimer domains (SLD names: barbenheimertee, shopbarbenheimer)*

(*Continued*)

(Continued)

The Barbenheimer phenomenon is also significant because of the degree to which it lent itself to counterfeiting as a potential infringement type. Accordingly, the proliferation of unofficial merchandise was also apparent across other channels, such as e-commerce marketplaces (Figure 8.8).

Figure 8.8 Examples of unofficial Barbenheimer products offered for sale on e-commerce marketplaces as of August 2023

Case Study 8.4: 'New Year' Domains 2023

The new year can be a popular time for brand owners to launch new products, campaigns, and marketing activity, and one way in which this can be promoted in a topical fashion is through the registration of new domains making explicit reference to the year. However, similar tactics can also be employed by bad actors, through the registration of desirable domain names. In some cases, these domains may be registered well in advance of the new year itself. This study considers activity associated with the registration of domains with names beginning or ending with the string *2023*, throughout the calendar year 2022.

Figure 8.9 shows the daily numbers of registrations of '2023-specific' domains throughout 2022, and the cumulative total number of such domains actively registered.

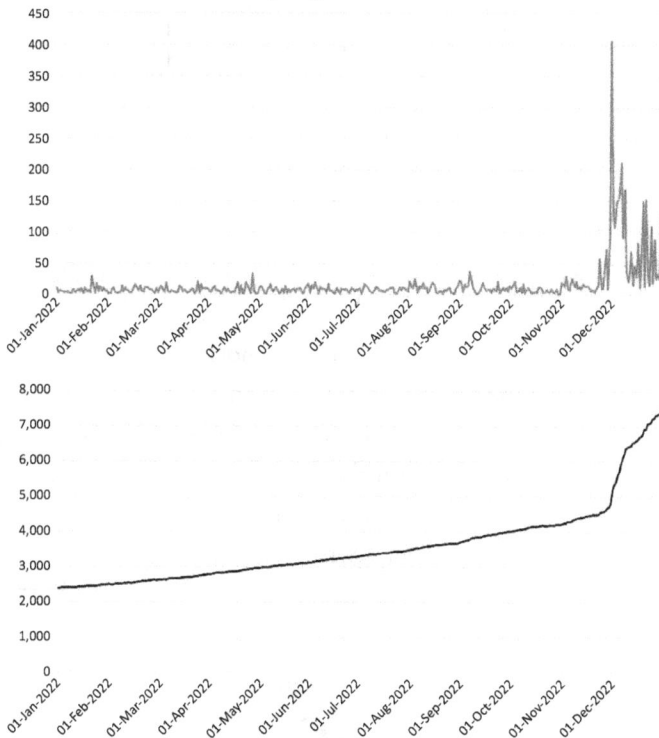

Figure 8.9 Daily numbers of registrations of domains with names beginning or ending with 2023 (top), and the cumulative number of active registrations (bottom) (January to December 2022)

(*Continued*)

(Continued)

The dataset shows a sharp increase in activity toward the end of 2022, but it is significant that registrations were taking place throughout the year, superimposed on a 'baseline' of over 2,000 2023-related registrations at the start of 2022.

Table 8.1 Top TLDs among the 2023-specific domains registered during 2022

TLD	No. Domains
.com	3,138
.cyou	1,748
.xyz	319
.org	227
.top	138
.net	104
.click	90
.online	58
.vip	52
.info	51
(others)	533

Considering the most popular TLDs utilized in the dataset of unique domain names, the popularity of new-gTLDs commonly associated with infringing activity is again notable (Table 8.1).

Considering the content of the associated websites, a range of potential infringements were identified, targeting a variety of well-known brands, indicating that the occurrence of the new year was commonly used as a 'hook' by bad actors to launch scams and promote their own content (Figure 8.10).

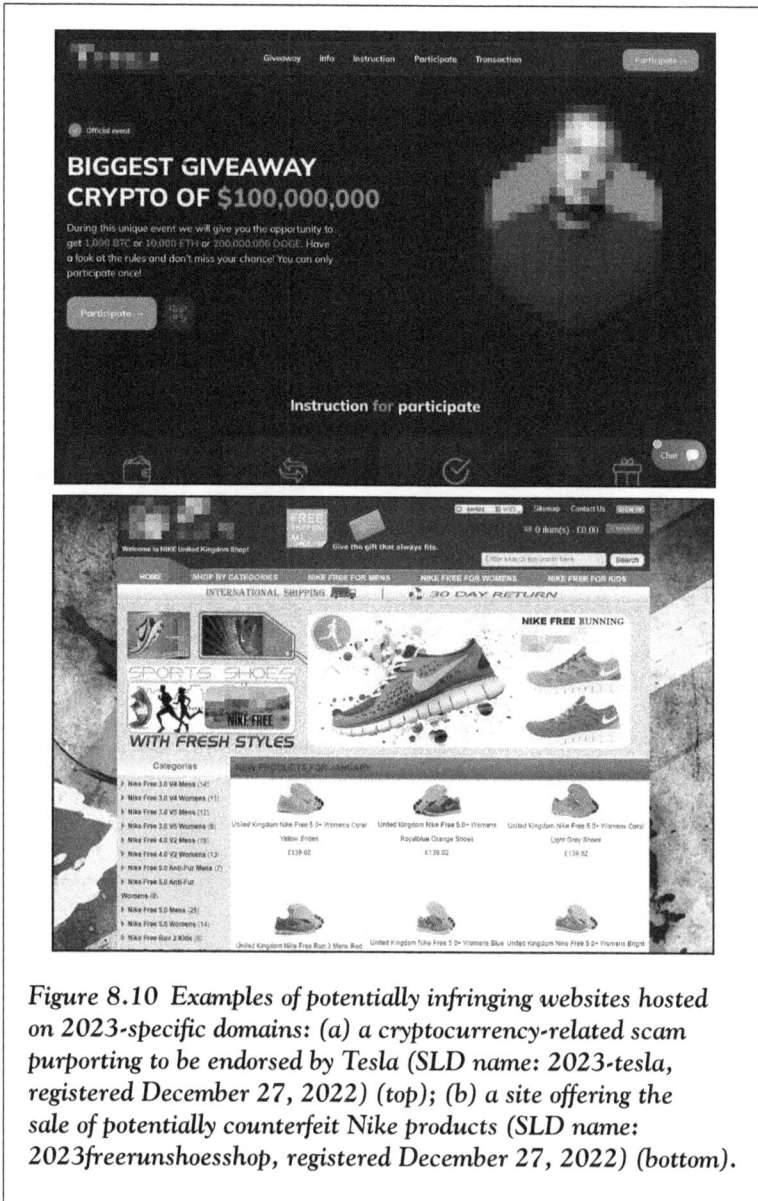

Figure 8.10 *Examples of potentially infringing websites hosted on 2023-specific domains: (a) a cryptocurrency-related scam purporting to be endorsed by Tesla (SLD name: 2023-tesla, registered December 27, 2022) (top); (b) a site offering the sale of potentially counterfeit Nike products (SLD name: 2023freerunshoesshop, registered December 27, 2022) (bottom).*

Case Study 8.5: Black Friday Domains[7]

In a similar vein to the 'New Year' domains (Case Study 8.4), a range of previous studies[8,9] have noted the existence of spikes of domain registrations related to the e-commerce shopping events Black Friday and Cyber Monday, and others such as Chinese Singles Day on November 11 (*11-11*). This case study considers registration activity for domains with names containing *black(-)friday* or *cyber(-)monday* (with optional hyphens in both cases; hereafter collectively referred to as '*Black Friday domains*') (analysis carried out as of September 2023).

The analysis—based on gTLD zone-file data—found 6,596 active examples of such domains and considered the dates of registration of these domains (Figure 8.11).

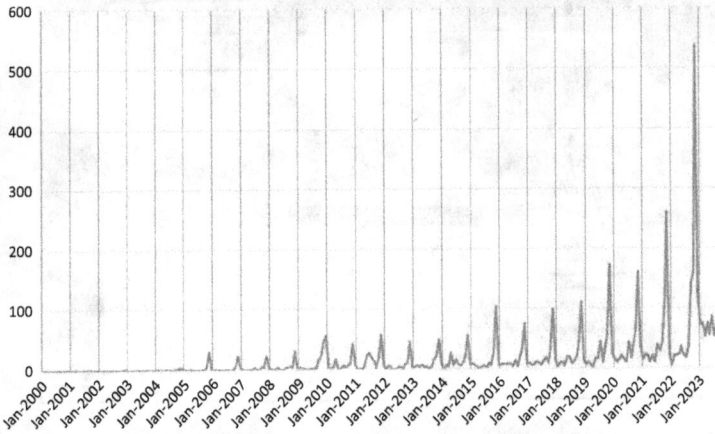

Figure 8.11 Numbers of Black Friday domains in the dataset, by month of registration (January 2000 to September 2023)

The dataset shows a striking annual cycle in the registration activity, with clear spikes in activity in the fourth quarter of each year, representing domains registered to be utilized over the Black Friday period.

---

[7] https://www.iamstobbs.com/opinion/web-dot-coms-but-once-a-year-holiday-shopping-activity-part-1-black-friday-domains

[8] https://www.cscdigitalbrand.services/blog/how-will-black-friday-ecommerce-domains-trend/

[9] https://www.cscdigitalbrand.services/blog/holiday-shopping-events-part-2/

Additionally, while a general visible upward trend year-on-year is also visible, this is not necessarily indicative in itself of an overall increase in registration activity over time (since many of the domains registered in previous years will have expired prior to the date of analysis).

Perhaps unsurprisingly, the dataset included significant numbers of domains with names also featuring additional terms specifically related to e-commerce, particular product types, and/or well-known brand names. It is also noteworthy that domain names of the form *blackfridayXXXX.com* and *cybermondayYYYY.com* have already been registered for every value of *XXXX* between 2009 and 2040 and between 2051 and 2070, and for every value of *YYYY* between 2009 and 2052.

It is also informative to consider the popularity of individual TLDs within the dataset, as a function of the total numbers of registered domains across the TLD (i.e., determining the *frequency* of Black Friday domains), to determine whether certain TLDs are disproportionately more utilized (and excluding all domains that appear to be owned by legitimate brands). This analysis is shown in Figure 8.12, where the solid line shows the 'expected' numbers of Black Friday registrations (as a function of the total number of

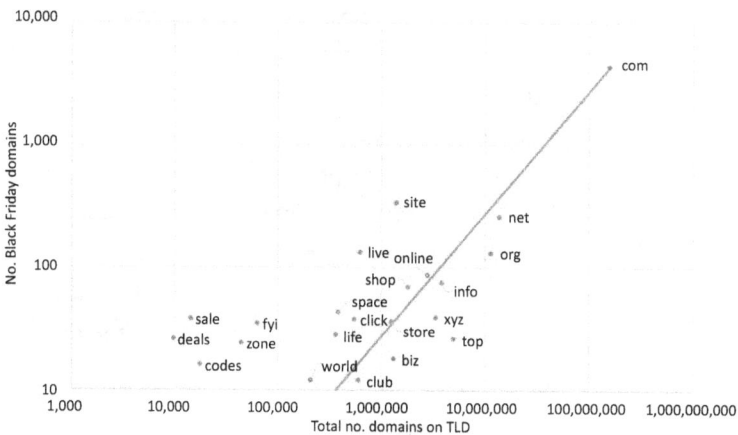

Figure 8.12 Total numbers of Black Friday domains on each TLD, compared with the total number of registered domains on the TLD

(*Continued*)

(Continued)

domains on each TLD), if all TLDs were utilized equally, and using the numbers for .com as a benchmark. Any TLDs that appear above this line (such as .site and .live) therefore appear disproportionately more frequently in the dataset than might be expected.

Table 8.2 shows the top TLDs, by frequency of occurrence (per million registered domains) of Black Friday domains.

Table 8.2 Top TLDs by frequency of occurrence (per million registered domains) of Black Friday domains (where N ≥ 5)

TLD	No. (N) of Black Friday Domains	Frequency Per Million Domains
.deals	26	2,762.70
.sale	38	2,633.59
.bargains	5	2,507.52
.codes	16	895.26
.fyi	35	556.07
.zone	24	540.48
.shopping	5	431.63
.site	331	236.43
.live	132	209.56
.space	43	109.86

It is striking (though perhaps not surprising) that five of the top ten TLDs are explicitly related to e-commerce. More generally, new-gTLDs that have been noted previously as being disproportionately utilized for fraudulent registrations (such as .xyz and .top) (see Table 5.1) are extensively represented within the dataset.

Figure 8.13 shows some examples of live domains from the dataset found to resolve to live, apparently infringing (e.g., the sale of counterfeits), or potentially illegal content.

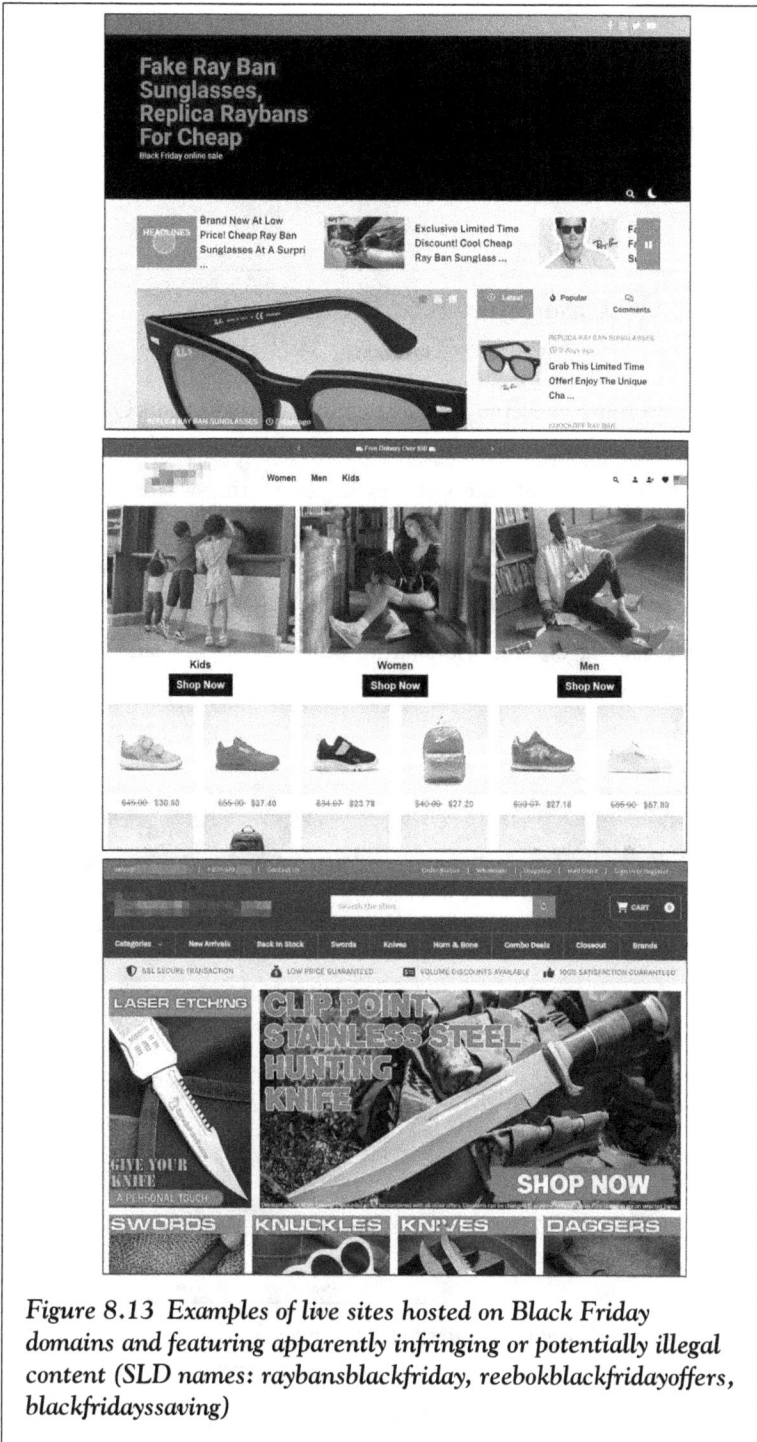

Figure 8.13 Examples of live sites hosted on Black Friday domains and featuring apparently infringing or potentially illegal content (SLD names: raybansblackfriday, reebokblackfridayoffers, blackfridayssaving)

Similar approaches can also be used to track trends over time in activity associated with individual infringement or fraud campaigns. Case Study 8.6 presents an overview of the analysis of a specific individual fraudulent website identified as being associated with a large-scale campaign involving the use of brand-specific domain registrations to create deceptive sites.

Case Study 8.6: Profiling a Scam Package-Tracking Website[10]

This case study concerns an investigation, carried out in Q1 2024, of a scam campaign involving the use of large numbers (potentially several thousands) of fake websites impersonating a range of well-known brands. The scam primarily targeted brands in the consumer goods industries and made use of domains featuring the name of the targeted brand, usually together with a country name (in English or local language), and also sharing other registration and hosting characteristics.

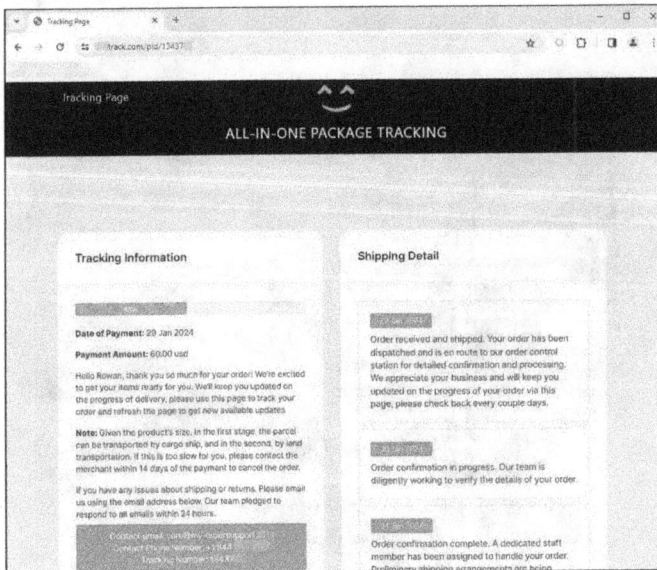

Figure 8.14 *Example of a user-specific page on the scam website*

---

10   https://www.iamstobbs.com/tracking-the-tracker-ebook

Further research, involving the use of test purchases, was then carried out into the method of operation of the campaign. This revealed that, following an attempted purchase, an email was sent to the customer directing them to a scam package-shipping tracking website (referred to in anonymized form in this study as ****track.com*). The site hosted a large number of victim-specific scam pages, each soliciting for payment (Figure 8.14).

The URL of each scam page included a string of digits (*xxxxxxx*), identical to the purported 'tracking number' displayed on the page (referred to in this case study as the *ID-number*), giving a URL of the form *https://***track.com/pid/xxxxxxx*. Further analysis showed that, by modifying of the string of digits in the URL, additional similar pages on the same site, but targeted at different recipients, were displayed. An initial check of 100 consecutive ID-numbers (encompassing the example identified initially; ID-number *13437xx*) showed that 35 (i.e., 35 percent) of the associated URLs generated live scam pages, displaying requested payment amounts of between $9.99 and $207.72 (USD). The 'inactive' ID-numbers generated a page displaying the message "*we could not find the order, maybe you have used the different email address?*" [*sic*].

A further in-depth analysis of groups of the pages available on the site (by varying the ID-number string) was then carried out, in order to gain an overview of the potential scale (in terms of total duration and financial impact) of the scam.

Noting that the ID-numbers appear to have been used in ascending order over time, Table 8.3 shows the dates on which each 100,000th ID-number (or the first subsequent example corresponding to an active scam page) appears to have been used, based on the '*date of payment*' shown on the page.

As of the date of the initial analysis (March 15, 2024), the campaign was still ongoing, with ID-number *1447000* having been used on that date. It is also noteworthy that the style of the pages changed slightly over time, in terms of the contact details displayed.

(*Continued*)

(Continued)

Table 8.3 Data for the first active scam page in each block of
100,000 ID-numbers

ID-Number	Date	Amount Requested on Page ($)	Days Since Previous 100,000th ID-Number
1	January 21, 2021	100.00	—
100000	October 25, 2021	125.98	277
200002	December 16, 2021	10.00	52
300000	February 25, 2022	68.52	71
400000	March 18, 2022	34.99	21
500000	April 2, 2022	43.00	15
600000	April 15, 2022	34.95	13
700000	September 30, 2022	100.00	168
800000	November 20, 2022	119.85	51
900000	March 29, 2023	69.00	129
1000002	August 13, 2023	115.00	137
1100000	September 5, 2023	90.00	23
1200000	October 18, 2023	12.50	43
1300007	January 12, 2024	72.50	86
1400010	February 23, 2024	50.00	42

The next phase of analysis considered the most recent complete set of 100,000 ID-numbers (i.e., the *13xxxxx* block, between *1300000* and *1399999*), covering a six-week period between January 12 and February 23, 2024. Within the block of associated URLs, 31,646 (of the 100,000, i.e., 31.6 percent) were found to resolve to active scam pages, with an average of 745 pages utilized each day. The currency was requested in USD in all but four cases (which instead used GBP), and the average amount requested per page was $59.50, giving a total of $1.88 million over the six-week period (i.e., $44,000 per day).

For comparison purposes, similar analyses were carried out for the *5xxxxx* block, and the first block of 100,000 ID-numbers (referred to as the *0xxxxx* block, although in practice the URLs do not incorporate leading zeroes in the ID-number string), as these are associated with (respectively) the shortest and longest durations of the utilization of all blocks in the overall dataset.

Table 8.4 **Summary statistics for the three analyzed blocks of 100,000 URLs/ID-numbers**

	0xxxxx Block	**5xxxxx Block**	**13xxxxx Block**
Start date	January 21, 2021	April 2, 2022	January 12, 2024
End date	October 25, 2021	April 15, 2022	February 23, 2024
Duration (days)	277	13	42
No. active scam pages	72,569	69,963	31,646
Pages utilized per day	262	5,700	745
Mean amount reqd. per page ($)	78.73	93.55	59.50
Mean total amount reqd. per day ($)	20,669	535,915	44,131
Total amount requested ($)	5,713,313	6,545,275	1,883,071

One possible explanation for the shorter duration of the *5xxxxx* block would be if a smaller proportion of the ID-numbers within the range were used for active scams, but the analysis shows this is not the case. Rather, actually, a *larger* proportion (69,963 or 70.0 percent) was associated with active pages, showing that this period exhibited a significantly higher rate of activity by the scammers. The summary statistics for the three blocks considered are shown in Table 8.4.

Overall, levels of activity and patterns of usage varied markedly over the period of utilization of the site, including changes in patterns of the target audience (as reflected by the currencies in which payment was requested, with 11 different currencies (USD, AUD, EUR, NZD, GBP, CAD, CHF, MAD, DKK, HRK, and HKD) referenced across the three blocks).

Figure 8.15 shows '*heat maps*' for each of the three analyzed blocks of 100,000 ID-numbers, representing the total numbers of active scam pages in each 'sub-block' of 50 adjacent ID-numbers (with darker shades denoting that a greater proportion of the ID-numbers in each sub-block were utilized for active scam pages). The high-level

(Continued)

(Continued)

Figure 8.15 Heat maps showing the total numbers of active scam pages in each sub-block of 50 adjacent ID-numbers (with darker shades indicating greater utilization of the available set of ID-numbers), for the 0xxxxx (top), 5xxxxx (middle), and 13xxxxx (bottom) blocks of 100,000 ID-numbers

observations are the facts that, in the earlier stages of the campaign: (i) overall, a greater proportion of the available ID-numbers were being utilized (shown by the fact that the top and middle figures appear generally darker overall than the bottom one) and (ii) there was a greater degree of variability over time in the extent of use of the available ID-numbers (shown by the marked variance between the dark and light areas in the top figure).

In extrapolating the above figures to provide an estimate of the total scale of the scam based on this initial sampling exercise, reasonable conservative assumptions might be that, across the full duration of the utilization of the site, approximately 50 percent of the possible available ID-numbers have been utilized for active scam pages, requesting an average of $50 per instance. On this basis, it would be possible to estimate that, between January 2021 and the date of analysis in March 2024, the site had been used to attempt to steal a total of 1.4 million (the ID-number range covered) × 50% × $50 = approximately $35 million.

Instead, however, it is also possible to carry out a full formal analysis, inspecting the URLs for all possible ID-numbers in the range

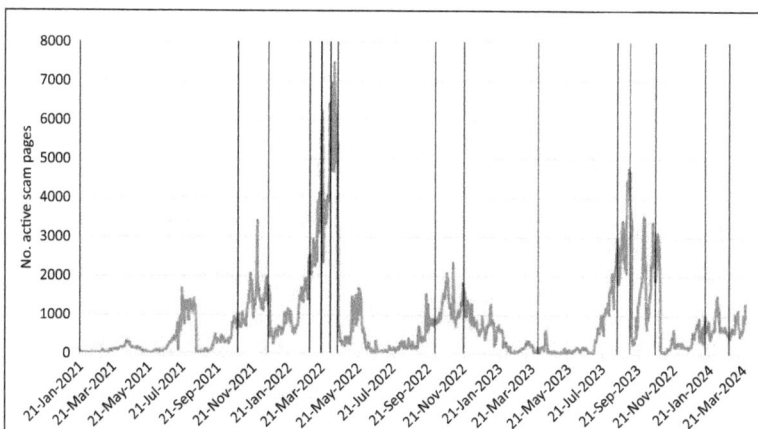

Figure 8.16 Daily numbers of active pages utilized on the scam site during the full duration of its period of use (vertical lines show the boundaries between the blocks of 100,000 ID-numbers)

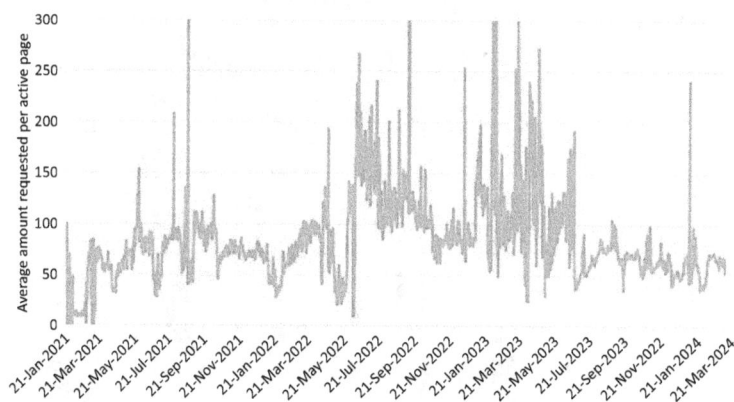

Figure 8.17 Daily mean payment requested per individual scam page, during the full duration of the period of use of the scam site

utilized up to the date of analysis (though this naturally requires a longer run-time for the automated analysis tool). A summary of the findings from this further research is shown in Figures 8.16 and 8.17.

Overall, 900,640 active scam pages were identified (out of a possible set of 1,465,505—the final ID-number to have been used on the date on which this second stage of analysis was carried out (March 25, 2024)—i.e., 61.5 percent). The average payment requested per page was in fact $85.33, or a total of $76.8 million. Among the

(*Continued*)

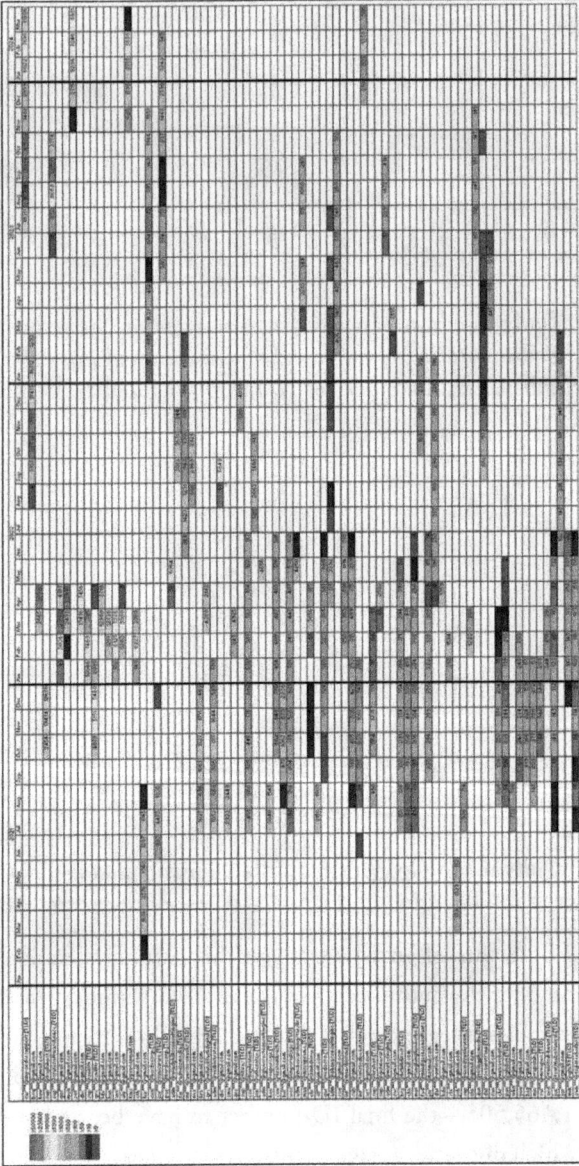

Figure 8.18 Timeline view showing the number of pages on which each of the top 80 overall most frequently used email addresses (obfuscated) was utilized, within each calendar month

other trends evident from the dataset are the facts that: (a) in many cases, there tends to be a drop off in daily activity (i.e., the numbers of active pages utilized) following the transition from one block of 100,000 ID-numbers to the next and (b) there was a large spike in total daily requested payment on September 15, 2022, corresponding to a significant number of pages requesting very large sums of money in each individual instance (up to $20,004 in one case), with an average per page for that day or $3,698, or a daily total of $5.7 million). It was also possible to establish that 485 distinct contact email addresses had been provided across the set of active scam pages, during the overall duration of the scam (Figure 8.18).

Assuming overall a conservative figure for the success rate of the campaign (particularly in view of the fact that it appears to have been specifically targeted, with the scam pages personalized to the recipient) of between 0.1 and 1 percent (i.e., equivalent to the statement that between one in a thousand and one in a hundred of those individuals targeted by the scam will ultimately have experienced a financial loss), the total funds successfully stolen through this single scam site may be in the range of $77,000 to $770,000.

Key Points

The key points from this chapter are as follows:

- High-profile events and news stories can often trigger corresponding spikes in activity relating to infringements targeting associated brands, as bad actors take advantage of increased levels of interest and searches by internet users, to drive traffic to their own content. This increased infringement activity can be apparent across a range of internet channels and content types.
- Depending on the brand, and the nature of the event triggering the increased activity, infringement types can cover the full range of categories relevant to brand

(Continued)

protection considerations generally. These may include instances of phishing and brand impersonation, misdirection of users to harmful or other third-party content, sale of counterfeit or otherwise infringing goods, digital piracy, false affiliation, and negative comment.

- Brand owners are advised to be vigilant, and to keep a closer focus on online activity, at times of heightened risk.
- In some cases, it may be possible to make estimates of the total amounts of revenue generated by a scam campaign, if specific financial information (such as payment amounts demanded) is included on any associated fraudulent website(s).

CHAPTER 9

Domain Landscape Analysis

Overview

This chapter will cover:

- A range of analyses illustrating how domain zone-file data can be used to provide insights into the domain-name landscape generally.
- An overview of the domain-name landscape, including information on the most popular TLDs and the state of the new-gTLD program.
- An overview of the adoption of dot-brand extensions, a special class of restricted new-gTLDs in which brand owners apply to act as the registry organization for their own, brand-specific TLD (and thereby retain control over all domains registered across that extension).
- An overview of the availability of unregistered domain names across the set of gTLD extensions.
- An introduction to internationalized domain names (IDNs), an overview of the IDN landscape, and an illustration of how IDNs can be used by bad actors to produce highly deceptive brand infringements.
- An introduction to the basic principles behind the generation of a domain-name management policy, providing guidance to brand owners on which domains should ideally be included in their official portfolio.

9.1 Introduction

As of the end of Q3, 2023, there were around 359 million registered domains and the number continues to grow, showing a year-on-year increase of around 8.5 million (+2.4%). These registrations are split across gTLDs (generic TLDs, such as .com, .net, and .org), ccTLDs (country-specific extensions), across which there were around 138 million domains, and new-gTLDs (the set of new extensions which have been launched in the period since 2012), which now account for around 30 million registrations. The top ten TLDs—by number of registered domains—as of this date were given as shown in Table 9.1.[1]

As noted previously, domain-name monitoring and analysis is a core component of many brand-protection programs due to the significance of domain names in intellectual property considerations, search-engine optimization, business-critical infrastructure, and ease of registration by infringers (and potential degree of deception and customer confusion). Accordingly, brand owners need to maintain a detailed overview of the domain-name landscape, both in terms of relevance to their own official registrations, and those of third parties.

Table 9.1 The top ten TLDs by number of registered domains, as of end-Q3, 2023 (source: Domain Name Industry Brief)

TLD	No. domains (millions)
.com	160.8
.cn	20.3
.de	17.6
.net	13.2
.uk	10.9
.org	10.8
.nl	6.3
.ru	5.8
.br	5.2
.au	4.3

---

[1] https://dnib.com/articles/the-domain-name-industry-brief-q3-2023

Fortunately, there is a rich suite of domain data generally available, by virtue of the availability (for certain TLDs) of zone-file data, and associated technical configuration and ownership details obtainable through standard look-ups.

This section presents examples of the types of insights which may be gained from detailed analysis of data regarding the overall domain landscape.

9.2 The New-gTLD Landscape

9.2.1 Overview[2]

In the second half of 2023, the Internet Corporation for Assigned Names and Numbers (ICANN) announced the proposal for a new round of new-gTLD applications to launch in Q2, 2026.[3] The original phase of the new-gTLD program launched in 2012, to add a series of new TLDs to the internet's Root Zone[4] (the highest level of DNS, and the basis for domain infrastructure), with the aim of "enhanc[ing] innovation, competition and consumer choice."[5,6] As part of the program, entities were invited to submit applications to act as registries for new TLDs. This would involve being responsible for maintaining the infrastructure, processing applications, and dealing with disputes for new domains, for the extension in question. Following the first round of applications in 2012—during which around 2,000 TLDs were proposed—and a subsequent period of assessment, the first new-gTLDs were delegated (added to the Root Zone) in October 2013. The new registries were categorized either as open (generally available for domain registrations), restricted (in which particular criteria had to be met for registrations to be permitted), or closed. The TLDs themselves are also grouped into types, with classes including generic, geographic, community, and brand, depending on their intended use. In some cases, brand owners have chosen to register

---

2 https://www.iamstobbs.com/opinion/the-new-new-gtlds
3 https://www.icann.org/newgtlds-next-round-en
4 https://www.iana.org/domains/root/db
5 https://newgtlds.icann.org/en/about/program
6 https://icannwiki.org/New_gTLD_Program

their brand name as a domain-name extension and maintain control of the TLD, so as to centralize ownership of their official websites and reduce customer confusion—so-called instances of *dot-brands*.

One of the main objectives of the program was a reduction in infringements and an increase in clarity for customers through the use of descriptive TLDs for websites—particularly through the use of restricted extensions such as .bank and .insurance.[7] As part of this initiative, the Trademark Clearing House (TMCH) scheme was introduced, through which brand owners were able to submit their trademarks for validation, granting them automatic rights to register the trademark as a new domain name upon the launch of a new TLD, and receive notice of any (exact-match) applications by third parties.[8] In addition, some new-gTLD registry organizations also offer blocking programs (such as the Domain Protected Marks List (DPML) originally offered by the Donuts organization[9]) which can be employed by brand owners.

Unfortunately, however, many of the registrations across the new-gTLDs have been associated with abuse, through a range of different types of infringement, from cybersquatting and brand impersonation, to phishing and malware distribution. Indeed many of the new-gTLDs are disproportionately *more* affected by infringements than the legacy extensions, despite in many cases having improved enforcement processes in place. The abuse is, in many cases, a reflection of low-cost registrations with lax requirements[10] (cf. Table 5.1). Overall levels of (legitimate) adoption have been rather lower than initially anticipated.[11]

Altogether a little over 1,200 new-gTLDs have been delegated since the start of the program,[12] with just over half have passed through the

---

[7] https://support.tppwholesale.com.au/hc/en-gb/articles/360008969518-Restricted-New-gTLDs

[8] https://newgtlds.icann.org/en/about/trademark-clearinghouse

[9] https://www.trademark-clearinghouse.com/content/donuts-dpml

[10] https://op.europa.eu/en/publication-detail/-/publication/7d16c267-7f1f-11ec-8c40-01aa75ed71a1

[11] https://www.hostdime.com/blog/2020-new-tlds-adoption/

[12] https://newgtlds.icann.org/en/program-status/delegated-strings

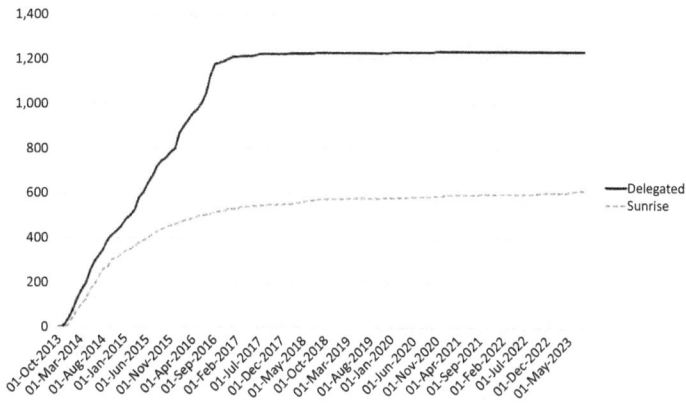

Figure 9.1 Growth in the cumulative number of new-gTLDs since the start of the program

start of their Sunrise period[13,14] (the initial launch phase, prior to General Availability, when brand owners are able to apply for new domains) (Figure 9.1).

For most of the new-gTLDs, the interval between delegation and Sunrise was less than a year, although there is a long tail of cases in which this period was significantly greater. Overall the vast majority of new-gTLDs were delegated within the first three years of the program, with many of those TLDs to have Sunrised most recently, therefore having seen extensive periods of time elapse since their initial delegation. In some cases, these delays may represent prolonged negotiations or discussions over the management or use-cases of the TLDs in question. One such example is the seven-year dispute between e-commerce giant Amazon and the South American member states of the Amazon Cooperation Treaty Organization, for control of the .amazon extension, which was eventually won by the Amazon corporation.[15,16,17]

---

[13] https://newgtlds.icann.org/en/program-status/sunrise-claims-periods

[14] https://newgtlds.icann.org/en/program-status/statistics

[15] https://www.licenseglobal.com/retail/amazon-wins-domain-dispute-sa-nations

[16] https://www.lexology.com/library/detail.aspx?g=85594134-7b40-436c-b5ac-a807d98d1b56

[17] https://www.ft.com/content/c8f227e6-7b0c-11e9-81d2-f785092ab560

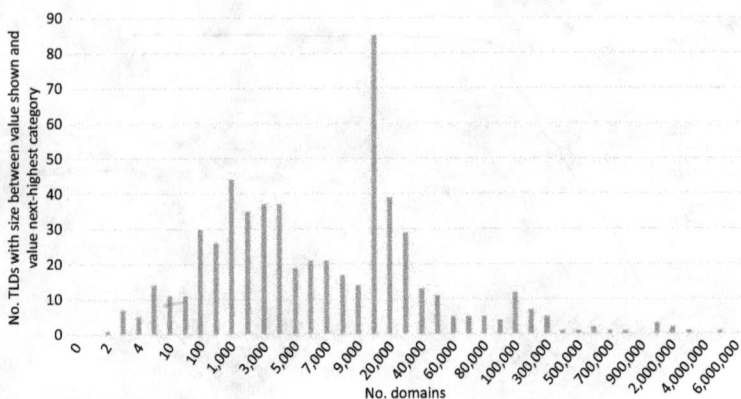

Figure 9.2 Numbers of new-gTLDs by TLD size (by number of registered domains) (November 2023)

As of the end of November 2023, 583 new-gTLDs have passed through the start of their Sunrise periods. The popularity of individual extensions varies greatly with a large range of number of registered domains across the set of TLDs (Figure 9.2 and Table 9.2).[18]

Overall there is no strong correlation between the age of an extension (i.e., the amount of elapsed time since its launch) and the number of

Table 9.2 Top ten new-gTLDs by TLD size (by number of registered domains) (November 2023)

New-gTLD	No. registered domains
.top	5,208,791
.xyz	3,342,289
.online	2,896,998
.shop	2,002,143
.site	1,428,703
.store	1,353,876
.app	1,320,994
.vip	827,725
.dev	797,403
.club	615,342

[18] https://www.iamstobbs.com/opinion/expert-.watches-.new-.online-.website-.news-.lol-a-review-of-the-current-state-of-the-new-gtld-programme

registrations across the TLD (Figure 9.3), indicating that the new-gTLDs vary widely in rate of uptake. There are a number of reasons why this is the case, with significant factors being that the new-gTLDs vary widely in terms of their availability, registration cost, and intended use-case.

These factors have a general impact on the desirability of particular extensions, including their use by bad actors. Indeed many of the most popular new-gTLDs (notably .app, .dev, .top, .page (with just under 100k

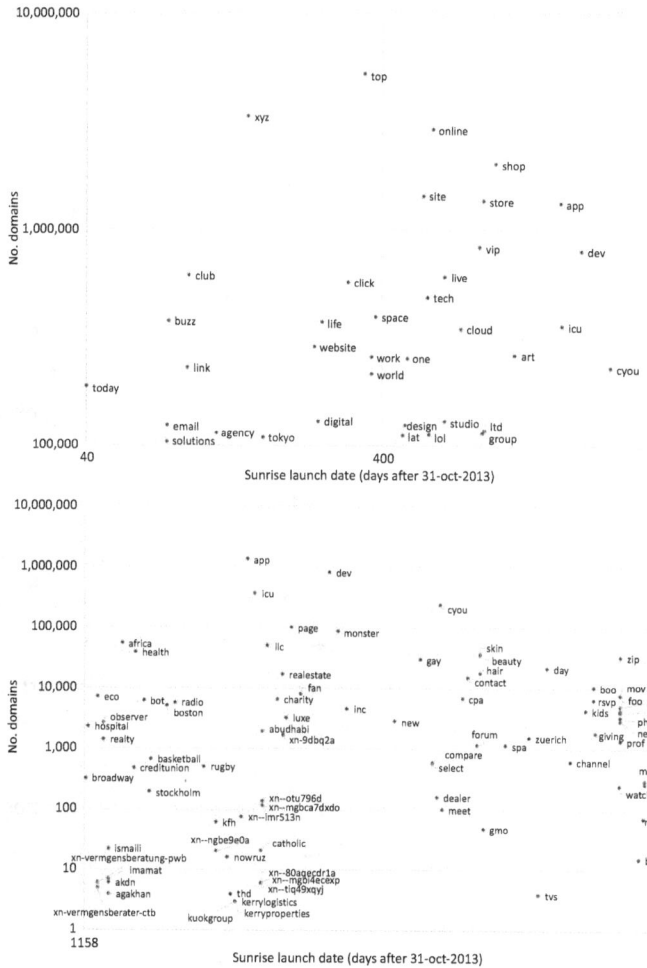

Figure 9.3 (Log-log) scatter plots of new-gTLD size (by number of registered domains) against date of start of Sunrise period (measured in days since October 31, 2013), for: (a) all new-gTLDs with more than 100,000 domain registrations (top); and (b) all new-gTLDs registered since the start of 2017 (bottom)

domains, at 99,499), .buzz, and .cyou) appear in the top 30 highest threat TLDs (Table 5.1) overall, and other popular new-gTLD extensions, such as .xyz, are also notorious for association with abuse.[19]

It is noteworthy that a significant proportion of the early adoption of new-gTLD domains arose in response to the availability of very low-cost registrations. In many cases, however, renewal rates of these domains were very low, with registrants often opting to move to an alternative registrar for a similar deal, at the point of domain expiry. Much of this activity was accounted for by high volumes of registrations of speculative brand infringements, a situation which has been mediated to some degree by the introduction of schemes (such as GlobalBlock[20]) allowing brand owners to block registrations matching protected terms, across particular TLDs.**

Of course, however, new-gTLD domains are also utilized for legit-imate purposes, and the set of most popular extensions also includes a number of examples which provide insight into the most popular use-cases. For example, the presence of .store and .shop in the list of top extensions suggests that the new-gTLDs are a popular choice for e-com-merce sites, and the inclusion of .app is consistent with the growth of mobile technologies.

9.2.2 Dot-Brands

It is also informative to consider the state of the *dot-brand* landscape.[21] Dot-brands are a special class of restricted new-gTLDs, where a brand owner has been granted the responsibility of overseeing the infrastructure of their own brand-specific domain extension, with examples including .barclays and .bmw. This can be an attractive prospect for an organiza-tion, as it gives them full control over all domains registered across the extension in question[22] and (providing they utilize the extension for all official websites and successfully communicate to their customer base that

---

[19] https://silicon.nyc/xyz-domain-problems-spam/
[20] https://www.iamstobbs.com/opinion/key-facts-about-the-globalblock-scheme-a-consideration-for-domain-management-and-online-brand-protection-clients
[21] https://www.iamstobbs.com/opinion/a-review-of-the-current-state-of-the-new-gtld-programme-dot-brands
[22] https://icannwiki.org/Brand_TLD

this is the case) can make it a much more difficult for fraudsters to create convincing fake sites. However, it is a costly enterprise (with just the initial evaluation fee reaching \$185,000[23] in the first phase of applications), whereby the brand owner needs to act as a domain registry in their own right, requiring extensive investment in the necessary technological infrastructure.[24] There are also other considerations, such as the requirements to 'rebuild' search-engine rankings when switching over to a new corporate domain name.[25] Overall these facts have led to a number of dot-brand applicants subsequently discontinuing use. Nevertheless for large corporates, it is a possibility worth considering, particularly with the new round of gTLD applications set to launch in 2026.

As of December 2023, there were 421 delegated dot-brand extensions. A significant study of the extent of their utilization has been carried out by management consultancy DOTZON, in the sixth edition of their Digital Company Brands report.[26] This study considers factors such as the number of registered domains on each extension, the extent of use for e-mail communication, the proportion of domains resolving to live sites, and other search-engine optimization statistics, to calculate a metric of the 'digitalness' of each company and its dot-brand TLD. The analysis gives the top ten as .leclerc, .schwarz, .audi, .weber, .mma, .google, .abbott, .cern, .lundbeck, and .allfinanz.[27] It is significant to note that European entities, particularly in Germany and France, feature highly in the list of dot-brand adopters, with insurance and finance as the top industries.[28]

A simple piece of analysis is just to consider the total number of registered domains across each of the dot-brand extensions (where zone-file data are available (334 extensions), which includes all of DOTZON's top

---

[23] https://newgtlds.icann.org/en/applicants/global-support/faqs/faqs-en

[24] https://circleid.com/posts/20200822-why-you-should-not-apply-for-a-dot-brand-new-gtld

[25] https://circleid.com/posts/20160927_seo_and_new_dot_brand_gtld

[26] https://dotzon.consulting/studien/

[27] https://circleid.com/posts/20231130-dotzon-study-digital-company-brands-2023

[28] https://www.worldipreview.com/contributed-article/global-adoption-of-dotbrand-domains

Table 9.3 Top dot-brand extensions, by number of registered domains (where data available)

TLD	Owner	No. domains
.ovh	OVH	94,090
.quest	Quest Software	38,918
.dvag	Deutsche Vermögensberatung	5,693
.kred	KredTLD	3,158
.giving	Giving Limited	1,845
.mma	MMA IARD	1,667
.allfinanz	Allfinanz Deutsche Vermögensberatung Aktiengesellschaft	1,264
.crs	Federated Co-operatives (Co-Operative Retailing System)	1,127
.leclerc	E.Leclerc	1,109
.gmx	1&1 Mail & Media (GMX, Global Message Exchange)	949

ten apart from .audi). The top ten extensions, by numbers of domains, are listed in Table 9.3.

Overall 48 of the extensions analyzed (i.e., 14%) have more than 100 domains registered. Conversely 160 of the extensions analyzed (48%) have ten registered domains or fewer.

Of course the total number of registered domains on a dot-brand extension is not, in itself, a measure of how 'well' a brand owner is utilizing the extension; it would be perfectly valid for a brand owner just to use (say) *www.[brand]* as their sole corporate website and nothing else (and, arguably, this presents the least risk of customer confusion). Nevertheless a dot-brand extension does provide a number of compelling use-cases for brand owners, including possibilities for region-, product-, or corporate-division-specific subsites. For example, .mma and .allfinanz use subdomain names for individual financial consultants, and .bmw and .audi do likewise for specific dealerships. Studies from the last few years have consistently found that around three-quarters of dot-brand domains tend to resolve to active websites.[29]

Significant insights are also available through consideration of the second-level domain names (SLDs) used with dot-brand extensions. Table

---

[29] https://www.cscdbs.com/en/resources-news/dot-brand-report/

Table 9.4 Most frequently used SLDs (for dot-brands where data available)

SLD	No. instances
www	63
home	61
go	42
my	39
mail	38
careers	34
global	33
api	32
cloud	31
jobs	28

9.4 shows the top ten most frequently used SLDs from analysis of zone-file information.

These trends are largely unchanged from a similar study carried out five years earlier,[30] from which the top five SLDs all still appear in the current top six (though now with the addition of *go*).

A special case is the two-character SLD; two-character strings are often used to denote country codes, and can be used in conjunction

Table 9.5 Most frequently used two-character SLDs (for dot-brands where data available)

SLD	No. instances
go	42
my	39
id	21
it	17
de	17
ai	17
uk	16
us	16
in	14
ru	13

---

[30] https://www.cscglobal.com/cscglobal/pdfs/DBS/CSC_Dot_Brand_Insights_Report_Jun2018.pdf

with dot-brand extensions to create regional subsites. The top ten two-character SLDs are shown in Table 9.5.

Many of these (particularly *de, uk, us, and ru*) are likely to be used most frequently to refer to their respective countries (i.e., Germany, UK, United States, and Russia), while others (*go, my*) are more likely to be intended for use as readable keywords. It is also striking that *ai* appears in the top ten, most likely a reflection of the growing popularity of artificial intelligence (AI) technologies, and their adoption by major corporations (see Section 14.1).

Insight into these frequently used keywords can be beneficial to organizations potentially looking to build out a dot-brand presence, providing guidance on common trends used to make websites navigable and avoid customer confusion, and also potentially to assist with conventions which may help to improve search-engine optimization strategies.

9.3 Domain-Name Availability

Throughout this section, the data pertaining to domain-name availability are based on the presence or absence of domains in the respective zone file.[31] However it is worth noting that the absence of a domain from the zone file does not *necessarily* mean that the name is unregistered and available; other factors (such as the domain having being put 'on hold', or having no associated nameservers) may also result in the name not being present.[32] Accordingly, the figures relating to the numbers of unregistered domains will actually be conservative (upper) estimates.

9.3.1 The .Com Namespace

As shown in Table 9.1, .com remains by far the most popular domain extension (with both brand owners and infringers alike), and retains the greatest familiarity with internet users generally. As such, .com registrations are very often the first choice to brand owners for their official

---

[31] https://www.iamstobbs.com/availability-of-domains-ebook
[32] https://serverfault.com/questions/1003729/expiry-of-domain-from-zone-file

corporate websites. However, the popularity of the extension also means that—although the total number of *possible* domain names, which (for 'classic' Web2 DNS) can be up to 63-characters in length, is enormous— by some measures, the TLD is beginning to 'run short' of capacity, with many of the short and memorable possible domain names already registered, leaving limited choice for entities seeking to launch a new brand identity.

Only three one-character .com domains are currently in existence (*x.com*—acquired by Elon Musk following Twitter's rebrand—plus *q.com* and *z.com*), with the majority of one-letter names having been explicitly reserved by the Internet Assigned Numbers Authority (IANA) in the early 1990s.[33] Many other short .com names are in active use by major corporations for their public-facing websites and e-mail infrastructure,[34] with numerous instances of multimillion dollar sales of two-letter domain names having been reported.[35] It has also been reported that the vast majority of dictionary terms up to (at least) five characters in length are no longer available.[36] Generally, domains are offered on a 'first come, first served' basis, meaning that (depending on IP protection), brands may often need to resort to acquisition processes in order the secure their preferred domain.[37]

More detailed insights are available from analysis of the .com zone file. For simplicity, the findings presented in this section pertain to domains consisting just of (Latin) *alphabetic* characters (with data correct as of September 2023). However, it is worth noting that numeric domain names are also popular, particularly in regions such as China, where their use can circumvent language barriers and certain numbers can have specific cultural significance.

---

[33] https://www.quora.com/Why-are-there-no-single-letter-domain-names

[34] https://smartbranding.com/ll-type-domains/

[35] https://www.globenewswire.com/en/newsrelease/2019/04/29/1811388/9865/en/Coveted-Two-Letter-Domain-Name-Potentially-Worth-Millions-to-Auction-Exclusively-on-NameJet.html

[36] https://www.quora.com/Have-all-5-character-com-domain-names-been-taken

[37] https://nz.news.yahoo.com/world-running-domain-names-gone-130011203.html

Table 9.6 Statistics for alphabetic .com domain names of SLD length n characters

n (SLD length)	Possible no.	No. registered	No. unregistered or absent from zone file	% registered
1	26	3	23	11.54%
2	676	674	2	99.70%
3	17,576	17,532	44	99.75%
4	456,976	455,325	1,651	99.64%
5	11,881,376	2,744,780	9,136,596	23.10%
6	308,915,776	5,779,635	303,136,141	1.87%
7	8.03×10^9	6,828,656	8.02×10^9	0.085%
8	2.09×10^{11}	8,482,121	2.09×10^{11}	0.0041%
9	5.43×10^{12}	9,609,092	5.43×10^{12}	0.00018%
10	1.41×10^{14}	10,658,182	1.41×10^{14}	0.0000076%
11	3.67×10^{15}	10,963,997	3.67×10^{15}	0.00000030%
12	9.54×10^{16}	10,843,645	9.54×10^{16}	0.000000011%

Table 9.6 shows the total number of registered domains for each domain (SLD) length. In each case, these values are also expressed as a proportion of the total 'pool' of possible domain names (of which the number, for a domain length of *n* characters, is equal to 26^n).

For two-, three-, and four-letter alphabetic domain names, over 99.6 percent of the available names are already registered (with several of the remainder also reserved or otherwise unavailable). Just under one-quarter of the five-letter domain names are taken, and beyond this, although the absolute *number* of registered domains continues to rise up to an SLD length of 11 characters, the *proportion* of the namespace which is registered drops off rapidly, due to the exponential growth in the *possible* number of names as SLD length increases.

For the two-letter domains, only two (*dm.com* and *jh.com*) (out of $26^2 = 676$) are not (as of the time of analysis) present in the zone file. However, both have active whois records, and are not available for registration.

With three letters, all but 44 combinations (out of a possible set of 26^3 = 17,576) are definitively registered.

The following is a list of all three-letter strings which are not currently present in the .com zone file:

baq	gdy	ndq	qgt	trc	zig
bfh	hfh	njq	qvz	ucl	zip
btz	ilq	nnr	qzk	wxa	zkb
bzg	jig	oys	rfc	xjz	zkn
ciz	jrx	pbq	ruu	xkd	
eth	kgr	pqk	sfj	xko	
exu	kkk	pwe	soe	ykn	
fkd	mag	qag	sok	ykz	

This means that all three-letter combinations beginning with (at least) *a, d, l,* and *v* are taken, but even the 44 listed above also have active registration records, according to whois look-ups. Among the inactive strings, some have particular relevance. *kkk.com*, for example, expired in October 2022 and was subsequently offered for sale via GoDaddy Auctions. By mid-November, the domain had received a high bid of nearly $100,000, before being withdrawn from sale and blocked, following concerns about the domain's possible association with the Ku Klux Klan.[38]

9.3.2 Availability of Short Domains Across the gTLD Landscape

It is instructive to extend the above analysis across all gTLDs for which zone files are publicly available (1,078 extensions as of September 11, 2023). Table 9.7 shows, for each of the top 40 gTLDs, the proportion of the set of all possible domain names which are currently already registered, for one- to six-character alphabetic domain names.

A number of top-level observations are apparent:

- Overall, .com is by far the most 'full' namespace, with 23.10 percent of all possible five-letter domains and 1.87 percent of

---

[38] https://domaininvesting.com/godaddy-cancels-kkk-com-expiry-auction/

Table 9.7 Proportion of the set of all possible domain names which are already registered, for each of the top 40 gTLDs (by total number of registered one- to six-character domains), as a function of SLD length (n characters)

	n = 1	n = 2	n = 3	n = 4	n = 5	n = 6
com	11.54%	99.70%	99.75%	99.64%	23.10%	1.87%
net	7.69%	98.96%	99.78%	55.93%	3.74%	0.22%
org	65.38%	98.22%	99.37%	42.23%	3.22%	0.15%
xyz	69.23%	29.44%	81.99%	21.58%	1.35%	0.07%
info	3.85%	0.74%	94.48%	30.77%	1.21%	0.06%
top	50.00%	11.83%	7.59%	15.03%	1.57%	0.07%
shop	0.00%	2.81%	3.03%	8.92%	0.75%	0.05%
online	0.00%	3.25%	17.16%	9.99%	0.71%	0.04%
site	15.38%	6.21%	6.22%	6.92%	0.50%	0.03%
biz	100.00%	98.96%	43.68%	6.09%	0.47%	0.03%
store	3.85%	3.40%	7.62%	6.01%	0.43%	0.03%
app	92.31%	66.42%	72.04%	7.00%	0.41%	0.02%
dev	3.85%	53.40%	31.61%	6.12%	0.33%	0.02%
tech	0.00%	9.32%	31.75%	6.12%	0.32%	0.02%
vip	96.15%	91.86%	53.43%	7.84%	0.28%	0.01%
club	96.15%	40.53%	14.20%	5.38%	0.34%	0.01%
link	38.46%	54.59%	20.57%	5.08%	0.42%	0.01%
pro	15.38%	1.18%	0.76%	5.16%	0.25%	0.01%
live	19.23%	61.54%	13.55%	4.36%	0.23%	0.01%
cloud	0.00%	0.74%	24.29%	3.64%	0.23%	0.01%
fun	3.85%	1.92%	6.33%	4.01%	0.24%	0.01%
life	80.77%	73.37%	52.05%	3.42%	0.24%	0.01%
one	0.00%	5.77%	64.58%	3.81%	0.17%	0.01%
space	7.69%	3.85%	9.64%	3.04%	0.21%	0.01%
asia	92.31%	9.62%	42.26%	4.03%	0.14%	0.01%
work	80.77%	78.85%	12.86%	3.24%	0.14%	0.01%
world	23.08%	86.83%	51.46%	2.93%	0.13%	0.01%
website	0.00%	1.33%	5.70%	1.91%	0.16%	0.01%
buzz	7.69%	5.92%	10.50%	1.24%	0.17%	0.01%
mobi	0.00%	1.33%	28.23%	2.05%	0.11%	0.01%
ltd	100.00%	2.96%	25.74%	3.06%	0.10%	0.00%
icu	100.00%	22.19%	45.91%	0.57%	0.13%	0.01%

	$n = 1$	$n = 2$	$n = 3$	$n = 4$	$n = 5$	$n = 6$
email	73.08%	51.33%	37.20%	2.10%	0.09%	0.00%
group	84.62%	13.46%	30.54%	2.34%	0.10%	0.00%
click	7.69%	12.13%	4.76%	0.31%	0.12%	0.01%
digital	100.00%	72.34%	35.80%	1.91%	0.09%	0.00%
monster	7.69%	1.78%	9.35%	6.08%	0.04%	0.00%
art	11.54%	1.33%	6.00%	1.23%	0.10%	0.01%
design	19.23%	46.89%	29.12%	1.80%	0.09%	0.00%
lol	65.38%	10.36%	22.26%	1.73%	0.09%	0.00%

Key:

	100%
	99%–100%
	98%–99%
	95%–98%
	90%–95%
	50%–90%

six-letter domains registered (followed next by .net in both cases, with 3.74 and 0.22 percent, respectively).

- For three-letter domain names, .net, .com, and .org are all more than 99 percent full; .net actually has even lower availability than .com (17,537 domains registered out of a possible 17,576 compared with 17,532 for .com).
- For two-letter domain names, the .com, .net, .org, and .biz namespaces are all at least 98 percent taken (in addition to .country (99.26 percent), .law (98.67 percent), and .amsterdam (98.22 percent)).
- There are 27 gTLDs for which *all* 26 possible one-letter domains are registered. These extensions are: .biz, .ltd, .icu, .digital, .company, .wtf, .fyi, .cool, .run, .capital, .berlin, .law, .casa, .beer, .fashion, .hamburg, .wales, .srl, .country, .wedding, .cymru, .garden, .luxury, .irish, .esq, .abogado, and .prof.

Considering *all* gTLDs together (total number, $T = 1,078$), it is also possible to calculate the total proportion of all possible domain names of

Table 9.8 Statistics for all gTLD domain names of SLD length n characters

n (SLD length)	Possible no.	No. registered	% registered
1	28,028	3,584	12.79%
2	728,728	51,322	7.04%
3	18,946,928	622,712	3.29%
4	492,620,128	2,394,695	0.49%
5	12,808,123,328	5,667,908	0.044%
6	333,011,206,528	9,549,608	0.0029%

length n which are registered (where the total number of possible names is $(26n \times T)$) (Table 9.8).

The analysis shows that, although there are some subsets of the domain-name landscape which are nearing capacity (notably .com, .net, and .org for two- and three-letter domains), the overall landscape is by no means full. Even for highly desirable three-letter domain names, only around 3 percent of all possible names are taken, when considering the full set of gTLDs.

Accordingly going forward, it may be wise for brand owners to begin considering TLDs other than .com for their primary website presence. A number of pre-existing TLDs are beginning to be 'repurposed' for alternative use, including .io (popularly being used for technology-related brands) .ai (for brands relating to AI), .tv (relating to television or streaming services), and .co (as an alternative to .com for company websites). As of 2024, the original phase of the new gTLD program (Section 9.2) is ongoing, with new TLDs continuing to be launched, and the next round of applications for new domain extensions is set to begin in 2026. Some brand owners may find it advantageous to consider applying to run a new dot-brand extension, giving them full control over all domains across the TLD in question. Failing this, utilization of programs such as the TMCH and registration-alert and blocking schemes can be an effective way of defending IP and receiving early warning of infringements. In addition, brand owners should consider registering relevant domain names defensively across key TLDs, where they are available. Furthermore it may also be advantageous to consider extending registration policies into the emerging Web3 landscape (Section 13.3). In particular, the blockchain domain ecosystem provides options covering both generic extensions and dot-brands.

An associated recommendation for potential new brand owners is to select a longer, unusual, and/or novel term for their brand name. This not only raises the possibility of the respective domain being available for registration but also makes it possible to secure stronger intellectual property protection, and makes the prospect of brand monitoring more straightforward (and less reliant on successful removal of false positives).

9.4 Internationalized Domain Names (IDNs)[39]

IDNs are domain names featuring characters in non-Latin scripts, including examples featuring accented characters (e.g., münchen.de) and those which are entirely written in alternative character sets (such as яндекс.рф —Yandex Russia). The availability of this infrastructure not only allows brand owners to create domain names in local languages and target content to specific markets but also provides potential for bad actors to create names which are deceptively similar to the official domain names of trusted brands (e.g., by substituting a character with a non-Latin equivalent appearing visually similar—a so-called homoglyph).

IDNs can also be represented in an encoded form (using Latin characters only) known as Punycode, which is denoted by a string beginning 'xn--', and is how IDNs are represented in plain text within domain-name zone files. The encoded version contains all Latin characters from the domain name and also includes a representation of all non-Latin characters and their relative positions within the string (e.g., *hermès.com* is represented in Punycode as *xn--herms7ra.com*).

This section provides an overview of the existing landscape of IDNs across the set of gTLD extensions, and gives examples of some of the ways in which these domains can be utilized by infringers. For the analysis, all Punycode domains are translated to their true IDN equivalents.

Overall (as of the end of September 2023) there are around 1.3 million gTLD IDNs, with 470 distinct TLDs having at least one registered IDN. Table 9.9 shows the most popular gTLDs for IDN registrations.

---

[39] https://www.iamstobbs.com/idns-ebook

Table 9.9 Top gTLDs by numbers of IDNs

TLD	No. of IDNs
.com	853,308
.net	135,775
. 在线 (.xn--3ds443g) (Chinese for 'online')	27,956
.top	24,988
.商标 (.xn--czr694b) (Chinese for 'trademark')	24,894
.公司 (.xn--55qx5d) (Chinese for 'company')	23,972
.org	22,470
.info	17,365
.网络 (.xn--io0a7i) (Chinese for 'network')	16,377
.online	15,670
(*Others*)	135,556

Table 9.10 shows the most popular languages of the SLD strings (based on Google's *DETECTLANGUAGE* functionality[40]).

Table 9.10 Top SLD languages by numbers of gTLD IDNs

Language code	Language[41,42]	No. of IDNs
zh	Chinese	505,952
ko	Korean	136,248
de	German	112,566
ja	Japanese	104,861
th	Thai	42,153
en	English	38,844
zh-Hant	Chinese (trad.)	35,952
tr	Turkish	34,859
es	Spanish	34,576
fr	French	32,802
(*Others*)	219,518

---

[40] https://support.google.com/docs/answer/3093278?hl=en

[41] https://developers.google.com/admin-sdk/directory/v1/languages

[42] https://www.w3schools.com/tags/ref_language_codes.asp

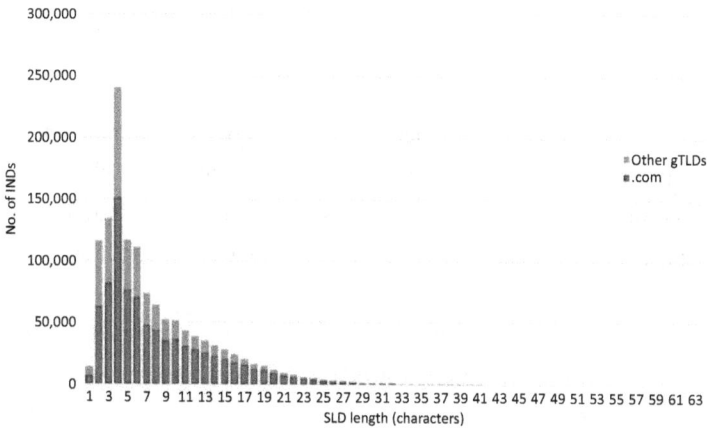

Figure 9.4 Distribution of IDN SLD lengths

The set of IDNs is (perhaps unsurprisingly) dominated by languages using entirely non-Latin alphabets, with four of the top five languages utilizing alternative character sets. In total, 125 different languages are represented within the dataset.

Figure 9.4 shows the distribution of SLD lengths (in characters) across the full dataset.

There is a wide range of SLD lengths present in the dataset of IDNs, from one character (over 14,000 instances) to 57 (one instance).

As an indicator of the likely level of infringements, and use of potentially deceptive domain names within the IDN dataset generally, it is instructive to consider the number of domains with SLDs similar to those of the main corporate domain names of each of the top ten most valuable global brands in 2023, as per the list provided by Kantar in their BrandZ analysis.[43] This analysis (presented as Case Study 9.1) considers homoglyph domains, that is, those in which one or more characters in the brand name has been replaced with a *non-Latin* character appearing visually similar, but with no additional keywords or other terms present in the domain name. Homoglyph domains comprise a specific subcategory of domains classified more generally as featuring brand variants (such as the examples considered in Case Study 7.1).

---

[43] https://www.kantar.com/inspiration/brands/revealed-the-worlds-most-valuable-brands-of-2023

Case Study 9.1: IDN Homoglyph Domains Targeting the Top Ten Most Valuable Global Brands

Table 9.11 shows the numbers of IDN homoglyph domains identified for the ten brands, also specifying the numbers which appear to be under the official ownership of the brand owner in question (e.g., defensive registrations or domains used for internal security purposes).

The visual similarity of some of these domains to the names of the official sites in question is striking, and presents very significant potential for the construction of deceptive sites. For example, the list of homoglyph domains for Google (the most heavily targeted top ten brand) is shown below (excluding official domains, and any examples where the whole SLD is in a *consistent* non-Latin script—e.g., γοογλε (Greek)—such that the domain may therefore simply

Table 9.11 Total numbers of IDN homoglyph domain names for each of the top ten most valuable global brands (shown in brackets are the numbers which appear to be under official ownership)

Brand string	.com	Other gTLDs	Total
apple	30 (10)	6 (1)	36 (11)
google	159 (44)	27 (6)	186 (50)
microsoft	34 (0)	7 (0)	41 (0)
amazon	82 (42)	17 (6)	99 (48)
mcdonalds	4 (0)	0	4 (0)
visa	5 (2)	0	5 (2)
tencent	1 (0)	0	1 (0)
louisvuitton	1 (0)	0	1 (0)
mastercard	10 (10)	0	10 (10)
coca(-)cola*	5 (0)	0	5 (0)
Total	331 (108)	57 (13)	388 (121)

* Hyphen optional

be intended for targeting toward a non-English market, rather than being explicitly deceptive):

google.com	googie.com	google.com	googlĕ.com	google.com
googlə.com	googɪe.com	google.com	googlē.com	googłe.com
googɪe.com	googɪə.com	GooGle.com	googlę.com	googłe.com
googíe.com	googiə.com	googlé.com	googlə.com	googłĕ.com
googīe.com	gœgle.com	googlĕ.com	googlə.com	googlę.com
googie.com	googʟe.com	googlê.com	googlɔ.com	google.com
googie.com	google.com	googlĕ.com	googľe.com	googlė.com
googlę.com	google.com	gŏŏgle.com	ɗoogle.com	Google.net
googlę.com	google.com	gŏŏgle.com	qoogle.com	googlé.net
google.com	goógle.com	gŏŏgle.com	google.com	googlĕ.net
googĺe.com	góógle.com	gŏogle.com	googlə.com	googlê.net
google.com	góóglĕ.com	gŏogle.com	gœglə.com	googlĕ.net
googlĕ.com	góóglę.com	gŏŏgle.com	googíə.com	googlə.net
googłe.com	góògle.com	gøøgle.com	googľə.com	googłe.net
googłe.com	góògle.com	gøøglé.com	googłə.com	góógle.net
googdle.com	góóglĕ.com	gøøgle.com	googłə.com	gòògle.net
google.com	gòògle.com	gøøgle.com	googlə.com	gôôgle.net
googole.com	góogle.com	gøøgle.com	googlə.com	gŏögle.net
google.com	góógle.com	google.com	googlə.com	gŏögle.net
googlé.com	góóglé.com	google.com	goóglə.com	gŏŏgle.net
googlé.com	góóglĕ.com	google.com	googlə.com	gøøgle.net
gòòglĕ.com	gôogle.com	gøøgle.com	googlə.com	google.net
goôglê.com	góôgle.com	gøøgle.com	góoglə.com	google.net
googðle.com	gôôglĕ.com	ğoogle.com	googlə.com	googłe.online
googðle.com	gôôglĕ.com	google.com	gooqle.com	gøøgle.online
gøøgle.com	gôôglĕ.com	google.com	góoqle.com	google.org
google.com	gôogle.com	googĺe.com	gooqlə.com	gøøgle.org
googlę.com	góógle.com	google.com	gŏögle.biz	góógle.xyz

Considering the full set of 267 nonofficial IDN homoglyph domains targeting the top ten brands (which have been registered over a long period of time, with the oldest examples dating back to 2001), 73 (27 percent) return a live website response. Furthermore a number of observations are consistent with the hypothesis that many

(Continued)

(*Continued*)

of these domains are likely to have been registered with fraudulent or infringing intent:

- 79 (30 percent) have active MX records, indicating that they have been configured to be able to send and receive e-mails and could therefore be associated with phishing activity. 53 of these have no active website and may be being used for their email functionality only.
- 128 (48 percent) explicitly make use of some sort of privacy-protection service in their whois record, as is often the case for domains registered for egregious use.
- The registrar breakdown is dominated by retail-grade providers, often popular with infringers (See Section 5.1.1), with the top three within the dataset found to be GoDaddy.com, LLC (102 domains), Squarespace Domains II LLC (38), and NameCheap, Inc. (25).

Among the domains resolving to live content, several examples of websites featuring brand infringements or other content of potential concern were identified, with content types including lookalike sites, unauthorized brand usage (Figure 9.5), instances of misdirection and potential piracy, in addition to a number of pages offering the domain name for sale or monetized through the inclusion of pay-per-click links.

The next phase of analysis considers the total number of replaced (i.e., non-Latin) characters in each of the domains (again excluding official domains and those where the whole SLD string is in a consistent non-Latin script). Table 9.12 shows the mean values for each of the ten brands, expressed both as an absolute number, and as a proportion of the whole brand string.

Across the full dataset, the average number of replaced characters in a homoglyph domain is 1.62 (26 percent of the whole string), highlighting the necessity for the use of detection technologies able

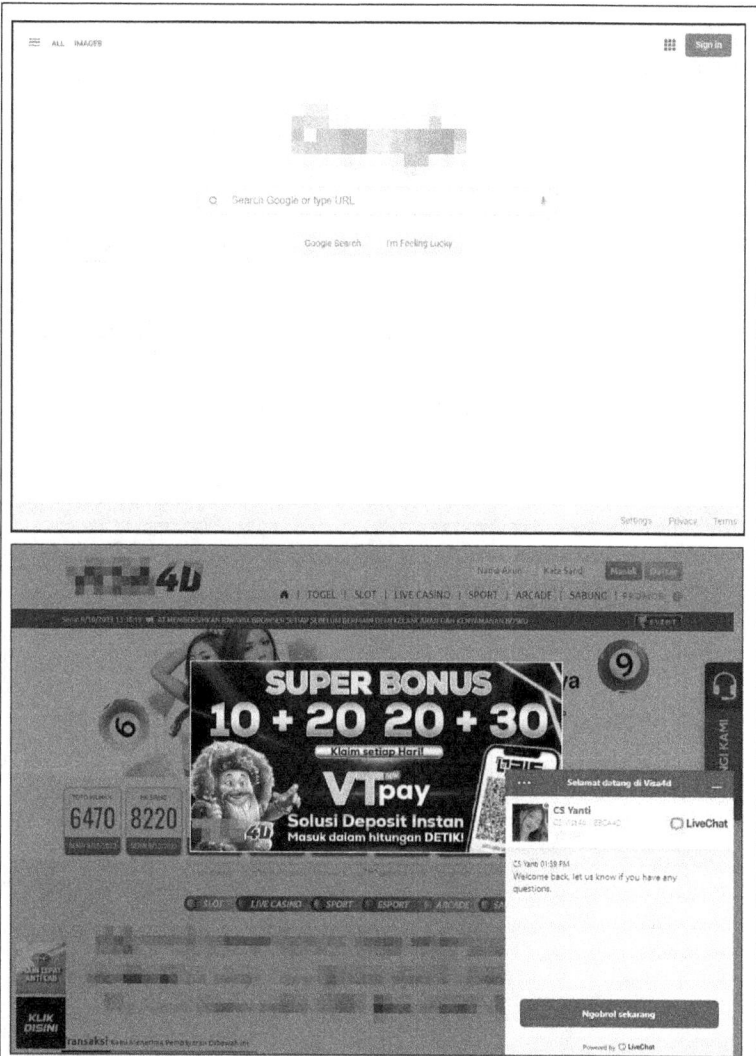

Figure 9.5 Examples of live sites of potential concern hosted on homoglyph domains: Lookalike site (SLD name: googℓe (xn--googe-m6a)), unauthorised use of brand (SLD name: visā (xn--vis-ola))

to analyze the full strings in order to detect visual similarity, rather than just identifying instances which differ from the official string by (say) a single character.

The dataset includes ten domains in which more than one-half of the characters in the string are replaced by non-Latin homoglyphs. These are listed in Table 9.13.

(Continued)

(Continued)

Table 9.12 *Mean number of replaced characters (also expressed as a proportion of the whole brand string) in the set of IDN homoglyph domains for each of the ten brands*

Brand string	No. domains	Mean no. of replaced characters	Mean % of replaced characters
apple	25	1.92	38%
google	135	1.67	28%
microsoft	41	1.39	15%
amazon	45	1.44	24%
mcdonalds	4	3.00	33%
visa	3	1.00	25%
tencent	1	2.00	29%
louisvuitton	1	2.00	17%
mastercard	0	–	–
coca(-)cola*	5	1.20	15%

* Hyphen optional

None of the domains resolved to any infringing content as of the time of analysis, although three (marked with a dagger) were found to have active MX records.

Table 9.13 *Domains in which more than half of the characters are replaced by non-Latin homoglyphs*

Domain name	Punycode representation	No. repl. characters	% repl. characters
APPLE.com	xn--spa916kwa0ea.com	5	100%
appie.com†	xn--80ak6aa4i.com	5	100%
appie.net†	xn--80ak6aa4i.net	5	100%
appie.com†	xn--80a6aa2gv8a.com	5	100%
apple.com	xn--80ak6aa92e.com	5	100%
MICROSOFT.com	xn--9na8b158j8ana8f5252lha.com	9	100%
MCDONALDS.com	xn--koa0gs43goafd4cs67392a.com	9	100%
AMAZON.com	xn--koa507ka5cl7i.com	6	100%
google.com	xn--le-igba3625aa.com	4	67%
google.com	xn--gg-9hb063ya97o.com	4	67%

Across the full homoglyph dataset (and also when considering examples targeting other brands), the .com TLD appears to be used by far the most frequently for this specific type of infringement, presumably a reflection of the frequency of use of .com for official corporate sites, and the corresponding potential for confusion.

For brands, the infinite scope for homoglyph-type variations means that a defensive domain registration approach *in isolation* will most likely prove to be only of limited effectiveness in preventing infringements (and may be costly); in cases where brands have been found to be holding portfolios of homoglyph domains for defensive purposes, there are typically at least as many equally convincing other variant domains available for registration, or currently held by third parties. Accordingly, a program of defensive registrations should always be accompanied by a proactive initiative of monitoring for third-party registrations.

9.5 Domain-Name Management Policy Construction[44]

As discussed in Section 1.3, a core component of a brand protection and IP-management initiative for a corporation is the maintenance of a portfolio of official (core plus tactical) domains. In many cases, a portfolio is specified on the basis of a domain-name management policy, which sets out the list of domain names required for inclusion in the portfolio, in terms of the brand (and other keyword) strings to feature as the SLD names, and the TLDs to be covered. Once a proposed portfolio has been specified, it can be constructed through a combination of domain purchases, acquisitions (where possible and appropriate), and lapses of domains no longer required.

In general terms, the construction of a policy will involve consideration of a number of factors, including levels of IP protection, geographical extent of business operations, brand protection budget, pre-existing infringement patterns, and overall level of risk aversion by the brand owner. As part of these considerations, it is often necessary to

---

[44] https://www.iamstobbs.com/opinion/strategies-for-constructing-a-domain-name-registration-and-management-policy

assign brands, sub-brands, and keyword strings into tiers, depending on their level of importance and protection, and generally specifying that higher-tier strings should be protected (through defensive registrations) across a wider range of TLDs and/or with a greater range of brand variants or relevance keywords. In addition, knowledge of the domain landscape and patterns of infringements (including insights into factors such as the higher-threat TLDs)—as discussed in previous sections—will help to inform the policy.

A desired domain portfolio can conveniently be specified in terms of a '*matrix*' of proposed domain names, in which the rows and columns represent the relevant brand terms/keyword strings (SLDs), and the TLDs, respectively. A schematic example of how this domain matrix may look in practice is shown in Table 9.14.

The construction of the policy matrix is based, in general, on considerations such as whether the focus should be on high-relevance domain names only (e.g., those which are likely to be directly utilizable for business purposes, such as cases where the SLD consists of just the brand name), or whether to build a broader defensive portfolio (e.g., incorporating variants containing product- or industry-related or geographical keywords), and the extent to which 'fuzzy' or typo-variations should be included.

A general recommendation is not to attempt to cover a range of typos or misspellings which is too broad, due to the potential for infinite variations of these types, and the corresponding possibility of rapidly escalating costs for domains which have little commercial value (see also Case Study 9.1). Instead a more efficient approach is to augment the domain management program with a brand-protection service which is able to identify these types of examples as they arise, and deal with them appropriately through an enforcement and domain-acquisition program.

Finally it may be appropriate to ensure that coverage encompasses keyword strings or patterns associated with known or repeated infringements.

When constructing the groups of TLDs to be covered, it is generally advisable to include those which:

- Are generally popular.
- Relate to those geographical regions in which the brand has current or planned business operations, and/or where IP protection (such as trademark registrations) are in place.

Table 9.14 Schematic example of a domain portfolio matrix for the fictitious (UK-based) luxury brand Luxurybrand, with tagline 'We Are Luxurybrand', offering a range of products: handbags (major product), shoes (intermediate), and perfume (minor)

Brand term / keyword string (SLD)	Popular		Geographically relevant			Industry-relevant new-gTLDs		High threat	
	.com only	Popular Group 1	UK (.uk, .co. uk, etc.)	EU	Rest of world	General (.shop, .store, .luxury, etc)	Product-type-specific	High threat Group 1 (highest threat)	High threat Group 2 (moderate threat)
luxurybrand	✓	✓	✓	✓	✓	✓	✓	✓	✓
weareluxurybrand	✓	✓	✓	✓	✓	✓	✓	✓	✓
we-are-luxurybrand	✓	✓	✓	✓	✓	✓	✓	✓	✓
luxurybrandhandbags	✓	✓	✓	✓	✓	✓	✓	✓	
luxurybrandbags	✓	✓	✓	✓	✓	✓	✓	✓	
luxurybrand-handbags	✓	✓	✓	✓	✓	✓	✓	✓	
luxurybrand-bags	✓	✓	✓	✓	✓	✓	✓	✓	
luxurybrandshoes	✓	✓	✓	✓			✓		
luxurybrandboots	✓	✓	✓	✓			✓		

(Continued)

(*Continued*)

Brand term / keyword string (SLD)	Popular		Geographically relevant			Industry-relevant new-gTLDs		High threat	
	.com only	Popular Group 1	UK (.uk, .co. uk, etc.)	EU	Rest of world	General (shop, .store, .luxury, etc)	Product-type-specific	High threat Group 1 (highest threat)	High threat Group 2 (moderate threat)
luxurybrandfootwear	✓	✓	✓	✓			✓		
luxurybrand-shoes	✓	✓	✓	✓			✓		
luxurybrand-boots	✓	✓	✓	✓			✓		
luxurybrand-footwear	✓	✓	✓	✓			✓		
luxurybrandperfume	✓		✓				✓		
luxurybrandfragrance	✓		✓				✓		
luxurybrand-perfume	✓		✓				✓		
luxurybrand-fragrance	✓		✓				✓		

Required TLDs

- Are commonly associated with infringing or fraudulent activity.
- (For new-gTLDs particularly), are industry-specific and relate to the business areas of the brand. As part of this assessment, it is important also to review new extensions as they approach their launch phases.

When attempting to construct the specified portfolio, it is important to note that it may not always be possible to acquire a domain currently under the ownership of a third party, depending on factors such as nature of use, prior rights, and levels of IP protection (see Section 11.2.2). In such instances, the suggested approach may simply be to monitor the site for changes to the content (so as to identify any appearance of infringing material).

Part of the portfolio consolidation process may also involve bringing all officially owned domains under centralized control (if, e.g., they have been registered by partners, affiliates, or franchise holders through outside providers).

Other general recommendations are also often applicable. One example might be to ensure that any official portfolio domains which are not under active use are configured to redirect to the brand owner's official transactional site, so as to maximize web traffic and minimize customer confusion. Additionally a significant component of effective domain management is the implementation of an effective domain security program utilizing an appropriate enterprise-class domain-name registrar, to ensure that official domains are protected from security threats such as site compromise and hacking.

Key points

The key points from this chapter are as follows:

- Domain-name analysis is of key importance for many brand protection and IP management considerations, due to the significance of domain names in maintenance of business-critical infrastructure and in third-party online infringements.

(Continued)

(Continued)

- Over 1,200 new domain-name extensions have been delegated (i.e., added to the internet Root Zone) since the start of the new-gTLD program in 2012. Within these, one special class of extension is the dot-brands, which are brand-specific extensions operated by the brand owner in question.
- Although the total number of possible unregistered domain names is extremely large, certain areas of the domain namespace (such as short and/or dictionary-word names across the .com, .net, and .org extensions) are beginning to run low on availability.
- Implications of this lack of availability may be a push toward brand owners selecting longer, unusual, or novel brand names, and/or exploring the use of alternative TLDs, or dot-brands (or, ultimately, Web3 alternatives) for their primary website presence.
- IDNs are domain names featuring characters in non-Latin scripts, which can alternatively be represented in an encoded form (using Latin characters only) known as Punycode.
- IDNs can be utilized by bad actors as a way of creating a highly deceptive infringing domain name and/or website.
- Domain-name management policies are a way of setting out recommendations for brand owners on the suggested names to be included in an official portfolio of core and tactical domains. The contents of a policy are dictated by levels of IP protection, geographical coverage of business operations, budget, and level of risk aversion, together with insights driven by an analysis of pre-existing patterns of infringements (such as information on brand terms typically used by bad actors, and data on high-threat TLDs).

CHAPTER 10

Brand Prominence and Sentiment

Overview

This chapter will cover:

- Formulations of simple metrics for quantifying the prominence and sense of sentiment (using a keyword-based approach) of the mentions of a brand, based on a representative sample of web pages.
- Ways in which these metrics can be applied in order to compare brands against each other and provide the basis for tracking changes over time.
- Exploration of how prominence and sentiment metrics can be linked to other relevant factors and parameters.

Measurement of the online **prominence** of brands provides insights into a number of areas, including search engine optimization (SEO) and web-traffic analysis, and brand valuation. Overall, it reflects the numbers of web pages on which brand references are present, and the degree of prominence of those mentions on the individual pages, within specific datasets of web pages. Frequently, these datasets are chosen to consist of those pages that are highly ranked by search engines in response to business-related query terms (i.e., the 'highest visibility' content). Brand prominence metrics usually cover all relevant content—both official and third-party—and thereby incorporate a reflection of the degree to which the brand is being targeted by infringers (and may be likely to be targeted in the future, working on the basis that infringers often favor brands which are popular and/or have an extensive pre-existing 'audience' or following).

A related idea is the concept of measurement of brand **sentiment**—that is, the sense (positive or negative) in which the brand is mentioned, for which quantification metrics can also be devised. Sentiment measurement can provide information on customer perception and brand value and can allow factors such as the impact of news stories and marketing initiatives to be tracked.

This section presents formulations of simple metrics through which measurements of prominence and sentiment can be quantified. Note that the analysis of sentiment as described here is built purely on a keyword-based approach (providing a straightforward and scalable framework). This methodology is distinct from more sophisticated approaches involving systems based on artificial intelligence and machine learning, for which the underlying algorithms have been 'trained' to correctly classify the content, based on datasets incorporating parameters that have initially been categorized manually (see Section 14.1).

Box 10.1 Formulation Definition—A Simple Metric for Quantifying Online Prominence[1,2]

The suggested metric for measuring brand prominence is based on the number of pages on which a brand mention is identified, and the number and prominence of the mentions on each page, from the analysis of a dataset of web pages.

In general, the most flexible approach is to identify brand mentions through analysis of the full HTML content of the web page (which includes material not necessarily present in the visible content), using technology able to match using *regular expressions* (*regex*). This formulation allows the type of matching to be 'tuned' as required. For example, it may or may not be appropriate to consider

---

[1] https://www.iamstobbs.com/measuring-brand-prominence-of-fashion-brands-ebook

[2] https://www.iamstobbs.com/online-brand-prominence-and-sentiment-ebook

brand appearances within longer strings (i.e., wildcard or *substring* matching)—for some brands, this may be desirable (e.g., for the AI brand *GPT*, it may be appropriate to include variations such as *ChatGPT* or *GPT4*), but for others this approach may generate false positives (e.g., for *Intel*, it would not be appropriate to consider a word such as *intelligence* to constitute a brand mention). In general, some element of wildcard matching is usually desirable (e.g., to identify references to the brand name in the URL of a page, in which the full URL is presented as a single string, with no spaces), so it may be appropriate to configure the matching such that, for example, the brand name must be prefixed and suffixed by any character *other* than an alphabetical character to be considered a relevant mention (e.g., *abc-intel-xyz*—where the brand name is embedded between hyphens—*would* be counted as a mention of *Intel*). However, the general principle, when comparing brands against each other, is to treat all brands similarly, as far as possible.

The next key point is that, when collecting the set of web pages for analysis, it is necessary *not* to explicitly search for any of the brand names under consideration. The reason for this is that—by definition—for any given query submitted to a search engine, all of the results will relate to the search term being used. Even if the analysis involves the collection of all such results, by continuing to paginate through until no further results are returned, this will usually only return a maximum number of results (typically a few hundred) for any given search engine and query. If, therefore, each brand name is simply searched separately, this will yield a relatively consistent number of results for each brand, and the brands will artificially appear to have similar online prominences. Instead, it is preferable to use *generic* search queries to bring back sets of pages relevant to the industry area of the brands in question (or to business in general) and measure the prominence of the brands based on the mentions that happen to be present in this overall representative sample of pages.

(Continued)

(Continued)

Once the dataset of web pages has been collected, the measurement of prominence is reliant on the calculation of the **brand content score** for each brand on each page, as defined in Chapter 3. This metric reflects both the number and prominence of the brand mentions on the page.

The overall prominence score for each brand can then simply be calculated as the mean of the individual brand content scores, across all pages analyzed. This simple approach also allows trends over time to be calculated, without needing to apply complex 'normalizations' to the data in order to compare one study to another.

Box 10.2 Formulation Definition—A Simple Metric for Quantifying Online Sentiment

Sentiment may most simply be quantified by identifying instances of brand mentions in proximity to any of a library of keywords implying positive or negative meaning (such as the lists provided by Hu and Liu, 2004).[3,4,††] Essentially, the approach is identical to that used for *issue monitoring*, involving the use of proximity-based keyword matching (as in Case Study 4.2), but where the sentiment keywords are here used in place of relevance keywords.

The most straightforward approach is where all keywords are treated equally (i.e., with equal weighting, implying that all the 'positive' keywords are equally strongly positive, and vice versa), such that (for each analyzed web page) the score contribution from each brand-keyword pair is a function only of the proximity between the two words (with instances where the words appear more closely together assigned a higher score). A brand reference near to a positive keyword is then assigned a positive score contribution and vice versa. The total positive (**S+**) and negative (**S-**) scores for each brand

---

[3] https://ptrckprry.com/course/ssd/data/positive-words.txt
[4] https://ptrckprry.com/course/ssd/data/negative-words.txt

can then be calculated, and the overall sentiment score (S_{page}) for the brand on the page in question is the difference between the two, that is:

$$S_{page} = S_+ - S_-$$

The overall sentiment score (S_{tot}) for the brand across the whole dataset of pages analyzed can then be defined as follows:

$$S_{tot} = \{[\sum_i^N (\sqrt[3]{S_{page\_i}})] / N\} \times \sqrt{N}$$

or equivalently:

$$S_{tot} = \{[\sum_i^N (\sqrt[3]{S_{page\_i}})] / \sqrt{N}$$

that is, the mean of the cube roots of the individual page sentiment scores, calculated across all (N) pages on which any reference to the brand was identified, multiplied by the square root of N (the number of contributing pages).

Notes:

- Taking the cube roots of the 'raw' sentiment scores reduces the impact of outliers (e.g., as may arise from 'junk' pages 'stuffed' with large numbers of random keywords), while retaining the 'sense' (positive or negative) of the individual page scores.
- The multiplication by √N provides a measure of significance, upweighting the score for brands where the mentions are *consistently* positive or negative, and downweighting it for brands for which the scores would otherwise be 'skewed' due to the fact that only a few relevant pages had been identified.

In some studies, it may be appropriate to edit the keyword lists (particularly if the brands or industry areas under consideration present the potential for confusion with any of the keywords in the lists*)

(Continued)

(Continued)

and/or utilize more focused or industry-specific sentiment keywords (reflecting the type of language and terminology likely to be used in the content being analyzed).

* Examples might include *limited* (presented in the standard library as a negative keyword (e.g., *options are limited*), but which may frequently be referenced in a neutral sense in business-related content—e.g., as part of a company name) and *cloud* (also presented as a negative keyword (e.g., *under a cloud*), but which may appear in reference to cloud technology providers, e.g.).

Case Study 10.1: Online Prominence and Sentiment of the Top 100 Most Valuable Global Brands

The first illustration of the general methodology outlined earlier concerns an analysis (as of November 2023) of the prominence and sentiment of references to the top 100 most valuable global brands in 2023. The case study considers a set of web pages from the first page of (approximately 100) results returned by google.com (from a UK IP address) in response to a series of searches for each of 50 words related generally to business (*business, company, employer, industry, profits, revenue*, etc.), giving a dataset of 4,376 unique URLs.

Where appropriate, additional brand *variations* are specified as being considered to be brand references (e.g., any regex (see Box 10.1) string of the form *tata.?consult.** (where '.?' is any optional one character, and '.*' is any number of characters) is considered to be a reference to Tata Consultancy Services). Additionally, for some of the most generic brand names, specific additional qualifiers are required, so as to avoid false positives (e.g., for JD, a brand reference is deemed to have been identified only if a match to *jd.?com* or *jingdong* explicitly is found; for TD, a match to *td.?bank* is required).

Beyond this (other than explicitly specifying that *start-ups* should not be considered a reference to UPS), no additional filtering is carried out to remove 'false positives' (such as references to *visa* in the generic sense, rather than as the brand name, or third-party usage of common brand names (such as BCA) by other entities). In more sophisticated formulations of this methodology, keyword-based filtering (Chapter 4) could be applied (though this would need to be on a per-brand basis, given that the brands cover a range of different industry areas). However, in an effort to treat all brands similarly as far as possible, filtering has not been applied in this case. Arguably, the fact that the overall scores reflect both *legitimate* brand references and *other* uses of the brand term does provide useful information on the extent to which the brand name is used online, and relates to issues such as brand distinctiveness and brand dilution.

The proximity matching for sentiment analysis uses a maximum score of 100 and a proximity 'half life' of one word.

The overall prominence scores for the top 30 most prominent brands are shown in Figure 10.1.

Figure 10.2 shows a comparison between the overall prominence score for the top 30 most prominent brands and their ranking in the Kantar list of most valuable brands.

Overall, Google is the most prominent brand within the set of web pages considered, by a significant margin, followed by Microsoft, LinkedIn, Amazon, and Facebook. There is also a weak correlation (coefficient = −0.30) between the Kantar ranking of the brands and their prominence scores, with many of the more highly ranked brands having higher prominences. For example, three of the top four most prominent brands (Google, Microsoft, and Amazon) appear in the top four of the Kantar index.

It is possible to consider a 'deeper dive' into the data, by first considering the relationship between brand prominence and absolute brand value (as also provided by Kantar), rather than just ranking, and also segmenting the brands by industry area, to determine whether any of the trends are sector specific. In order to do so, the 100 brands are assigned to 11 industry categories (a simplified version of the 18 groups used by Kantar). The findings are shown in Figure 10.3.

(*Continued*)

(*Continued*)

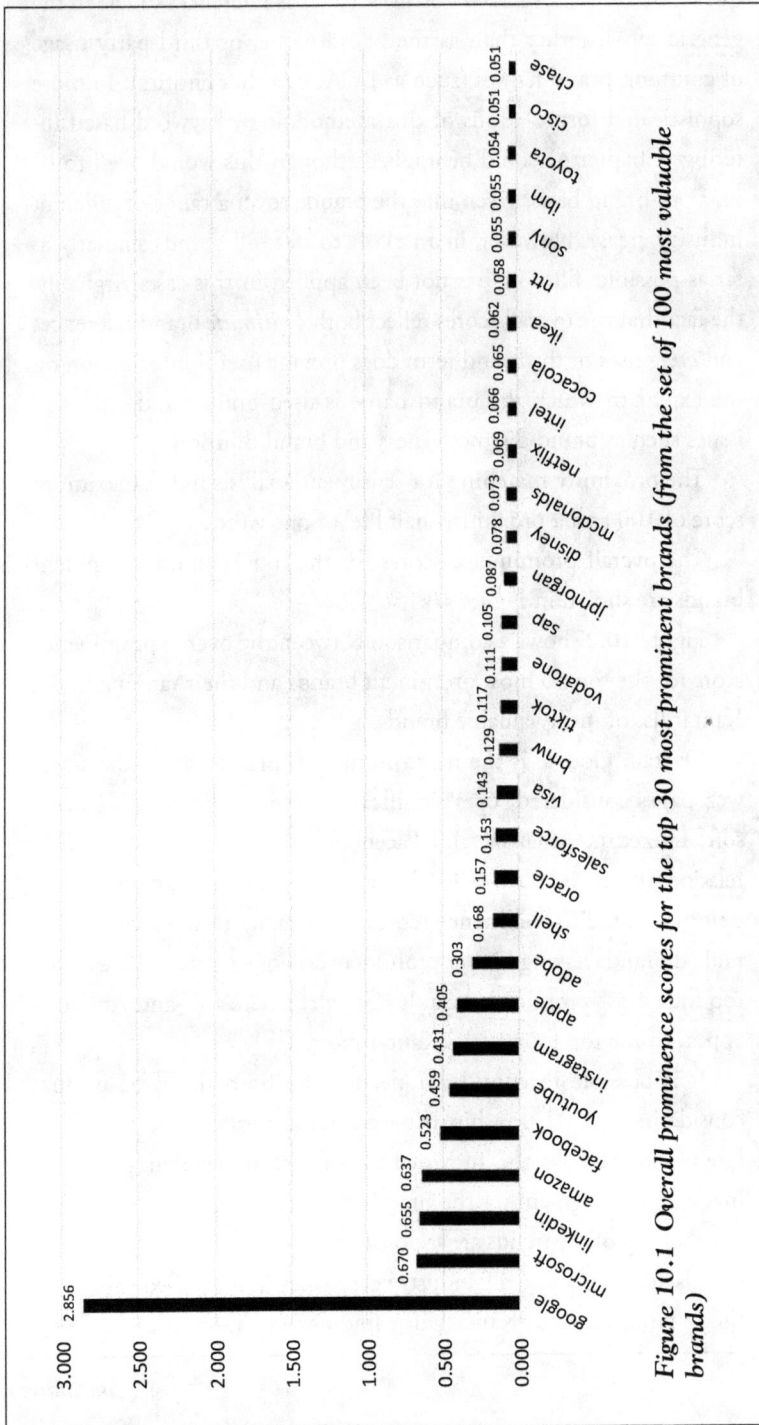

Figure 10.1 Overall prominence scores for the top 30 most prominent brands (from the set of 100 most valuable brands)

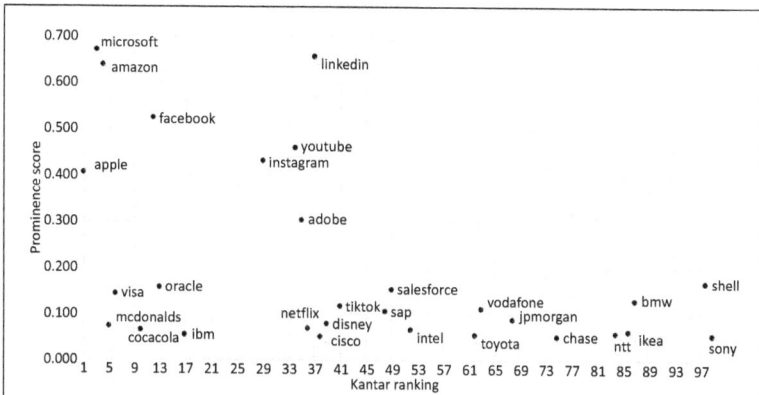

Figure 10.2 Comparison of overall prominence score with Kantar ranking for the top 30 most prominent brands (excluding Google; second in the Kantar list)

Overall, there is a general positive (though relatively weak) correlation between brand value and prominence score (correlation coefficient = +0.61). The following additional trends are also noteworthy:

- The group of brands that are disproportionately more prominent than would be expected by virtue of their brand value (i.e., those appearing toward the bottom-right of the graphs in Figure 10.3) is dominated by those in the media and entertainment sector (especially the social media and search brands Google, Facebook, LinkedIn, Instagram, and YouTube) and the technology sector (specifically Oracle, Salesforce, and SAP). This observation may be reflective of the online ubiquitous nature of the former set of brands, and the frequency with which the latter set of business-service brands are referenced in general business-related content.
- The set of brands that are disproportionately less prominent than might be expected (i.e., those appearing toward the top-left of the graphs in Figure 10.3) is more varied, but it is notable that many of the luxury brands

(Continued)

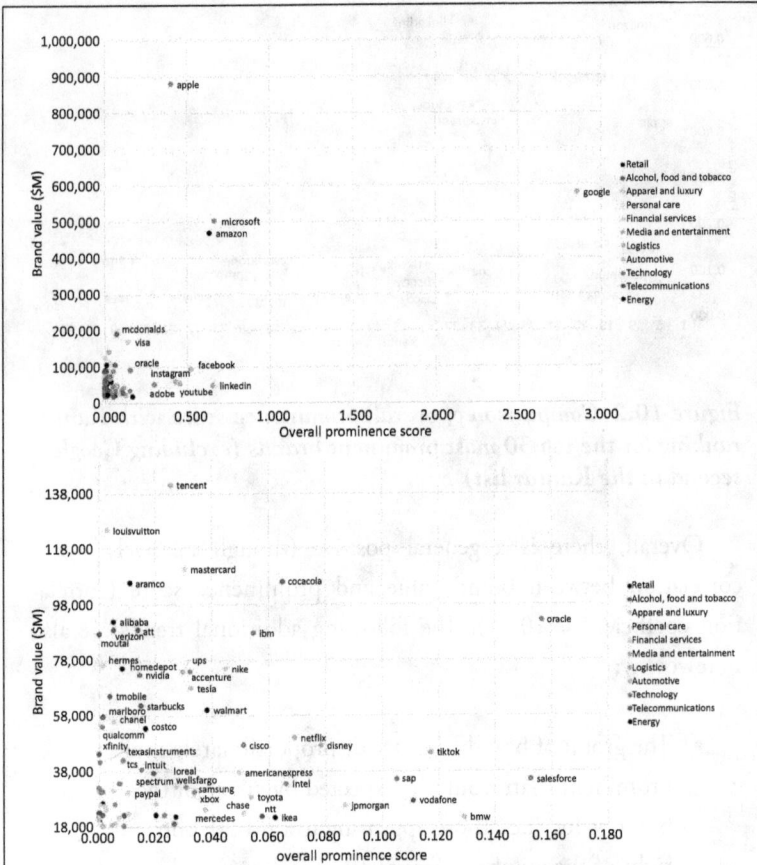

Figure 10.3 *Comparison of overall prominence score with brand value, for the top 100 brands, split by industry area (top: full dataset; bottom: detailed zoom of lower prominence/ lower brand value area)*

(Louis Vuitton, Hermes, Chanel) appear in this area. This may be reflective both of the high value of these brands generally, and the extent to which they perhaps need to be less reliant on SEO techniques, relying instead on reputation to drive traffic to their online content.

The overall weakness of the correlation is likely due to the fact that Kantar's overall formulation of brand value takes into account a number of factors beyond simple online prominence, such as current demand, price premium, and future demand and price.

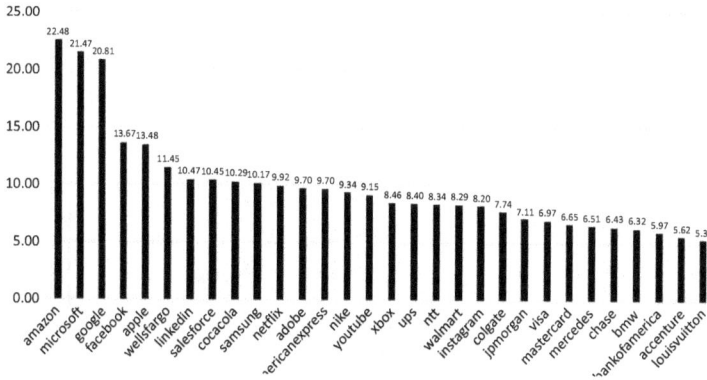

Figure 10.4 *Overall sentiment scores for the top 30 most positively referenced brands (from the set of 100 most valuable brands)*

The overall sentiment scores for the top 30 most positively referenced brands are shown in Figure 10.4.

It is noteworthy that the top four most valuable brands (Apple, Google, Microsoft, Amazon) (as per the Kantar rankings) all appear in the top five brands which are most positively referenced overall, with Amazon achieving the most highly positive sentiment score. Part of the reason for this top ranking is the fact that the dataset actually includes several pages from the official Amazon website, together with other sites that are affiliated with the brand, or provide brand-specific information (such as *amazonworkspaces.com* and *aboutamazon.com*).

An example of one of the highly scored pages for Amazon is shown in Figure 10.5, showing that it can be manually verified as including positive phraseology (i.e., consistent with the assertion that the methodology is generating meaningful results).

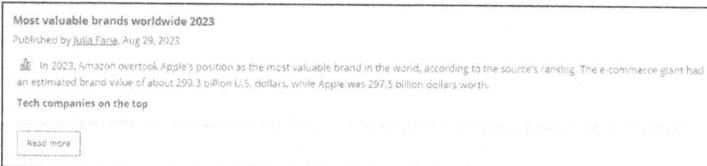

Figure 10.5 *Example of an extract from a web page assigned a highly positive sentiment score for Amazon (score = +100)*

(Continued)

Conversely, the bottom (most negatively referenced) brand in this analysis is ICBC, which appears to be—at least in part—due to news stories surrounding a cyberattack against the brand[5] which took place shortly prior to the analysis (Figure 10.6).

News in-depth US Treasury bonds

Cyber attack shines light on role of China's largest lender in US Treasury market

Disruption caused by hack of ICBC shows how bank has become an important link in $26tn market

Figure 10.6 Example of an extract from a web page assigned a highly negative sentiment score for ICBC (score = −56)

Case Study 10.2: Further Explorations in Brand Perception

Case Study 10.1 considered a set of web pages drawn from a series of generic, business-related search terms and may accordingly be more likely to incorporate pages that are overall relatively *neutral* or *positive* (specifically in cases where official or affiliated sites are featured). It might be possible to gain more meaningful insights into customer comments (i.e., 'true' perception) through the use of more focused search terms, potentially including the types of terminology that might be expected to appear on pages of reviews or product discussions.

As a follow-up, it is instructive to carry out an analysis of a set of web pages sourced using search terms specifically selected to focus on content pertaining to brand commentary (*popular, best, worst,*

---

[5] https://www.ft.com/content/d3c7259c-0ea6-414b-9013-ac615b1a8177

favourite, favorite, hated, loved, review, reviews, boycott, NPS; combined with each of: *company, companies, brand, brands, product, products, service, services*). The case study focuses on a set of approximately 100 brands selected from a range of online sources listing companies that are generally considered to be viewed particularly favorably or unfavorably.

Tables 10.1 and 10.2 show the top ten and bottom ten brands from the dataset, by overall sentiment score.

Table 10.1 Top ten brands by overall sentiment score

Brand	Sentiment Score
Amazon	+54.85
Google	+28.40
Facebook	+28.31
Apple	+27.81
Netflix	+23.09
TikTok	+19.10
Samsung	+18.44
Boots	+18.08
Twitter	+17.77
Gucci	+16.44

Table 10.2 Bottom ten brands by overall sentiment score

Brand	Sentiment Score
Equifax	−8.15
Nestlé	−2.63
Bitcoin	−2.62
Caterpillar	−2.35
Trump	−1.41
Hyundai	−1.05
Goldman Sachs	−0.79
Cigna	−0.69
FTX	−0.58
Spirit Airlines	−0.50

(Continued)

(Continued)

Note: of the 341 pages assigned positive sentiment scores for Amazon (the top brand in the rankings), 46 are URLs from an official Amazon website (amazon.com or amazon.co.uk), and the analysis may be picking up keywords pertaining to positive references to *other* brands featured on the pages (noting that the dataset includes URLs such as *amazon.co.uk/trending-products/* and *amazon.co.uk/Customers-Most-Loved-Popular-Brands-Fashion/*— actually the top two highest-scored pages for the Amazon brand itself). If all pages from official Amazon websites are removed from the sentiment calculation for the brand, its overall sentiment score decreases to +42.35.

The list of most positively referenced brands is dominated by brands that are large and popular generally. While a proportion of the identified references undoubtedly consists of genuine positive comments relating to these brands, a contributing factor to their high scores is likely to be their significant online prominence generally (reflected through the inclusion of the scaling factor of $\sqrt{N}$ (N = no. of contributing pages) in the calculation (Box 10.2)). It is also true, particularly for relatively ubiquitous online brands such as Google and Facebook, that brand mentions will be common on web pages containing positive comments in *other* contexts.

The list of most negatively referenced ('unpopular') brands is probably somewhat more meaningful, including many of the brands that are commonly subject to criticism and negative comments online. A series of examples of some of the highly negatively scored pages for brands in the bottom five are presented below, as an illustration of the types of negative comments being detected.

- Equifax
  - *https://observer.com/2018/01/equifax-most-hated-financial-services-company-data-breach/* (score = −271)
  - *https://www.ctpboston.com/latest/blog/the-6-worst-brand-apologies-and-what-should-have-been-done/* (score = −257):

"#4 Equifax: When your 'deep regret' is followed by a Congressional investigation, millions in consumer settlements and a CEO resig-

nation, it's pretty clear you missed the mark. That's what happened to Equifax after a massive data breach in 2017…. The credit reporting company responsible, in part, for protecting its consumers' financial information from the bad guys, had the personal data of 147 million people stolen from under their noses over a period of several months. It then took more than a month for Equifax to tell its customers and government agencies about it. In the meantime, three executives sold off nearly $2 million in company stock. So when the apology from CEO Richard Smith came—in the form of what looks like a hostage video and an Op-Ed in USA Today— the best apology would have been a new CEO apologizing for the decisions of the company and Smith. That came two weeks later. Crisis communications isn't simply about saying the right things and acting contrite. It's being transparent, doing the right thing to fix the problem, supporting those who were wronged and doing it all without delay. Equifax badly missed on all fronts"

- Nestlé
  - *https://www.babymilkaction.org/nestle-boycott-list* (score = −492)
  - *http://www.infactcanada.ca/nestle_boycott_product.htm* (score = −407)
- Trump
  - *https://mosthated33.com/collections/all* (score = −207) (Figure 10.7)
  - *https://commetric.com/2020/09/30/consumer-boycotts-the-5-most-controversial-brands-in-the-media-right-now/* (score = −187): "Over the last 10-15 years, boycotts have exploded in popularity, and the anti-Trump #GrabYourWallet campaign alone put almost 50 companies with ties to the president in activists sites."

It is also interesting to note that the brands taken from the (*positive*) lists of brands that are generally viewed favorably tend to sit

(*Continued*)

Figure 10.7 *Example of an extract from a web page assigned a highly negative sentiment score for Trump*

within a higher sentiment score range than those from the (*negative*) lists of unfavorable brands (although there is a significant amount of overlap, and numerous brands that feature in *both* sets of lists—including all of the top five by overall sentiment score) (Figure 10.8).

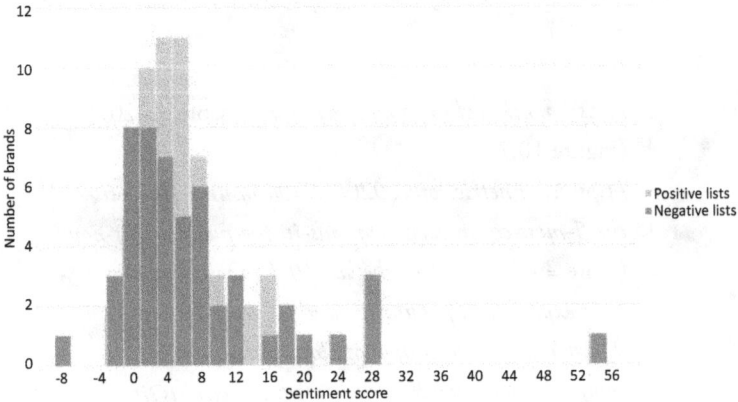

Figure 10.8 *Distributions of sentiment scores for those brands taken from the positive lists and those from the negative lists*

Case Study 10.3: The Relationship Between Prominence and Market Capitalization of the Top 20 Cryptocurrencies[6]

The following case study considers a group of 'brands' within a single industry area (in this case, the names of the top 20 cryptocurrencies by market capitalization, or total value) (as of December 2023), with a view to determining the extent of any correlation between these values and the online prominence of the cryptocurrencies.

The analysis utilizes a set of approximately 500 web pages highly ranked on Google in response to any of a series of generic, cryptocurrency-related keywords. A reference to a cryptocurrency is deemed to have been identified if either its name or its currency abbreviation (Table 10.3) appears in the web page content, with all match strings required to be prefixed and suffixed by nonalphabetic characters, to remove instances of false-positive *substring* matching (see Box 10.1), and in an effort to treat all currencies equally.

Figure 10.9 shows the relationship between the overall prominence scores and the market capitalization of the cryptocurrencies in question.

For the cryptocurrency brands, the correlation between online prominence and market capitalization is striking (coefficient = +0.984), such that the cryptocurrencies with the greatest degree of online presence are those that are most valuable overall. It is also noteworthy that this is a much stronger relationship than was seen in Case Study 7.1, where the brands occupied a range of different industry sectors, and it was therefore much more difficult to assemble a set of web pages for analysis on which the brands could be compared on a like-for-like basis.

(Continued)

---

[6] https://www.iamstobbs.com/opinion/coining-success-trends-in-the-online-brand-prominence-and-overall-value-of-cryptocurrencies

(Continued)

Table 10.3 *Top 20 cryptocurrencies by market capitalization,
and the terms used to identify a mention of each cryptocurrency
on a web page*

Cryptocurrency	Market Cap.*	Match String†	Currency Abbreviation
Bitcoin	$857,939,715,290	bitcoin	BTC
Ethereum	$267,706,465,184	ethereum	ETH
Tether USDt	$91,025,367,583	tether	USDT
BNB Binance Coin	$40,758,382,493	binance	BNB
Solana	$37,346,263,893	solana	SOL
XRP Ripple	$33,340,695,353	ripple	XRP
US Dollar Coin	$24,870,321,970	dollar.?coin	USDC
Cardano	$21,316,170,372	cardano	ADA
Avalanche	$16,855,482,028	avalanche	AVAX
Dogecoin	$13,112,069,070	dogecoin	DOGE
Polkadot	$9,434,536,158	polkadot	DOT
TRON	$9,214,721,890	tron	TRX
Chainlink	$8,357,572,900	chainlink	LINK
Toncoin	$7,730,417,709	toncoin	TON
Polygon	$7,550,523,318	polygon	MATIC
Shiba Inu	$6,100,389,245	shiba	SHIB
Dai	$5,346,962,992	dai	DAI
Litecoin	$5,186,612,825	litecoin	LTC
Bitcoin Cash[7]	$4,534,932,853	bitcoin.?cash	BCH
Cosmos	$4,097,217,773	cosmos	ATOM

* as of 21-Dec-2023[8]

† '.?' denotes any or no (i.e. optional) additional single character

---

[7] References to 'Bitcoin Cash' are <u>also</u> counted as references to 'Bitcoin' unless the brand is referenced specifically as 'BitcoinCash' (with no space) or 'BCH'. If the analysis were to be adapted to add a 'correction' to account for this double counting, the worst-case scenario would be where <u>all</u> references to 'Bitcoin Cash' are double counted in this way. If this were the case, it would be possible to adjust the brand content score for Bitcoin for each page, by subtracting the score for Bitcoin Cash, before calculating the mean. Applying this adjustment gives an overall prominence score for Bitcoin of 10.500, compared with the calculated value of 10.693 (i.e., a difference of under 2 percent)—and, in reality, the most representative score for Bitcoin will actually be somewhere between these two values. In the analysis as presented, however, the adjustment has <u>not</u> been applied, since it is reasonable to make the case that any reference to Bitcoin Cash <u>should</u> also be counted as a reference to Bitcoin, since the name of the former cryptocurrency is derived from that of the latter. https://www.independent.co.uk/tech/bitcoin-cash-cryptocurrency-roger-ver-a8346816.html

[8] https://coinmarketcap.com/

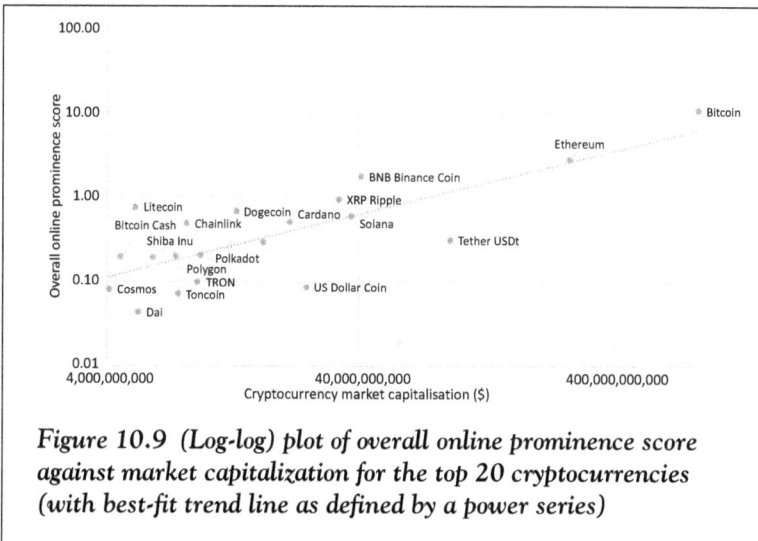

Figure 10.9 (Log-log) plot of overall online prominence score against market capitalization for the top 20 cryptocurrencies (with best-fit trend line as defined by a power series)

Key Points

The key points from this chapter are as follows:

- Brand **prominence** on a sample of web pages can simply be measured through an application of the brand content scoring approach (Chapter 3); a simple approach for measuring **sentiment** involves the identification of mentions of the brand in proximity to any of a library of keywords deemed to convey positive or negative meaning (with a closer proximity giving a greater weighting to the score).

- Prominence and sentiment measurements provide a basis for comparing brands against each other, and for tracking trends over time (e.g., for assessing the impact of news stories or marketing initiatives).

- Prominence and sentiment metrics may be related to other factors, including parameters relating to SEO, web-traffic analysis, and brand value (see Section 11.3.3 and Chapter 12).

CHAPTER 11

Quantifying Brand Protection Return-on-Investment[1,2,3]

Overview

This chapter will cover:

- The reasons why it is desirable to be able to quantify the return-on-investment (ROI) of a brand protection program and the factors contributing to the value of a program.
- Scenarios where simple standard calculations of ROI can be formulated, specifically cases of domain recovery and e-commerce marketplace takedowns.
- Ways in which basic ROI calculations can be extended to take account of other factors, such as consideration of variable substitution rates (reflecting the proportion of customers who will buy a legitimate item once an infringing version is made unavailable), quantification of long-term changes to the infringement landscape in response to a brand protection program, impacts on brand value, and the effects of proactive measures such as cybersecurity initiatives.

---

[1] https://www.iamstobbs.com/brand-protection-return-on-investment-ebook

[2] https://www.worldtrademarkreview.com/anti-counterfeiting/return-investment-proving-protection-pays

[3] https://www.circleid.com/posts/20201112-brand-abuse-and-ip-infringements-part-2-return-on-investment/

11.1 The Significance of Return-on-Investment (ROI)

The execution of a brand protection program can entail significant costs for brand owners. Aside from the investment in monitoring technologies and analyst resources, there are also typically a number of other requirements from appropriate stakeholders on the brand owner's side. These might include a requirement to oversee the brand protection program generally, liaising with any service provider and collating the prerequisite information for service configuration, and maintaining an appropriate portfolio of protected IP. Overall, there is therefore often a requirement to quantify the 'value' of a brand protection program, which can also be a prerequisite for justifying corporate spend on its implementation.

Formulation of an ROI calculation framework needs to take account of the act that, in general, a brand protection program will aim to address a range of issues, including:

- Areas where there are direct, quantitative impacts of brand infringements (including instances of lost sales, traffic misdirection, stolen funds and payments, etc.).
- Issues with impacts that superficially appear qualitative (damage to reputation, brand value, etc.), although—as will be outlined below—there are established methodologies for quantifying these effects.
- Other factors that may not (directly) be revenue generators (such as regulatory requirements for having a brand protection program in place).

Overall, the calculation of ROI aims to convert measurements of the actions *taken* into measurements of the corresponding *impact*. In many cases, this is most meaningfully quantified as the amount of revenue that can be recovered following the removal of infringing content via an enforcement (takedown) process.

11.2 Basic ROI Calculation Types

11.2.1 Introduction

There are a small number of areas in which there exist standard established methodologies for quantifying the ROI of a brand-protection initiative, although the underlying ideas (with appropriate modifications and data proxies) can often be adapted to be applicable to actions of other types. In this section, an overview is provided of two key areas (domain recovery (acquisition) and e-commerce marketplace enforcements) for which standardized methodologies can relatively simply be formulated.

11.2.2 Domain Recovery

The first model considers a case where a brand owner is able to reclaim an infringing brand-related domain name from a third party via some sort of dispute process (such as the UDRP). In general, this scenario will be most applicable in cases where the domain name contains the brand owner's trademark (or, depending on the type of name and nature of the dispute process, it may be sufficient for only a *similar* string to have been used—e.g., as in the DRS process used for .uk domains), and where the brand owner wishes to take ownership of the domain name. The domain must also qualify for eligibility for recovery through the dispute process. In general, this requires:

- The brand owner's trademark rights to predate the creation of the domain name.
- The domain name to be *confusingly similar* to the mark.
- The current owner not to have rights to, or legitimate interests in, the domain name.
- Indications of *bad faith* being present.

The ROI calculation can then be formulated on the basis that, following successful acquisition of the domain name, all web traffic to the infringing domain can be redirected to the brand owner's official transactional website and, accordingly, a proportion of this traffic can be 'converted' (for example, monetized) to generate revenue for the brand owner.

There are, however, a number of caveats to the applicability of this approach, including the following points:

- The 'value' of a domain name (by virtue of its associated incoming traffic) may vary depending on the nature of the search engine queries through which users are directed to the site; search terms that are more relevant to the business area of the brand owner are likely to result in a higher *conversion rate* (i.e., translating visitors into revenue).

- Postacquisition redirection to the official site may not be appropriate in all cases and can lead to the impression of affiliation between the parties and/or may produce an undesirable brand association. Accordingly, a common alternative strategy is to hold the domain in an inactive state for a period of time, so as to reduce its domain 'authority' (i.e., explicitly aim to decrease its search engine ranking— and thereby also its levels of web traffic—and then assess its potential value simply as a component of the brand owner's official domain portfolio (either as an active website, or a strategic or defensive registration), in accordance with a domain registration and management policy (Section 9.5).

The ROI calculation itself requires a number of inputs (some of which must be assumed or extrapolated from other information, or may require data sourced directly from the brand owner), including:

- The **web traffic** (number of visitors) to the site—this information is most usually obtained (preacquisition) from third-party data sources, though this is often based just on a sample (deemed to be representative) of web users and is only possible if traffic levels are high enough for these sources to have information on the domain in question. Post-acquisition, it may be possible to determine levels of traffic through analysis of webserver data (i.e., once the technical infrastructure of the domain is under the control of the brand owner).
- The **conversion rate** for visitors to the brand owner's official site (i.e., the proportion of visitors who will then go on to make a purchase/become a customer).
- The average **customer 'value'**, or spend—the assumed figures for these latter two points are most usually determined based on discussion with the brand owner.

The basic principles behind the calculation are as follows:

- Web traffic (for which the data are normally provided in terms of the number of visitors to the website per day) can be converted to a number of unique visitors per year, by making an assumption regarding the proportion of this traffic that constitutes 'repeat' visitors on distinct days, aggregated over the year.
- An assumed business conversion rate can then be used to determine the proportion of unique visitors who will make a spend on the brand owner's official website (on the assumption that all traffic to the recovered domain is redirected to the official site, following successful acquisition).
- Finally, an assumed average spend per customer will allow the 'value' associated with the traffic to the domain to be calculated.

A schematic representation of how the calculation can be formulated in practice, including example values for the data inputs, is shown in Figure 11.1.

It is also worth noting that this approach is most meaningful for websites whose primary function is related to e-commerce; for other types of site content, other approaches may be more appropriate (e.g., for a

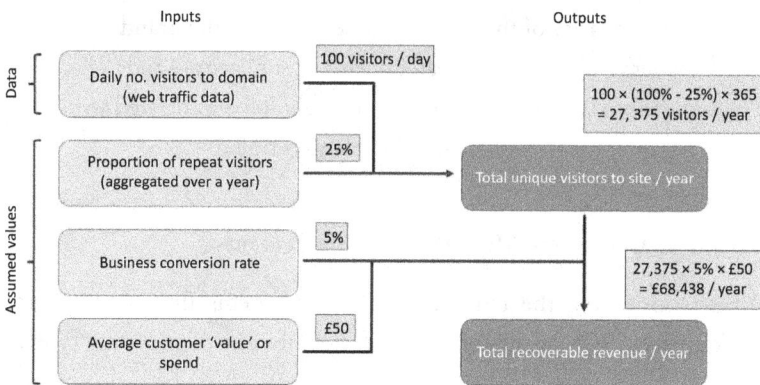

Figure 11.1 Illustration of an ROI calculation for a domain recovery case

phishing site, the 'value' may be more reasonably determined by considering assumed values for the numbers of victims, and the average financial loss per victim).

Similar approaches can be used for other types of domain enforcement action, even where the domain is not recovered (i.e., where not all of its traffic can be 'reclaimed' and monetized). Examples of such cases may be:

- The deactivation (only) of an e-commerce site selling infringing goods.
- The removal of pay-per-click links from the parking page associated with an infringing domain name.

In these instances, it is necessary to make a further assumption regarding the *proportion* of the site's traffic that can be reclaimed following successful enforcement. This may be dependent on a number of factors, such as:

- The range of brands featured on the infringing site (e.g., for a *mono-brand* site—that is, one on which only a single brand is infringed—it is reasonable to make the case that the majority of the traffic to the site is 'intended' for the brand in question; conversely, where multiple brands are featured, it is likely that only a proportion of the site's traffic relates to any one of the specific individual brands).
- The similarity of the domain name to that of the brand owner's official site; a greater degree of similarity—and therefore customer confusion—is likely to be associated with a greater proportion of reclaimable web traffic.

11.2.3 E-Commerce Marketplace Enforcement

When considering the removal of infringing items from e-commerce marketplaces, ROI calculations broadly fall into one of two main types:

- Advance (or *a priori*) calculations—these estimate the potential ROI from a brand protection program that is not yet in place.

- Post-enforcement ROI calculations—these quantify the
'value' of goods removed through an enforcement (takedown)
program (and, potentially, the proportion of lost revenue that
may be reclaimable).

The first type, carried out before any enforcements have yet taken place, is generally formulated on the basis of a 'sweep' (or series of searches) across a range of key marketplaces, to identify the number of results returned in response to a search for the brand (and/or other relevant keywords). The calculation also requires a number of assumptions; specifically (for each marketplace site):

- The numbers of items typically offered per individual listing.
- The proportion of listings that typically feature infringing
(e.g., counterfeit) goods—that is, those for which takedowns
are possible/appropriate.

In both cases (for brand protection service providers), these assumptions are usually made on the basis of prior experience of monitoring and enforcing on the marketplaces in question for a range of customers. Typically, it will only be meaningful to specify these values within an order of magnitude (at best), and they may also vary according to factors such as product type.

The basic principles behind the calculation are as follows:

- For each marketplace site, the number of results (i.e., listings)
returned by the search is multiplied by the assumed number
of items per listing and the proportion of listings that are
typically infringing, to give the potential number of infringing
listings to be removed.
- The recoverable revenue is then calculated by determining the
number of customers who will buy a legitimate item once the
infringing version is made unavailable and specifying their
spend (i.e., the price of a genuine product). This first variable
requires the specification of an overall **substitution rate**,
which takes account of two main component factors:

o The proportion of customers who will buy a legitimate item once the infringing version is made unavailable (i.e., the 'true' substitution rate).

o The 'conversion' between the number of items available and the number of associated sales (i.e., accounting for the fact that not all available items translate to a sale)—this component is analogous to the 'conversion rate' used in the calculation in Section 11.2.2.

In some formulations of this calculation, these components are specified separately. However, for simplicity, the formulation presented here utilizes a single number that encompasses both components (i.e., an overall substitution rate).

A schematic representation of this calculation, including example values, is shown in Figure 11.2.

Similar ideas can be applied to calculate recoverable revenue in a *post*-enforcement style of calculation (i.e., after a series of takedowns has actually been carried out) (see Case Study 11.1). The main difference in this case is that the calculation can be based on the *actual* numbers and values (prices) of the items removed, rather than having to rely on assumptions. This type of calculation is in many ways preferable since it represents a truer reflection of the content that is genuinely infringing (and actionable). Additionally, it is typically often possible to make use of data from brand-monitoring tools, which will usually automatically

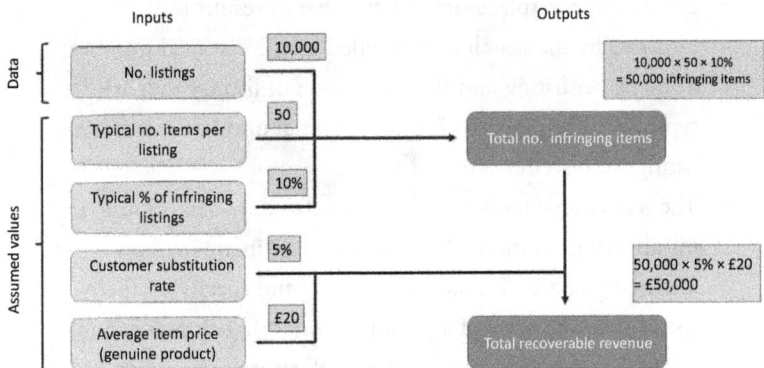

Figure 11.2 Illustration of an ROI calculation for an e-commerce marketplace enforcement program (a priori calculation)

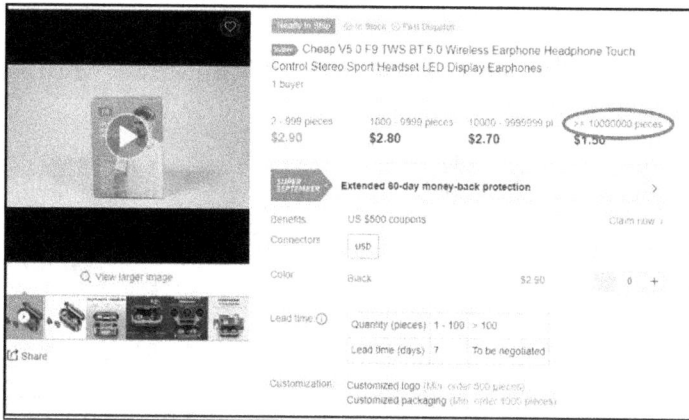

Figure 11.3 Example of an e-commerce marketplace listing offering an unrealistically high quantity of items

extract (i.e., 'scrape') key pieces of information (such as prices and quantities) from the e-commerce listings (see Section 2.4).

One other point to note is that it is often appropriate to apply a data *cap* to the quantity of information given in the listings. This is necessary because the quoted availabilities are sometimes unrealistically large (Figure 11.3). In such cases, the numbers are often simply intended to imply that the seller can manufacture on demand as many items as required, rather than giving a true reflection of the numbers held in inventory. Utilization of a data cap involves specifying an upper limit to the quantities deemed to be on offer in the listings, so as to avoid the calculated recoverable revenue values being unrealistically high.

Case Study 11.1: A Sample Post-enforcement E-Commerce Marketplace ROI Calculation

This case study presents a very simple example of the way in which a ROI calculation might typically be presented, formulated in terms of the 'reclaimable revenue' following a period of marketplace enforcement for a series of brand-owner clients in a range of different industry (i.e., product-type) areas. The figures (Table 11.1) are based on a year's worth of enforcements carried out over approximately 100 marketplaces by a brand-protection service provider for ten of their clients.

(Continued)

(*Continued*)

Table 11.1 *Outputs from a simplified ROI calculation based on marketplace enforcement actions*

Industry Area	No. Clients Featured	Total No. Listings Removed	Reclaimable Revenue
Automotive	4	105,725	$2,643,125
Fashion	3	201,913	$5,047,825
Food	1	43,473	$1,086,825
Software	1	56,553	$1,413,825
TOTAL	10	436,213	$10,905,325

In this case, the calculation is based *just* on the number of listings enforced, with some simple (conservative) 'across-the-board' assumptions made for the other parameters:

- No. items per listing = 5
- Genuine item price = $50
- Customer substitution rate = 10 percent

This type of highly simplified, conservative approach is often favored by brand owners looking to produce an ROI management report, which is easy to understand and justify. The formulation is such that the assumed parameters can easily be varied and the outputs updated (e.g., by having alternative scenarios where the substitution rates are set at, say, 5 or 1 percent).

In addition, more granular data can easily be factored in, such as using the true (scraped) quantity (i.e., items per listing) values for each individual listing, or subdividing the listings by product type, and using distinct corresponding legitimate item prices in each case. It is also possible to easily investigate the impact of data caps—for example, for one of the fashion brands considered in the above calculation, the application of a cap of 100 units was found to decrease the reclaimable revenue figure by 27 percent.

11.2.4 Other Calculation Types

The above general approaches are not specific to domain and marketplace enforcements and similar approaches can be used to carry out ROI calculations in other contexts, providing appropriate data are available or can be assumed.

Furthermore, for some channel types, 'classic' web traffic data may not be available or meaningful, but it may instead be possible to use other metrics as *proxies* for the number of visitors to (or popularity of) a piece of content. Examples might include:

- (For social media,) the number of followers or 'likes' of a profile or posting.
- (For mobile apps,) the number of downloads.
- (For instances of piracy or filesharing of digital content,) the number of individuals involved in sharing the content (e.g., *seeds* and *leechers* with protocols such as BitTorrent).

Additionally, in some cases, it may be possible to incorporate other data to provide a measure of lost and/or recoverable revenue. Examples might be information on the volumes of goods being sold via third-party infringing e-commerce websites, such as data sourced from trade or import/export databases, or from open-source investigations.

11.3 Extending the Ideas

This section explores a number of ideas that can be used to extend the concepts discussed above and tailor the approaches to situations that are more complex and/or take account of additional factors.

11.3.1 Variable Substitution Rates

11.3.1.1 Foundational Ideas

The concept of a substitution rate (Section 11.2.3) takes account of the proportion of customers who will buy a legitimate item once an infringing version is made unavailable (via a takedown process).

In reality, substitution rates will vary markedly, with a strong dependence on the nature and price of the infringing item. For example, the substitution rate may be much lower for an obvious counterfeit with a very low price point (i.e., where the buyer is likely to be much more aware that they are not buying a legitimate product, and will constitute part of a very different customer market to that of the legitimate, high-priced original).‡‡ Similarly, the substitution rate is likely to vary depending on whether the customers are knowingly visiting a nonlegitimate e-commerce site, or whether they intend to visit a genuine supplier but have been misdirected via some sort of IP abuse. Substitution rates are also likely to be dependent on platform type; for example, takedowns from business-to-business e-commerce platforms are likely to impact on an earlier stage in the supply chain and may be more significant for controlling the proliferation of items on other (say, business-to-consumer) platforms, rather than directly translating to recoverable revenue.

In general, it is possible to account for these ideas using a variable substitution rate. In one such formulation,[4] the substitution rate is assumed to decrease as the unit price of the item in question increases; however, it may be more realistic to reformulate this idea in terms of the price *differential* between the infringing and legitimate goods, rather than its absolute value (Figure 11.4).

It is also worth pointing out that this formulation may not be appropriate for very low-priced items; for example, there is a little significant distinction (in terms of absolute value, and therefore customer preference)

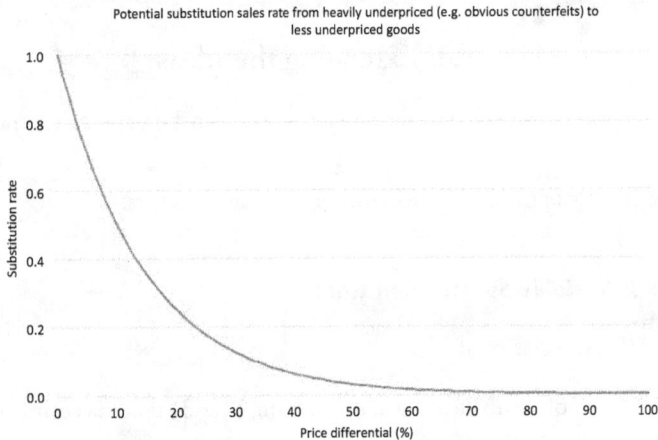

Figure 11.4 *Example of the suggested relationship between substitution rate and price differential (between infringing and legitimate goods) (after an original version by C. Abrahams)*

---

[4] https://circleid.com/posts/20220726-calculating-the-return-on-investment-of-online-brand-protection-projects

between a £2 legitimate product and a £1 infringement, even though the price differential as a *factor* (i.e., 50 percent) is significant.

There are also a number of additional caveats and considerations associated with this simple type of approach. First, low substitution rates (as might be appropriate for takedowns of counterfeit versions of high-end luxury items) do not necessarily imply that the enforcement itself is of low 'value', since a proactive takedown program can have positive impacts on brand reputation and value (Section 11.3.3).

In general, a number of related factors will be important. Some brands are very adversely affected (in terms of damage to their prestige and image) by high levels of counterfeiting, while others are able to retain their desirability. Part of this difference may be due to factors such as pre-existing brand value and the quality of marketing.

Other relevant points to consider in the formulation of these calculations are:

- The level of customer confusion between real and counterfeit goods.
- The degree of overlap in customer base for real and counterfeit goods.
- The level and type of communication by the brand to customers regarding counterfeits (where, in general, brand owners will tend to sit somewhere in a 'spectrum' between those who choose not to acknowledge the issue, and those who operate extensive programs of communication about the potential dangers of counterfeit items).

11.3.1.2 An Overview of Previous Research Into Substitution Rates

Literature review

In the simplest formulation of a brand protection ROI calculation, the substitution rate can be assumed to be a fixed value 'across the board', with the least sophisticated models simply using a value of 1 (i.e. 100 percent, or a one-to-one substitution). However, as discussed in Section 11.3.1.1, this assumption is likely to be highly unrealistic, with a truer reflection of substitution rate being one which varies according to a range of different factors (relative price point, product type, type of sales channel, degree of customer deception, etc.). Some analyses suggest that the substitution rate is best calculated as a simple function of the ratio between the price of the counterfeit and the ('market') price of the legitimate item.[5]

The article from which Figure 11.4 is taken also states (without citation) that "*around 20% of 'well-intentioned' online buyers would end up being offered a non-genuine experience, and it is these sales that the brand owner would hope to gain if they can remove the fake offer,*" which may be a useful benchmark as a fixed assumed substitution rate. It is also noteworthy that a similar figure is given by another study[§§] (using data from 2003), looking at a rather distinct type of infringement and finding that illegal music downloads reduce legitimate purchases by 20 percent (i.e., every five music downloads substitutes one legitimate purchase).[6] However, the figures vary markedly between studies. One analysis[7] assumed a 'conservative' figure of 10 percent for sales of recorded music, another[8] cited a study assuming a 5 percent rate for digital piracy and 10 percent for physical piracy—though stated that these figures are small compared with industry reports, while yet another study[§§,9] found that 45 percent of consumers of pirated DVDs would purchase an authorized version if the copy were unavailable. At the other end of the scale, a figure of around 65 percent (stated as being consistent with a survey-based range of 40 to 70 percent) was cited in a further

---

[5] https://uibm.mise.gov.it/attachments/category/225/Counterfeiting_Scope,%20characteristics%20and%20analyses%202012.pdf

[6] For additional comparison, a substitution rate of 20 percent is the figure favored by the International Federation of the Phonographic Industry (IFPI), when calculating potential damages from infringing websites. However, the issue with using a simple estimate in calculations for music sales is that distribution models have moved away from being dominated by discrete physical sales, toward an environment where streaming subscriptions are much more common, making damages much more difficult to calculate (D. Price, IFPI, pers. comm. 20-May-2024).

[7] https://www.asisonline.org/security-management-magazine/articles/2010/07/counterfeiting-and-piracy-at-what-cost/

[8] https://www.usitc.gov/publications/332/pub4199.pdf

[9] https://www.inta.org/wp-content/uploads/public-files/perspectives/industry-research/2017_Frontier_Report.pdf

piece of research***, in which a substitution rate was derived from data on the sales of pirated units and the price of legitimate goods.

Looking at the contributing factors in more detail, WIPO states in their Advisory Committee of Enforcement[10] that, as alluded to above, a one-to-one substitution rate is only appropriate if three conditions are met:

1. The infringing item is essentially identical in quality to the legitimate one.
2. The consumer is paying the full retail price for the infringing item.
3. The consumer is unaware they are purchasing a nonlegitimate product.

Where these factors do not hold true, the substitution rate will be lower than 100 percent. The degree of deception of consumers purchasing infringing goods (i.e., relating to point 3 above) is likely to vary according to a number of factors, but product type may be particularly important. For example, sales of fake pharmaceutical products are likely to involve a high degree of deception (since customers are generally less willing to buy counterfeits of these types of products), and the substitution rate is therefore likely to be high. A similar principle holds true for food, with one study[11,12] citing a high conversion rate (57 percent) for meat products (although, even for food and beverages, there is also a customer market for products known to be counterfeit, and for which the substitution rate will be correspondingly lower—one study (USITC, 2010) gives a value of 2 percent for the United Kingdom). Similarly, for other consumer product types where the deliberate purchase of counterfeits may be more common (especially if the legitimate sales channels are more markedly separated from the counterfeit ones), the substitution rates will again be low. In some studies, the difference between 'knowing'

---

[10] https://www.wipo.int/edocs/mdocs/enforcement/en/wipo_ace_6/wipo_ace_6_4.pdf
[11] https://www.theglobeandmail.com/report-on-business/robcommentary/counterfeit-products-threatening-the-food-industrys-delicate-balance/article29220689/
[12] https://canadiangrocer.com/food-fraud-catch-me-if-you-can

and 'unknowing' purchase of counterfeits is referred to as the distinction between the *primary* market (i.e., consumers attempting to purchase genuine products) and the *secondary* market (for intentional purchasers of counterfeits). Similar comments on the effect of substitution rate also appear in other studies.[13]

One particularly significant study is the UK IPO Counterfeit Goods Research (Wave 3) (2023).[14] In particular, Part 3 of the study[15] (based on an extensive survey) includes the proportions of respondents who answered, for each product category type, "*if [the counterfeit products] weren't available, they would buy the product directly from the brand.*" Though this is not an explicit equivalence of substitution rate (since the respondents in this part of the study are *intentional* purchasers of counterfeits—in many cases, for considerations of price—and therefore comprise just a subset of the full customer market), it does provide some useful insights (and it can be assumed that, if *nonintentional* purchasers of counterfeits were also

Table 11.2 Proportion of intentional purchasers of counterfeit goods who would buy a legitimate item if the counterfeits were unavailable, for a range of product types (source: UK IPO)

Product Category	Proportion of Respondents (%)
Cosmetics and toiletry products	28
Hygiene products	38
Clothing products (excluding sportswear)	19
Footwear/shoes (excluding sports footwear)	25
Accessories (excluding watches)	19
Watches (including smartwatches)	35
Regular sportswear	24
Sportswear from clubs/franchises	34
Toys	20
Electrical accessories	25
Alcohol products	36
Cosmetics and toiletry products	28

[13] https://www.gao.gov/assets/gao-10-423.pdf
[14] https://www.gov.uk/government/publications/ipo-counterfeit-goods-research-wave-3
[15] https://www.gov.uk/government/publications/ipo-counterfeit-goods-research-wave-3/ipo-counterfeit-goods-research-wave-3-part-3-categories

included, the substitution rates would be *higher*). These values are shown in Table 11.2.

The study shows that product type can have a marked impact on substitution rate. For example, sales of counterfeit versions of products such as clothing and accessories may translate to legitimate sales to a lower degree (i.e., lower substitution rates), for a number of reasons. These might include the perceived reasonable quality of counterfeits, the high price of legitimate items (and the associated greater level of fear by customers of theft of their purchases), and the view of many big brands as unethical.

It is also noteworthy that the study found 11 percent of unintentional buyers of fake products expressed anger at the *brand* whose product they thought they were buying, thereby also highlighting the potential impacts of counterfeiting on reputation and brand value.

The research also includes some significant other analysis, looking at individuals who had stated an openness to purchasing counterfeits, and finding what they would consider to be the optimum price for a counterfeit (compared to the legitimate item). Below this price point, respondents would doubt the product quality; above it, price begins to become a concern (compared with that of the legitimate item). For a counterfeit bottle of perfume (legitimate item price: £70), the optimum price was found to £25 (36 percent of the genuine item); for a counterfeit handbag (legitimate item price: £1,500), the optimum price was £101 (7 percent of the genuine)[16] (Figure 11.5).

This part of the analysis does not, of course, translate easily into insights regarding substitution rate as a function of price, other than to say that, at these optimum price ratios (i.e., where the counterfeit item is most favorably viewed as an alternative to the legitimate version), the substitution rate is likely to be low.

Other surveys also give comparable numbers to those shown in Table 11.2. A 2007 study by the ACG,[17,18] for example, found that 27 percent of purchasers of fake watches would have bought a genuine alternative

---

[16] https://www.gov.uk/government/publications/ipo-counterfeit-goods-research-wave-3/ipo-counterfeit-goods-research-wave-3-part-2-trends
[17] https://www.wipo.int/ip-outreach/en/tools/research/details.jsp?id=691
[18] Original link: http://www.a-cg.org/guest/pdf/surveywatches.pdf

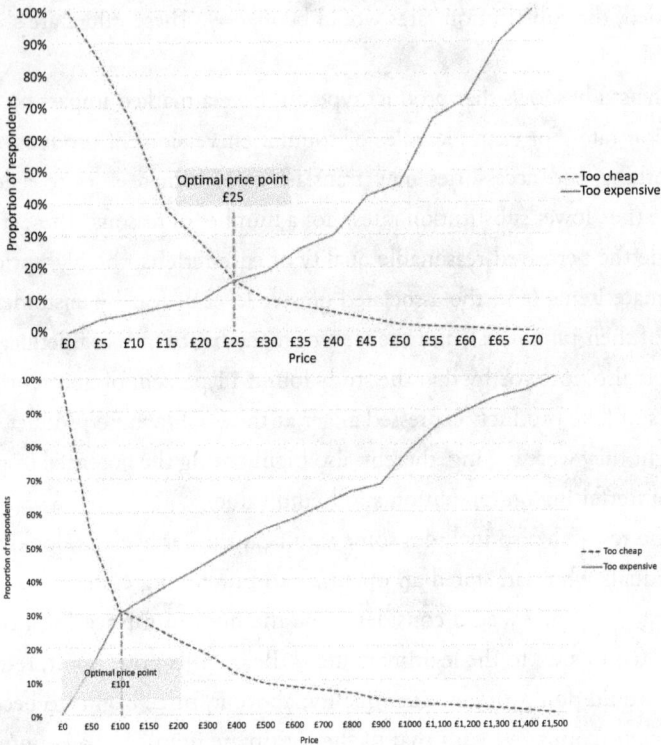

Figure 11.5 Perceptions of price for a counterfeit version of a bottle of perfume (£70) (top) and a handbag (£1,500) (bottom) (after original versions by UK IPO)

if the fake was unavailable, with over a quarter of the consumers having bought the counterfeit unintentionally.

The substitution rates shown in Table 11.3, derived from the previously mentioned study and an additional piece of research,[†††] have been cited in multiple overviews and analyses.[19,20]

Other sectors are referenced in alternative studies. For example, one review[21] cites substitution rates of 20 percent for movie piracy, 10 to 50

---

[19] https://www.prv.se/globalassets/dokument/english/piracy/counterfeiting-and-piracy-and-the-swedish-economy-2019.pdf (also available at https://read.oecdilibrary.org/governance/counterfeiting-and-piracy-and-the-swedish-economy_eb300f5b-en)

[20] https://www.ige.ch/fileadmin/user_upload/geistiges-eigentum/faelschungen-piraterie/Study_counterfeiting-piracy-and-the-swiss-economy_EN_01.pdf

[21] https://www.google.co.uk/books/edition/The_Global_Regime_for_the_Enforcement_of/1ew0DwAAQBAJ

Table 11.3 Substitution rates based on studies by ACG and Tom et al.

Product Sector	Substitution Rate (%)
Perfumery and cosmetics	49
Watches and jewelry	27
Clothing and accessories	39
Other sectors	30

percent for music, 0 to 70 percent for plant seeds, and up to 100 percent for books. The overview also states that some researchers view substitution rates for IP infringements *generally* as close to zero, stating that digital piracy serves mainly just to increase awareness of the works of the content creator.

The ACG study also gives some useful information on the proportion of purchases of fake items that are made knowingly, as a function of product type, ranging from 20 percent for automotive spare parts to 55 percent for perfumery and cosmetics.

Other factors are also likely to be relevant. For example, substitution rates are likely to be low in developing economies, where consumers generally have lower purchasing power, but the price of legitimate goods may be comparable to other geographies. This effect may be accentuated if the region has ready access to facilities for the low-cost production of counterfeits.[22]

Summary

The substitution rate (i.e., the factor for converting counterfeit sales into legitimate sales) is a key piece of data for any brand owner looking to quantify recoverable revenue as part of a brand protection ROI analysis. However, there has been relatively little previous work to satisfactorily quantify this parameter—not least because it is extremely difficult to prove.

However, it does seem that, for many classes of product, a value in the range of roughly 20 to 40 percent may be appropriate. Therefore—all other factors being equal—a conservative figure of 20 percent (i.e., a gain of one sale for every five infringements removed) might be appropriate for

---

[22] https://infojustice.org/archives/3214

an 'across-the-board' single-figure estimation (as may be appropriate for brand owners wishing to construct the simplest type of formulation for their calculations) in many cases.

In practice, however, the most realistic estimation of substitution rate may vary significantly from this figure, depending on a range of factors. These are likely to include at least the following:

- **Price differential** between the infringing and the legitimate item—a larger price discrepancy is likely to imply a lower substitution rate (e.g., customers purchasing a very low-priced version of a normally expensive item are less likely to buy the legitimate item if the infringement is unavailable).
- The **degree of deception** involved in the sale—a higher degree of deception (e.g., involving customer misdirection and/or high-quality counterfeits) will imply a higher substitution rate (e.g., customers already believing they are purchasing a legitimate item will be more likely to purchase that legitimate item if the infringing version is made unavailable).
- The **product type**—counterfeit versions of some types of products (such as pharmaceuticals and food) are less likely to be viewed as favorable options by consumers and will therefore be associated with higher substitution rates (i.e., customers will be more inclined to buy legitimate versions). Conversely, for other product types (such as clothing), where health considerations are less of a factor, and the high price and high desirability (where purely *appearance* may be the primary consideration) of the legitimate items are more relevant, counterfeit versions may be much more favorably viewed relative to the legitimate item (implying lower substitution rates).
- The nature of the **consumer market**—markets in which consumers generally have lower spending power will generally be more likely to have lower substitution rates, particularly if there is a strong capability for the low-cost production of counterfeits in-region.

Overall, there is no satisfactory *'one-size-fits-all'* approach for the estimation of substitution rate. In general, it is most reasonable to consider the characteristics of each enforcement program on a case-by-case basis, ideally incorporating analysis of the data in a granular way. The most rigorous assessment should consider price, product, market, and channel type, the way in which buyers are drawn to the point of sale, and the way in which the items are presented.

11.3.2 Quantifying the Long-Term Landscape Impact of a Brand Protection Program

The aim of many brand protection programs is a long-term change to the infringement landscape, and the value of the initiative is more usefully quantified in terms of this overall impact, rather than simply considering numbers of takedowns on an ongoing basis. Examples of these types of long-term goals might include:

- A general decrease in the numbers of active infringements over time (as may result from the actions of a proactive enforcement program making the brand a less attractive target to infringers and causing them to instead target other brands).
- 'Cleaning' the set of results returned in response to brand-specific searches (e.g., on marketplaces or search engines), so that only legitimate channels and partners are displayed on (say) the first few pages of results)—essentially, decreasing the 'visibility' of infringements.
- Gaining *'ownership of the buy button'*—this objective is related to the above point, and essentially means that, on platforms where multiple sellers can be returned in response to a particular query, the official channel(s) is returned as the top or default result.

Figure 11.6 shows an example of the profile over time of the monthly numbers of enforcements carried out for an effective brand protection program. In this case, an initial high level of infringements has been successfully addressed, such that only low levels of enforcement are required after a period of time (in this case, approximately 18 months) to tackle just the smaller numbers of new infringements as they arise.

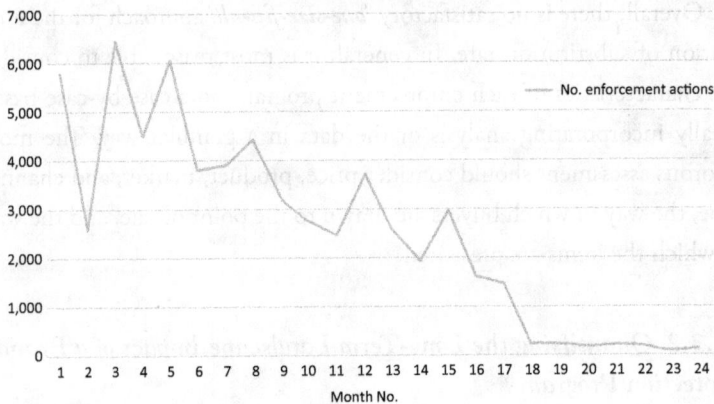

Figure 11.6 Example of the enforcement profile (monthly numbers of enforcements) over time for a successful brand protection program

However, it is important to judge the success of a brand protection program not just on a decrease over time in the numbers of enforcements (considered as a proxy for an apparent decrease in the number of infringements). It is common for infringers to simply change tactics in response to a brand protection program by the brand owner, and it is therefore important to monitor for changes to the landscape more generally, to ensure that significant findings are not being missed by simply retaining a consistent approach over time. Examples of changes in approach by infringers—and which, in general, will require associated modifications to monitoring focuses or techniques in order to capture the findings—might include:

- Moving to alternative or emerging sales platforms.
- Changing the ways in which infringing items are described, such as via the use of brand variations (e.g., abbreviations or deliberate misspellings; Figure 11.7) or using generic keywords only (rather than the brand name itself), in an effort to circumvent detection.
- Targeting alternative products or sub-brands.
- Changing the types or styles of infringements offered—for example, moving to higher-quality counterfeits which may be more difficult to distinguish from the legitimate item.

Even excluding any changes in behavior by the infringers themselves, the absolute numbers of takedowns do not necessarily provide the full

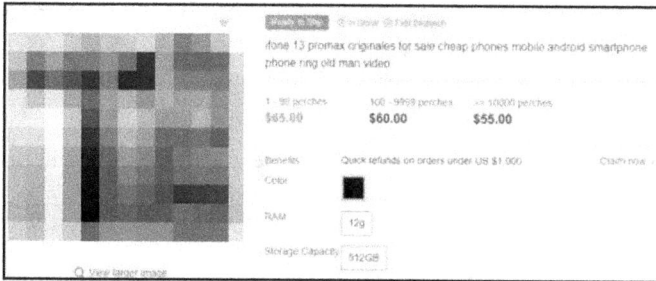

Figure 11.7 Example of a marketplace listing utilizing a deliberate misspelling ("ifone") of the iPhone brand name

picture. For example, it is not uncommon for the types of infringements tackled by a brand protection program to need to change over time; it may be practical to begin with the higher-impact or easier takedowns, before moving on to more complex (and time-consuming)—and thereby often lower-volume—enforcements as the program evolves.

However, although it is necessary to take note of all these caveats, it is possible to formulate a methodology framework for ROI calculations to take account of a general decrease over time in infringement activity (and the resulting required numbers of enforcement actions).

In order to construct this formulation,[23] it is useful to consider changes in the infringement landscape over time for the case of a newly launched brand (Figure 11.8).

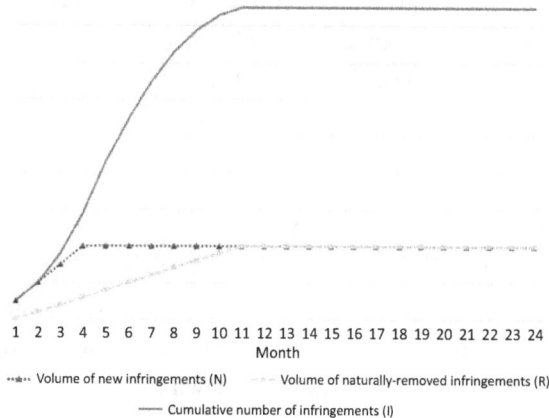

Figure 11.8 An illustration of the possible infringement landscape over time for a newly launched brand

---

[23] https://www.linkedin.com/pulse/calculation-return-investment-brand-pro-tection-thoughts-david-barnett/

The framework is constructed by making the following assumptions:

- After launch, the numbers of infringements (**N**; dotted line, triangular markers) ramp up, to a constant level.
- Even in the absence of any enforcement actions, there will be a 'natural removal' of infringements from the internet, arising from factors such as:
  - o Content being deactivated or expiring after a period of use.
  - o Older content dropping down search engine rankings.
    The level of this natural removal (**R**; dashed line, square markers) will also increase over time (though more slowly than **N**).
- The net effect is that the overall numbers of active infringements (**I**; solid line) will also increase over time (with the monthly increase ($\Delta\mathbf{I}$) in **I** equal to the difference between the monthly values of **N** and **R**)—that is, $\Delta\mathbf{I} = \mathbf{N} - \mathbf{R}$.

The formulation works on the basis of it being unrealistic that the number of active infringements will rise *indefinitely* but is instead more likely eventually to reach some sort of steady state (though the levels and timescales for this may vary significantly, depending on a range of factors). This implies that **R** will eventually catch up with **N**, or **N** will ultimately drop off (or both).

The next stage assumes that the brand owner begins a program of monitoring and enforcement at some point (say, in Month 12). The effect on the landscape is illustrated in Figure 11.9.

This formulation is constructed on the following basis:

- The brand protection program includes a monthly number of enforcements (**E**; long-dashed line, circular markers), which must be greater than **N** in order for the program to be successful.
- After the commencement of active enforcement, the rate of natural removal of infringements (**R**) drops off to zero (i.e., the infringements are being taken down more quickly than they naturally disappear).
- Since initially **E** > **N**, the number of active infringements (**I**) drops off (over a '*ramp-down*' phase) to a steady state*, such that

a point is reached (after month 18 in Figure 11.9) where the monthly number of enforcements simply needs to 'keep pace' with the rate of appearance of new infringements (the '*whackamole*' phase, i.e., **E** = **N**). Note: *whackamole* in this context is taken just to imply that infringements are taken down as quickly as they appear, rather than suggesting a random or disordered approach.

* Note: the value of **I** could equivalently be written as zero at this point if its value were calculated at the *end* of the month (i.e., *post*-enforcement) rather than at the *start*.

For a 'classic' ROI calculation (such as that described in Section 11.2.3), the value of a brand protection program is generally described in terms of the number of enforcements carried out within a given period—that is, a calculation formulated along the lines of:

$$\textbf{ROI} = \textbf{C} \times \textbf{E}$$

where **C** is the 'cost' of an infringement being active (or, equivalently, the 'value' of removing it), and **E** is the number of enforcements carried in that period (i.e., a value of **X** during the 'mature' stage of the brand protection program shown in Figure 11.9).

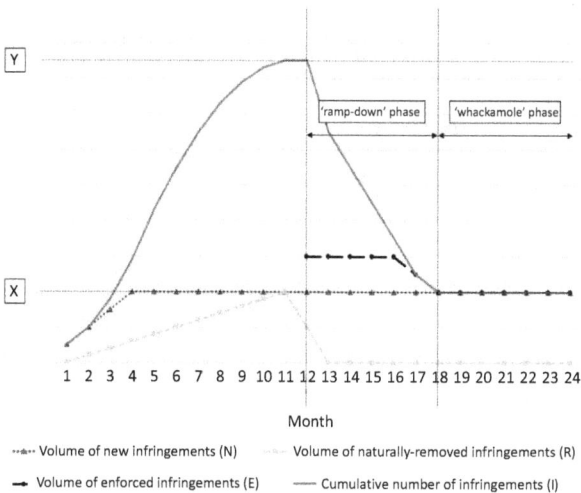

Figure 11.9 An illustration of the possible infringement landscape over time for a newly launched brand, with the introduction of a brand protection program in month 12

However, the updated model is based on the suggestion that it is preferable to consider the difference in the landscape which has arisen in response to the implementation of the brand protection program (or, equivalently, the effect of stopping the program). Accordingly, rather than calculating ROI as some function of $\mathbf{X}$ (which can be denoted as $\mathbf{ROI} = f(\mathbf{X})$), it is instead expressed in terms of the difference between $\mathbf{Y}$ and $\mathbf{X}$ (i.e., $\mathbf{ROI} = f(\mathbf{Y} - \mathbf{X})$), reflecting the difference in the number of active infringements compared with that which would have been present if the program were not being carried out (i.e., the *impact* of the program).

This model can be further expanded to account for external changes in the industry landscape (i.e., changes that are assumed would have occurred even in the *absence* of a brand protection program). In order to quantify this point, it is necessary to benchmark against a competitor brand (or, more realistically, a *group* of competitor brands) for which (it is assumed) no enforcement actions are being carried out (Figure 11.10).

In the situation shown, an increase in the level of infringements for the benchmark brand(s) is seen across the monitoring period, which is assumed to be representative of the industry landscape in general (perhaps driven by some sort of external event driving an overall increase in infringement activity). The calculation framework then assumes that, in the absence of a brand protection program, the numbers of infringements for the brand under consideration would also have increased by the same

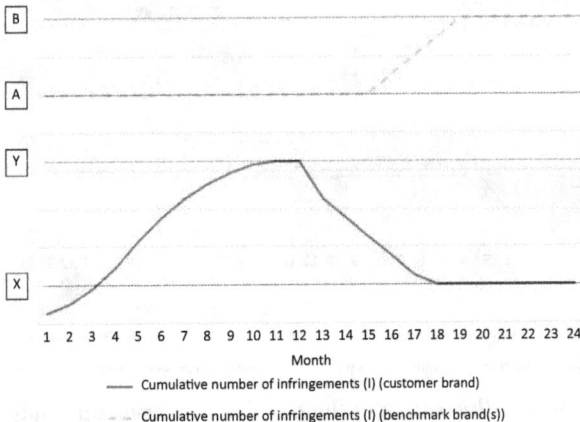

Figure 11.10 *An illustration of the possible infringement landscape over time for a newly launched brand, with the introduction of a brand protection program in Month 12 (as in Figure 11.9), and for a competitor 'benchmark' (control) brand*

proportion (equal to (**B/A**)). Therefore, the ROI calculation is based on the difference between the final level of infringements (**X**) and the level which *would have been* in place in the *absence* of the brand protection program, but *also* taking into account the changes in the industry landscape (i.e., a value of (**B/A**) × **Y**)—accordingly, in the notation used above:

$$ROI = f\{ [(\mathbf{B} / \mathbf{A}) \times \mathbf{Y}] - \mathbf{X} \}$$

Even in this most complex formulation, however, there are also other caveats to consider; for example, it is difficult to separate industry developments from the effects of *brand-specific* changes (such as simple variations in its popularity) over time.

11.3.3 The Role of Brand Value

A key area that is often neglected in classic brand protection ROI calculations is the impact of a successful brand protection program on brand value.

The intellectual property associated with a brand has an intrinsic value[24,25,‡‡‡] including its potential to generate future revenue.[26] A related idea is the concept of brand equity, the value of products and services associated with the brand. There are well-established approaches for calculating brand value, taking account of factors such as the costs to create the brand assets initially, consideration of planned or natural brand obsolescence, and the use of *royalty relief* methodology (which considers the equivalent cost for licensing the IP if it were not owned by the brand). These parameters are affected by brand visibility (customer awareness, market perception, etc.) and customer loyalty (which drives the potential to generate income).[27] Accordingly, there is the potential for infringements and other instances of brand abuse to adversely affect brand value. Damaging factors might typically include:

---

[24] https://www.iamstobbs.com/opinion/adding-value-to-the-determination-of-brand-protection-return-on-investment

[25] https://www.circleid.com/posts/20201110-brand-abuse-and-ip-infringements-part-1-brand-impact/

[26] https://www.ipwatchdog.com/2018/04/24/intellectual-property-valued-selling-business/id=96098/

[27] https://www.prophet.com/2016/09/brand-equity-vs-brand-value/

- Unauthorized use of IP (e.g., sale of counterfeits, instances of fraudulent websites, false claims of affiliation, etc.).
- Brand dilution or genericism (i.e., the evolution of a brand name into a generic descriptor of the product type in question), or the sale of lookalike products or brands.
- Reputational damage (as might result from boycott activity and activism, brand association with undesirable content, etc.).

There are also additional complicating factors, such as the fact that higher levels of abuse could be taken to imply that the brand is a desirable one, and therefore actually has an intrinsic *greater* brand value.

In order to further consider these points, it is instructive to consider a global study[28] looking (year-on-year) at the total global enterprise value of listed companies (Figure 11.11).

The principal components of overall company value are:

- Net tangible assets (*bottom bars*)—that is, property and so on.
- Intangible assets disclosed on the corporate balance sheet— for example, assets (including brands) pertaining to company acquisitions, patents held, customer contracts, and so on (*second-from-bottom bars*), and acquired *goodwill* (*second-from-top bars*).
- Other (principally undisclosed) intangible assets (*top bars*)— the difference between the corporate 'net book' value of balance-sheet assets and the enterprise value as determined by the financial market, encompassing factors such as internally generated brand value, goodwill, and so on; that is, the 'premium' on the business.

Overall, almost 50 percent of global enterprise value is *intangible*, of which only a small proportion is reflected on the balance sheet. The

---

[28] https://static.brandirectory.com/reports/brand-finance-gift-2022-full-report.pdf

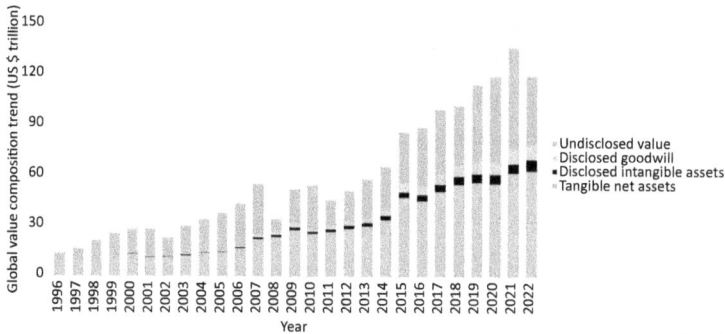

Figure 11.11 Total global enterprise value of listed companies (1996 to 2022) and its constituent components (after an original version by Brand Finance plc)

internally generated brand value itself typically represents a significant part of enterprise value and naturally varies by industry type but is potentially around 20 percent on average across all sectors.

The significant value of brand—noting that the numbers in Figure 11.11 are in trillions of U.S. dollars—highlights the importance of adequate investment in, and management and protection of, company brands.

A trademark targeted by high volumes of unauthorized use will be affected through both *brand* and *financial* impacts (essentially, the *value at risk*), largely driven by changes in customer perception and behaviors. Conversely, steps taken by the brand owner to invest in and improve brand (and IP) protection can significantly improve brand performance and economic value.

Some of the positive impacts arising from an effective program of brand protection might typically include:

- **Brand impacts**
  - Improved brand awareness/familiarity/loyalty
  - Growth of brand perception/reputation
- **Financial impacts**
  - Increased sales volume/value (including forecasted values)
  - Enhanced brand growth opportunities

o Reduced customer churn

o Lower cost of capital (brand risk)

o Lower operating costs required to address the issues (e.g., enforcement actions, customer education, brand re-designs and marketing, additional product innovation, market research, and so on)

The interplay between these factors is illustrated by the schematic in Figure 11.12.

Starting with a particular brand valuation, Figure 11.12 considers the case where the brand owner makes a spend (*investment*) on a brand protection program, which might typically be calculated as a percentage of brand value or sales (shown as a cost, i.e., as a downward bar). Following the brand protection program, an uplift in both brand strength and financial factors, as discussed above, can be expected. These have a positive additive effect, resulting in a final brand valuation (shown as the bar on the right). If the brand protection program has been successful, the uplifts will be greater than the spend (i.e., a positive ROI) and the final brand value will be greater than the initial one (by a net *uplift* value).

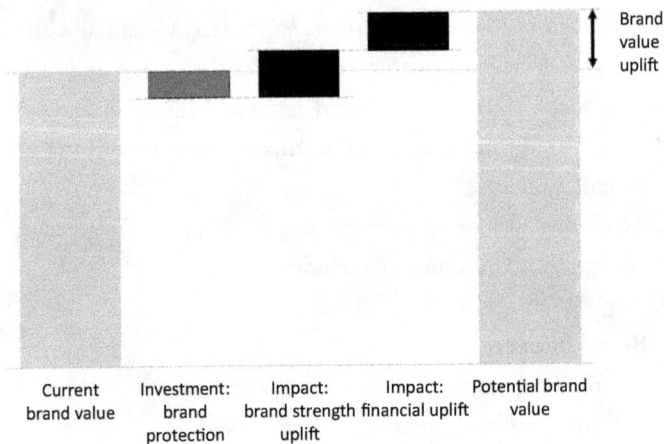

Figure 11.12 Schematic of the impact on brand value of a successful brand protection program

11.3.4 Quantifying the Impact of Proactive Measures— Cybersecurity ROI

As the importance of a strong cybersecurity posture becomes increasingly appreciated by brand owners, it may also prove useful to be able to construct ROI-style calculations to illustrate the value of implementing security measures (such as domain security products and technologies).

In these cases, the measures are generally proactive, rather than reactive, meaning the metrics will need to reflect the effects of a security initiative on the probability of a cyberattack which has not yet happened. However, when such breaches do occur, they can be highly damaging from both a financial and reputational point of view, meaning the potential returns from decreasing the likelihood of an attack can be significant.

Using simple probability theory,[29] it is possible to express the expected financial loss per year (L) due to a cyberattack as follows:

$$L = p \times C$$

where p is the probability of an attack during the year, and C is the financial cost (or 'damage') of an attack. If, therefore, the probability of an attack can be decreased from p_{before} to p_{after} through the implementation of cybersecurity measures, the expected saving (S) (per year) to the organization can be expressed as:

$$S = (p_{before} - p_{after}) \times C$$

In reality, these values are extremely difficult to quantify. However, some relevant figures are available from previous work; a 2022 study[30] showed that 88 percent of organizations were subject to some form of DNS attack in 2021, with each attack costing the enterprise an average of almost $1 million. On the basis, therefore, of the (conservative) assumption that the annual probability of an attack can be reduced through the introduction of cybersecurity measures from 10 to 1 percent, the

---

[29] The formulation is based on the principle that the expected value (E_x) of a variable (X) is given by

$$E_x = \Sigma_i [p(X_i) \times X]$$

where $p(X_i)$ is the probability of X taking the ith value.

[30] https://www.efficientip.com/wp-content/uploads/2022/05/IDC-EUR149048522-EfficientIP-infobrief_FINAL.pdf

equivalent annual saving to the company will be of the order of $90k. If the cost of implementing these measures is less than this value, the ROI will be positive. The size of the ROI will also likely be augmented by other factors, such as reduced costs for accessing cyber insurance cover, and positive impacts on brand value and reputation.

11.4 Other Factors to Consider

In practice, there are an almost limitless number of ways to construct an ROI calculation, and the specifics will vary from case to case, with the brand owner ultimately responsible for deciding on the particular assumptions to be applied. Wherever additional relevant information is available, it is sensible to incorporate it into the formulation of the final versions of the calculations used to quantify the value of an organization's brand protection initiative. Some examples of other possible inputs into these calculations might include data concerning the following areas:

- Changes in numbers of visitors to physical stores or volumes of traffic to official websites (e.g., as determined from the brand owner's webserver data).
- Changes in volumes of sales directly through the 'buy button' on e-commerce marketplaces.
- Fines/damages recovered through enforcement approaches such as legal actions.
- Information from 'on-the-ground'/offline actions (e.g., numbers of products removed from the supply chain via customs seizures, etc.).

In addition, it may be appropriate to make adjustments to the calculation (e.g., where assumptions are made relating to substitution rates), based on a classification of type of infringement—for example, counterfeit, grey market/parallel import, or trademark abuse (misdirection, etc.).

Even where their effects are not easily quantifiable, other brand protection approaches may also prove valuable to brand owners. Examples might include the use of product verification tools (allowing customers to verify the legitimacy of official goods) and customer education programs (such as those highlighting the dangers associated with the purchase of counterfeits).

In general, any approach to the calculation of ROI will require a number of assumptions and will be associated with a range of caveats. Some of the most significant points to bear in mind are as follows.

- Brand protection (i.e., the combination of monitoring and enforcement) can be considered just one component of a broader strategy of IP management—parts of which are business operation costs rather than revenue generators in their own right. Examples of other IP management tasks might typically include the construction and maintenance of a trademark portfolio and the acquisition of domains for possible future use (brand 'futureproofing').

- Some (not easily quantifiable) types of enforcement (such as sending notices or taking legal actions resulting in assurances by infringers not to reoffend or taking actions on channels where volume data are not readily available) may have greater impacts than simple (marketplace) takedowns (the so-called 'high-impact' enforcement approach). When considering the 'value' of such actions, it may be appropriate to formulate calculations based on the volumes of infringements *avoided* in the future.

- While the numbers produced as outputs from ROI calculations provide some measure of the 'value' of the brand protection program, they may not equate to 'real' recoverable revenue, even in cases where the program is perfectly constructed and implemented. Instead, it may be better to think of the outputs in more *qualitative* terms, viewing them as comparisons or 'points systems', measuring the (relative) success of the program.

Key Points

The key points from this chapter are as follows:

- Calculations of brand protection ROI aim to quantify the impact of actions taken in the program.
- Many simple formulations of ROI aim to reflect increases in revenue which can result from successful enforcement actions, such as recovery of infringing domains (and redirection of their web traffic to the brand owner's official site) and takedown of infringing goods from e-commerce marketplaces (resulting in increased sales of legitimate items once the infringing versions are no longer available).
- More sophisticated calculations may incorporate the use of substitution rates (i.e., the proportion of customers who will instead purchase a legitimate item following successful enforcement against an infringement), which are assumed to vary according to other relevant factors. These factors might typically include the price differential between infringing and legitimate items, the degree of customer deception involved in the sale of the infringement, the product type, and the nature of the customer market.
- The long-term impact of a brand protection program can be reflected in an ROI calculation by comparing the stable ongoing level of infringements during a mature program with the level from prior to its inception (deemed to be that which would still exist in the *absence* of the program). In practice, quantification might typically involve benchmarking against comparable competitor brands.
- Calculation of factors relating to brand value can also provide a means of demonstrating the ROI of a brand protection program. This is discussed further in the context of brand benchmarking (Chapter 12).

- ROI of proactive measures, such as cybersecurity initiatives, can be calculated based on the reduction in risk associated with the implementation of the measures.
- Overall, there is no *correct* way of calculating ROI, as all formulations require a range of assumptions and feature a number of caveats. ROI calculations are probably best viewed as a way of simply comparing brand protection programs against each other (providing a consistent approach is applied), and it is also important to appreciate that some of the benefits of brand protection are not quantifiable, or may simply be viewed as ways of reducing the levels of *future* infringements, and it may be appropriate to view the initiatives (at least in part) simply as general business operation costs.

CHAPTER 12

Brand Benchmarking[1]

Overview

This chapter will cover:

- A framework for benchmarking the effectiveness of a brand protection program.
- Construction of the framework of a calculation to quantify brand strength, which incorporates metrics derived from brand protection program benchmarking, together with other marketing, brand perception, and commercial factors, and which is typically carried out as the first phase of a formal brand valuation project.
- The construction of a brand strength 'scorecard' serves as a means of visualizing those program components that are most or least effective and identifying areas where improvements in individual initiatives can be made.

12.1 Brand Protection Program Benchmarking

Measurement and benchmarking (against peer companies) of the quality of an organization's brand protection program can be a useful exercise, helping to identify the constituents of a 'best-in-class' program, identifying gaps in a brand owner's current program, and building a case for internal stakeholder 'buy-in' for future initiatives.

---

[1] https://www.iamstobbs.com/opinion/my-brands-bigger-than-your-brand-quantifying-brand-strength-using-benchmarking-analyses

Table 12.1 Typical factors to be considered in a brand protection program benchmarking exercise

Category	Overall Aim	Areas for Consideration
Online program	Effectively detect and remove infringements from a comprehensive set of digital channels	Domain names
		General internet content
		E-commerce marketplaces
		Social media
		Mobile apps
Offline program	Effectively disrupt the physical supply chain for infringing items, through seizures, legal actions, and partnerships with customs and law enforcement	Litigation (against infringers)
		'On-the-ground' programs (e.g., partnerships with customs, law enforcement)
IP rights portfolio	Have sufficient rights protection to allow effective enforcement against infringements in key online and offline locations	Coverage allowing effective online enforcement
		Coverage allowing effective offline enforcement
		Presence of IP 'squatters' in at-risk territories
Public relations (PR)/marketing	Promote positive brand messaging and improve enforcement outcomes and ROI through collaborative efforts with industry partners	Media coverage
		Trade association partnerships and memberships

Assessment of a program will generally take account of some or all of the areas shown in Table 12.1 (which includes offline (Chapter 15), as well as online, initiatives), for which the ultimate aim is to express the effectiveness of each component as a numerical metric.

The primary factors to be considered for each of the relevant areas might typically include the following:

- **Online**
  - o **Domain names**
    - Numbers of brand-specific, third-party domain registrations, and breakdown by content type/level of threat.
    - Enforcement and dispute resolution procedure history.

- ▪ Extent of consolidation of the official domain portfolio with an enterprise-class (corporate) registrar.
  - o **General internet content**
    - ▪ Numbers and types of infringements present, particularly across pages that are highly ranked by search engines in response to relevant query terms.
  - o **E-commerce marketplaces**
    - ▪ Numbers of brand-related listings on a range of key marketplaces, and breakdown by type (e.g., genuine versus potential counterfeit).
  - o **Social media**
    - ▪ Numbers of brand-related posts and accounts on a range of key platforms and proportion that are unofficial/infringing.
    - ▪ Extent of control by the brand owner of key handles/usernames.
    - ▪ Extent of verification of official/authorized accounts.
  - o **Mobile apps**
    - ▪ Numbers of brand-related apps available on a range of key app stores and standalone app websites and proportion that are unofficial/infringing.
- • **Offline**
  - o **Litigation**
    - ▪ Numbers and levels of success of litigation measures against infringers, to deter future infringements and recover damages or lost revenue.
  - o **'On-the-ground' programs**
    - ▪ Extent of registration of core marks with customs representatives in key destination and source locations, to disrupt the transport of infringing goods.
- • **IP rights**
  - o **Coverage for online enforcement**
    - ▪ Extent of protection of core marks (e.g., by appropriate registered trademarks) in key jurisdictions related to online infringements.

- o **Coverage for offline enforcement**
  - ▪ Extent of protection of core marks in key jurisdictions (source, transit, and destination locations) related to the transport of infringing goods.
- o **Presence of IP 'squatters' in at-risk territories**
  - ▪ Extent of registration of relevant trademarks by third parties in high-risk jurisdictions (e.g., locations of manufacture and distribution of infringing goods).
- • **Public relations/marketing**
- o **Media coverage**
  - ▪ Levels of communication of positive brand messaging to, and by, credible media outlets with relevant audience demographics.
- o **Trade association partnerships and memberships**
  - ▪ Numbers and types of collaborations trade associations and platform-specific IP-protection programs.

For any given component, it may be appropriate to consider (and metricize) both the quality of the brand protection *strategy* itself (e.g., sufficient coverage to maintain an awareness of existing threats and an ability to identify emerging threats) and the level of effectiveness of the *execution* of that strategy (i.e., demonstrable success in mitigating threats). Once these parameters have individually been quantified, it is possible to benchmark brand owners against each other by plotting their positions on a matrix, of which a schematic is shown in Figure 12.1.

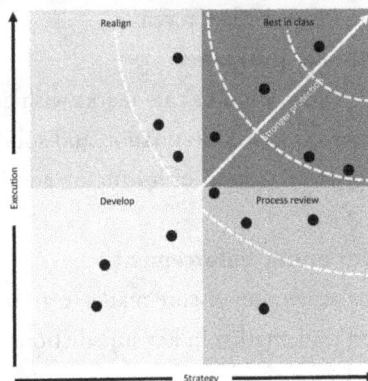

Figure 12.1 Schematic of a strategy/execution matrix for brand protection programs

Generally speaking, brands with the most effective brand protection programs will appear at the top-right of the plot area. Broadly, the matrix makes it possible to assign the program effectiveness into one of four high-level categories:

- **Best in class (top right)**—a best-in-class program is one where there is a well-executed, effective strategy (though it will still require ongoing oversight, to allow for responsiveness to emerging threats).
- **Requiring realignment (top left)**—this situation might typically arise in cases where a previously effective and well-executed strategy has not been sufficiently updated as required.
- **Requiring process review (bottom right)**—this categorization indicates a program for which there are shortcomings in the execution of a strategy that is appropriate in principle and may reflect an overall lack of investment in the program, or a requirement to focus on higher priority areas.
- **Requiring development (bottom left)**—this category shows shortcomings in both the strategy and its execution and might typically arise in cases where there has been insufficient stakeholder buy-in by the brand owner.

A further step is often the tracking of performance over time, which generally involves the construction of a series of brand protection key performance indicators (KPIs) aiming to measure the actions taken, and levels of success, relating to the factors listed previously. Examples might typically include: (online) numbers of enforcements, compliance rates for takedown notices, and ROI measures (Chapter 11); (offline) numbers of litigations, volumes and values of infringing items seized, numbers of trademarks filed, and numbers of trademarks of concern held by third parties; in addition to other business metrics such as sales volumes and revenues.

12.2 Brand Strength Measurement

Brand protection program effectiveness scores, as discussed in the previous section, can be used as one input into formulations to quantify brand *strength*. Brand strength has an impact on factors such as *royalty rate* (used as an input for *royalty relief* methodology—see Section 11.3.3) and can ultimately affect customer behaviors and revenue, thereby acting as a driver for overall brand value. Measurement of brand strength is often the first stage of a formal brand valuation analysis, which itself has a number of applications, including giving the ability to better inform trademark protection and licensing strategies, assisting with investment planning and budgeting, quantifying brand damages arising through IP abuse, facilitating access to financial credit, and as part of general valuation projects necessary for tax considerations or mergers and acquisitions.

Overall, quantification of brand strength involves consideration of a number of factors beyond just measurements of the effectiveness of any brand protection program. The range of relevant areas might typically include:

- **Direct actions by the brand owner**
  - o **Effectiveness of brand protection program**
    - Quality of online/offline program
    - Coverage of IP rights portfolio
  - o **Effectiveness of brand PR/marketing program**
    - Marketing budget
    - Social media use and policies
    - **Factors relating to (external) stakeholder impact**
  - o **Customer brand perception**
    - 'Top-of-mind' and prompted brand awareness
    - Net promoter score—a measure of likelihood of customer recommendation
    - Brand perception—including consideration of the factors driving the likelihood of customer recommendation (such as product features/performance, brand attributes, emotional drivers, etc.), as collected through, for example, consumer research and surveys
  - o **Media**
    - Online prominence and sentiment (Chapter 10)
  - o **Corporate and social responsibility**
    - Environmental, social, and governance measurements

- **Commercial performance**
  - **Financial performance**
    - Revenue
    - Revenue growth
    - Profitability

In a formal analysis, each parameter is expressed as a numerical metric (with a higher score denoting a more successful initiative), which can conveniently be displayed collectively as a brand strength *scorecard* (of which an example is shown in Figure 12.2). Each component can then also be weighted, controlling the extent of its contribution to the overall brand strength index. This formulation makes it possible to compare the scores for the individual components, in order to identify specific areas where program improvements can be made, and also provides a framework by which brands can be compared against their peers and/or competitors. It can also be insightful to carry out analysis on a more granular (e.g., per-country) basis (see Case Study 12.1).

Furthermore, there are particular characteristics of the measurement metrics that would be expected to be associated with a well-performing brand (i.e., one where the brand strength is high). Examples might include high online prominence and (positive) sentiment, and low levels of infringements. Accordingly, it is important that the calculation framework is constructed in such a way as to correctly reflect these points. For example, measurement of infringement levels should take account of the overall landscape (e.g., by reflecting changes in long-term trends arising from the implementation of a brand-protection program; see Section 11.3.2), rather than simply considering ongoing numbers of enforcements.

Case Study 12.1: A 'Mock-Up' of a Brand Strength Analysis

This case study presents an anonymized and 'sanitized' version of a brand strength measurement project, based on a real piece of work carried out for a brand owner client. The key elements of the methodology used in this particular case are:

(Continued)

(*Continued*)

- Each individual metric (reflecting the effectiveness of the corresponding brand initiative) is expressed as a value between 0 (least effective) and 10 (most effective).
- Each metric is assigned a *weighting*, reflecting its contribution to the total brand strength score, such that the contributions to the total of the three main areas (*brand owner actions, stakeholder impact,* and *commercial performance*) are 25, 50, and 25 percent, respectively.
- The analysis is carried out on a granular, per-country basis, allowing the effectiveness of the individual program components in the distinct business markets to be quantified.
- For each country, the total brand strength score (S_B) is calculated as the sum of the individual component scores (C), multiplied by their respective weightings (W), that is:

$$S_B = \Sigma_i \, C_i \times W_i$$

This also gives a total score between 0 and 10 (since the weightings, W_i, are expressed as percentages), but this value is then 'renormalized' (for convenience) by multiplying by 10, to give a final score between 0 and 100. This final score is often conveniently expressed as an overall brand 'rating'—e.g. AAA(-) to AAA(+) ("extremely strong") for a score between 81 and 100; AA(-) to AA(+) ("very strong") for a score between 71 and 80, and so on.

The algorithms used for calculating the metrics for the individual program components will differ depending on the nature of the initiative. For elements relating to brand perception, for example, the analysis may be based on the results of surveys to understand the drivers (such as product performance, identification with the brand, etc.) behind brand recommendation.

The individual component and total scores for each analyzed country can then be presented as a *scorecard*, as shown in Figure 12.2.

	Weighting		Weighting			Weighting	Country									
							UK	DE	FR	IT	ES	US	NZ	CN	ZA	HK
Brand owner actions	25.0%	Brand protection	15.0%	Online / offline programme	Execution	5.0%	5.0	5.0	6.0	8.0	7.0	8.0	7.0	6.0	6.0	5.0
				IP rights portfolio	Strategy	5.0%	6.0	5.0	6.0	8.0	6.0	5.0	7.0	4.0	5.0	5.0
		Brand marketing	10.0%	Marketing budget		5.0%	8.0	8.0	8.0	8.0	8.0	8.0	8.0	8.0	8.0	8.0
				Social media		5.0%	8.9	5.7	6.8	7.3	6.6	6.4	6.4	5.4	5.2	5.2
Stakeholder impact	50.0%	Customers	40.0%	Top-of-mind awareness		6.7%	6.9	6.9	6.9	5.9	6.9	6.9	6.3	6.9	6.9	6.9
				Prompted awareness		6.7%	8.8	5.8	5.8	6.6	7.4	5.1	8.6	5.0	7.1	5.3
				NPS		6.7%	8.0	6.4	6.3	7.3	7.5	5.2	6.3	5.5	7.7	5.8
				Brand perception	Product features / performance	6.7%	8.1	7.9	8.0	8.5	8.6	5.0	7.6	6.5	6.7	7.0
					Brand attributes	6.7%	8.0	7.8	8.0	8.3	8.1	7.2	7.5	7.8	6.5	7.1
					Emotional drivers	6.7%	7.9	7.6	7.9	8.1	8.2	7.0	7.7	7.9	8.4	7.0
		Media	5.0%	Online prominence		2.5%	6.8	6.2	6.6	6.8	7.0	6.6	6.6	7.9	7.6	6.5
				Online sentiment		2.5%	7.7	7.7	7.7	7.7	7.7	7.7	7.7	7.7	7.7	7.7
		CSR	5.0%	ESG		5.0%	9.0	9.0	9.0	9.0	9.0	9.0	9.0	9.0	9.0	9.0
Commercial performance	25.0%	Financial performance	25.0%	Revenue		8.3%	8.9	6.7	6.8	7.1	6.6	6.4	6.4	5.4	5.2	9.2
				Revenue growth		8.3%	5.7	6.9	6.2	5.8	6.2	8.6	6.4	6.8	6.5	8.7
				Profitability		8.3%	5.2	6.4	6.6	6.8	6.5	5.6	6.2	4.9	5.1	6.1
	100.0%		100.0%			100.0%	77.9	67.9	70.5	69.8	73.3	69.1	73.2	67.2	70.2	66.2

Figure 12.2 *Example of a scorecard used for a brand strength calculation (with analysis carried out on a per-country basis), showing example weightings and scores (expressed on a scale of 0 to 10 for individual components and on a normalized scale of 0 to 100 for the overall scores)*

(Continued)

(Continued)

Analysis of the scorecard allows the brand strength, and the effectiveness of the individual program initiatives, to be assessed in each distinct region. For example, from the results shown in Figure 12.2, it can be seen that improvements to the online/offline brand protection program might be warranted, particularly in Germany (DE), Italy (IT), and China (CN).

Key Points

The key points from this chapter are as follows:

- The effectiveness of a brand protection program can be metricized (measured), as a basis for comparison against those implemented by other organizations, by taking account of the quality of the online (monitoring and enforcement) and offline (disruption of the physical supply chain) programs, the extent of coverage of IP rights protection, and the quality of PR (including marketing activity and trade association relationships).
- For any given component of the program, it can be instructive to consider both the quality of the strategy and the level of effectiveness of its execution.
- Following the assessment of effectiveness, it can be advantageous to construct brand protection KPIs, allowing trends over time to be tracked.
- The metrics derived from brand protection program benchmarking can serve as one input into a brand strength calculation, which also takes account of other factors, such as brand perception and commercial factors, and which often serves as the initial phase of a formal brand value calculation.
- The findings from these calculations can be represented using a brand strength *scorecard*, which provides a visual representation of the effectiveness of the individual components, and can help identify areas where improvements can be made.

CHAPTER 13

Analyzing Trends in Web3

Overview

This chapter will cover:

- Definitions of key ideas relating to Web3, including non-fungible tokens (NFTs) and blockchain domains.
- Trends and patterns in blockchain domain registrations, including consideration of brand infringements in the Web3 landscape, and other patterns of use (including the emergence of collectible and graphical artwork blockchain domain names).

13.1 Introduction to Web3

Web3 is a general term referring to decentralized content on the internet (i.e., organized on a peer-to-peer basis and without reliance on authoritative hosting providers), with a particular focus on blockchain technologies. The term is often taken to reflect the emergence of new technologies that provide immersive experiences for users and encourage freedom of speech.

A blockchain is a publicly accessible digital ledger in which transactions are recorded. It is cryptographically sealed and cannot be modified after its contents are recorded. Blockchains form the basis of many digital currencies (such as Bitcoin) but also have a number of other applications, such as supply chain control by brand owners (Oriekhoe et al. 2024).[§§§]

A related project is the formation of the Aura Blockchain Consortium by the luxury groups Prada, LVMH, and Cartier in 2021.[1]

In terms of brand protection considerations, two Web3 concepts—non-fungible tokens (NFTs) and blockchain domains—are of particular relevance and are discussed below.

13.2 NFTs[2]

NFTs are cryptographic collectibles comprising any of several types of assets or media. Any digital file can be converted into an NFT through a process known as minting, whereby ownership is recorded on a block-chain. NFTs can take a number of different forms but are most commonly associated with graphics files (e.g., artworks, branded imagery, etc.) and other types of digital content (such as audio or music files). Brand owners are increasingly incorporating NFTs into their business models, through initiatives such as the production and trade of virtual branded items (e.g., items to be worn by avatars in virtual-reality environments—part of the *metaverse*, the generalized name given to a connected environment of 3D virtual worlds).

Trade of NFTs most commonly takes place through dedicated online marketplaces, of which a number of well-known examples are OpenSea, Rarible, Nifty Gateway, Binance, and SuperRare. From a brand owner's point of view, one of the current areas of greatest potential concern is the trade of NFTs featuring IP-protected content (such as counterfeit virtual items) (Figure 13.1). Some relevant early legal cases included the action by Hermès for trademark infringement against digital designer Mason Rothschild, following his release of a series of 100 *MetaBirkin* virtual handbag designs,[3,4] and the lawsuit by Nike against shopping platform

---

[1] https://www.pradagroup.com/en/news-media/news-section/aura-blockchain-consortium.html
[2] https://www.linkedin.com/pulse/rise-nft-david-barnett
[3] https://www.elle.com/uk/fashion/a38536774/birkin-bag-nft/
[4] https://www.businessoffashion.com/news/luxury/hermes-sues-nft-creator-over-metabirkin-sales/

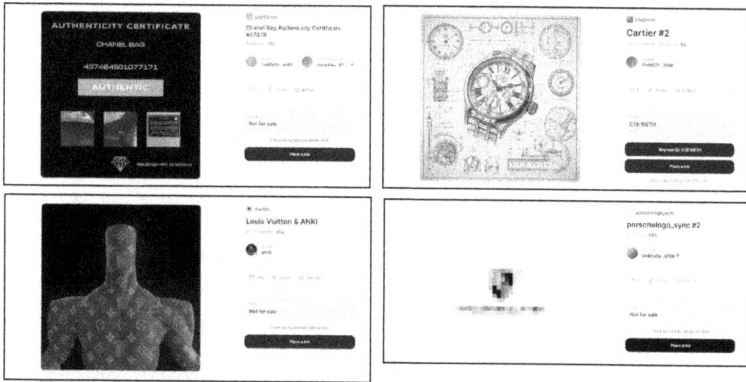

Figure 13.1 Examples of NFT marketplace listings for items featuring branded content

StockX for distributing *vault NFTs* featuring their logo and branding, intended to be redeemed for physical items.[5,6]

13.3 Blockchain Domains

13.3.1 Introduction to Blockchain Domains[7]

Like regular domains, blockchain domains consist of a second-level domain name and an extension (with specific examples including .eth, .crypto, and .bit) and can be utilized in a number of different ways. Common use-cases include the construction of decentralized websites (though these have special access requirements, and can only be viewed using a dedicated (Web3-enabled) browser such as Brave, or a browser plug-in), as memorable wallet addresses for sending and receiving cryptocurrency,

---

[5] https://brandequity.economictimes.indiatimes.com/amp/news/business-of-brands/can-hermes-and-nike-stop-unauthorised-nfts/89365547

[6] https://www.theverge.com/2022/2/10/22925252/nike-stockx-shoe-lawsuit-vault-nft-trademark-infringement

[7] https://www.iamstobbs.com/opinion/trends-in-web3-part-1-a-look-at-blockchain-domains

or as providing hosting infrastructure for programs to be run as apps. Blockchain domains are recorded, together with their ownership details, on a blockchain (i.e., are not hosted on a server or recorded in a regular registry zone file) and, unlike regular domain names, are not governed or regulated by the Internet Corporation for Assigned Names and Numbers (ICANN). They are offered by specialist providers and, although the costs may be higher than for traditional domains, are in many cases offered for registration for longer periods than gTLD domains, or may involve only a one-off cost to be owned in perpetuity.

Blockchain domains are attractive to many users because of the inherent security associated with the blockchain infrastructure, and their resistance against traditional blocking or censorship methods. For those with interests in other areas of the Web3 ecosystem, the use of blockchain domains may be a natural choice. Additionally, increasing restrictions of access to ('Web2') content by platform operators across a variety of channels (particularly on social media), in response to the use of data by AI developers for training their models,[8,9] may itself drive further adoption of Web3 technologies, which are inherently less prone to regulation and restriction.[10]

From a brand monitoring point of view, blockchain domains are generally difficult to identify, both because of the absence of zone files and because of the specific website access requirements. One commonly used detection technique can be to search for references to the blockchain domain names being traded in NFT marketplaces, and some blockchain domain providers also provide searchable databases of registered domains. However, more robust methods are likely to require direct monitoring of the content of the blockchains themselves, or searches across databases of transactions that have occurred on a specific blockchain.

Enforcement options are also currently limited, with one option being just to take down infringing listings offering the sale of a blockchain domain from the Web3 marketplace. However, this does not deactivate the domain name itself or change its ownership. Some blockchain

---

[8] https://techcrunch.com/2023/04/18/reddit-will-begin-charging-for-access-to-its-api/
[9] https://www.bbc.co.uk/news/technology-66093324
[10] https://cointelegraph.com/news/how-adoption-of-a-decentralized-internet-can-improve-digital-ownership

domain providers are becoming more mindful of the risks posed by cybersquatters[11] and offer brand owners the ability to block third-party registrations (similar to the Trademark Clearinghouse program for new gTLDs) or to claim ownership of trademarked names. However, these blocks are at the discretion of the domain providers, making them subject to change.

Additionally, information on the wallet addresses associated with the owners of blockchain domains or NFTs—as might be available through public records, Web3 marketplaces, or blockchain domain providers—can be used as the basis of an investigation to identify additional associated information relating to the entity in question and is a key piece of data in any attempt to 'cluster' findings within Web3 environments (see Case Study 14.3). In some cases, it may also be possible to submit a court order to the service provider for the disclosure of collected data.

As a further brand protection initiative, brand owners may also wish to consider proactive defensive registration of key domain names across relevant extensions. This approach is generally more cost-effective than attempting to subsequently acquire domain names of interest.

13.3.2 Trends and Patterns in Blockchain Domain Registrations

As of the start of 2024, there are around seven million active blockchain domains, with the majority registered through two major providers: 2.1 million through Ethereum Name Service[12] (*ENS*, which offers .eth registrations on the same blockchain as is used for the Ethereum cryptocurrency) and 3.8 million through Unstoppable Domains,[13] which offers registrations across more than ten extensions.

In the absence of zone files, comprehensive analysis of this domain dataset is not straightforward, but there are public sources for significant volumes of data. One example is Dune Analytics, which provides a range of tools and dashboards for the analysis of those .eth domains registered through ENS, and which is the source of the data for Case Study 13.1.

---

[11] https://www.brandsec.com.au/blockchain-domains-and-cybersquatting/
[12] https://ens.domains/
[13] https://unstoppabledomains.com/

Case Study 13.1: An Analysis of One Year of ENS .eth Blockchain Domain Registrations[14]

This case study concerns the analysis of the set of .eth blockchain domains registered through ENS, as a proxy for the wider blockchain domain landscape, and is based on information from Dune Analytics.[15,16] As of July 17, 2023, there were 2,719,569 such domains. At the time of analysis, granular data on the individual domain registrations was available for the previous year of activity, encompassing 1.47 million domains.

Figure 13.2 shows the daily numbers of registrations across the one-year period, and the median (SLD) length of the domains registered on each day.

Figure 13.1 shows a large spike in registration activity during the latter part of 2022. This may reflect the peak period of adoption of

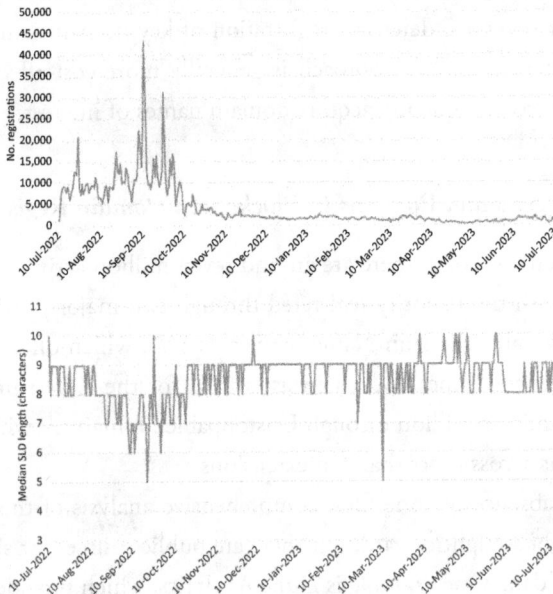

Figure 13.2 Daily numbers of .eth blockchain domain registrations via ENS (top) and the median SLD lengths of the sets of daily registrations (bottom) (July 2022 to July 2023)

---

[14] https://www.iamstobbs.com/trends-in-web3-ebook

[15] https://dune.com/makoto/ens

[16] https://dune.com/makoto/ens-released-to-be-released-names

blockchain domains, with the observed simultaneous drop in median domain name length consistent with this being the timeframe over which the bulk of short, desirable names were being registered.

A Deeper Dive Into the Data

Blockchain Domains Targeting the Top Ten Most Valuable Global Brands

The first deeper piece of analysis is to consider the prevalence of domains containing the names of each of the top ten most valuable global brands in 2023 (according to Kantar, as used in Case Study 10.1) (Figure 13.3). The assumption is that an analysis of these popular valuable brands will serve as an indicator of the likely level of brand infringements across the blockchain domain landscape more generally.[17,18]

The key finding is simply that there are large numbers of registrations targeting these brands, with over 3,500 registrations identified across the ten brands during the one-year monitoring period. Many

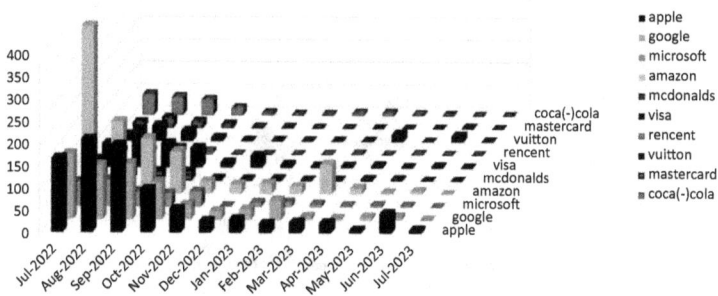

Figure 13.3 Monthly numbers of .eth blockchain domain registrations containing the names of each of the top ten most valuable global brands in 2023 (July 2022 to July 2023)

(Continued)

---

[17] https://dnsrf.org/blog/brand-names-in-blockchain-domains---new-frontier-for-brand-owners/index.html

[18] https://www.thefashionlaw.com/the-rise-in-blockchain-domains-presents-risks-opportunities-for-brands/

(Continued)

amazon 🛒 🛍 .eth

apple ▦ .eth

https://www.coca-cola.com/.eth

google🅿ay.eth

⬤ ◍ mastercard.eth

👊 mcdonalds®.eth

microsoft ▓ pro.eth

•tencent.eth

@visa.eth

louisvuitton♥.eth

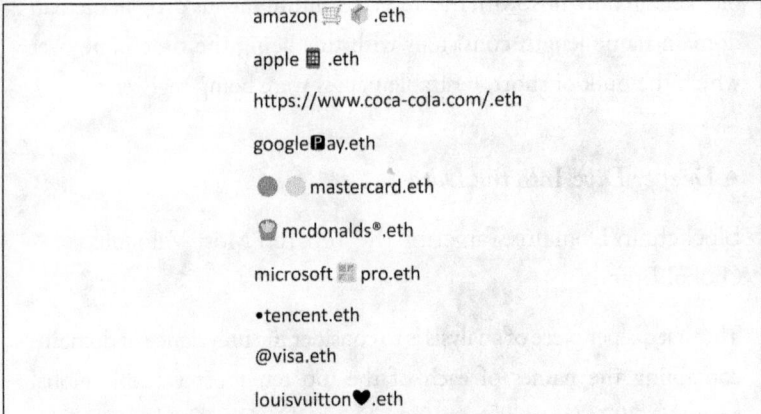

Figure 13.4 Examples of .eth blockchain domains containing the names of the top ten most valuable global brands in 2023 (and including special characters)

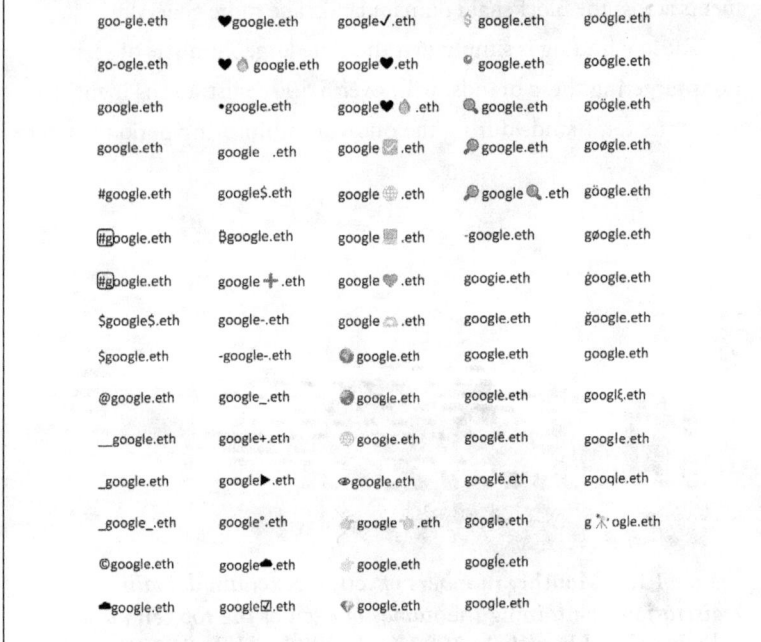

goo-gle.eth	♥google.eth	google✓.eth	$ google.eth	goógle.eth
go-ogle.eth	♥ 🔥 google.eth	google♥.eth	© google.eth	goógle.eth
google.eth	•google.eth	google♥ 🔥 .eth	🔍 google.eth	goögle.eth
google.eth	google .eth	google 🖼 .eth	🔍 google.eth	goøgle.eth
#google.eth	google$.eth	google 🌐 .eth	🔍 google 🔍 .eth	göogle.eth
#google.eth	₿google.eth	google 🖼 .eth	-google.eth	gøogle.eth
#google.eth	google ✚ .eth	google 💟 .eth	googie.eth	ğoogle.eth
$google$.eth	google-.eth	google 🗨 .eth	google.eth	ğoogle.eth
$google.eth	-google-.eth	🌐 google.eth	google.eth	qoogle.eth
@google.eth	google_.eth	🌐 google.eth	googlè.eth	googlξ.eth
__google.eth	google+.eth	🌐 google.eth	googlē.eth	google.eth
_google.eth	google▶.eth	⊛google.eth	googlĕ.eth	qooqle.eth
google.eth	google".eth	✈ google 🔵 .eth	googlə.eth	g 🚶 ogle.eth
©google.eth	google☁.eth	✈ google.eth	googlê.eth	google.eth
☁google.eth	google☑.eth	☘ google.eth	google.eth	google.eth

Figure 13.5 Examples of .eth blockchain domain names containing exact or fuzzy matches to Google

of the registrations—which can incorporate special characters such as emojis—present significant potential for confusion with official domain names (Figure 13.4), and the numbers are vastly increased if 'fuzzy matches' (i.e., misspellings and variations) to the brand names are also considered (Figure 13.5) (cf. Case Study 7.1). These observations strongly suggest that a significant proportion have been registered with the explicit intention of deceptive use, such as the creation of fake sites (although only a very small number resolved to any live content as of the time of analysis).

Very Long Blockchain Domain Names

Although the previous analyses have concentrated primarily on short domain names (with, in fact, 99.8 percent of the dataset having SLD lengths of 32 characters or fewer), there exists a very long tail of much longer blockchain domain names within the dataset (as their lengths are not limited in the same way as 'classic' (Web2) domains). The longest domains were found to have SLD lengths of 38,894 characters (three instances) (Figure 13.6).

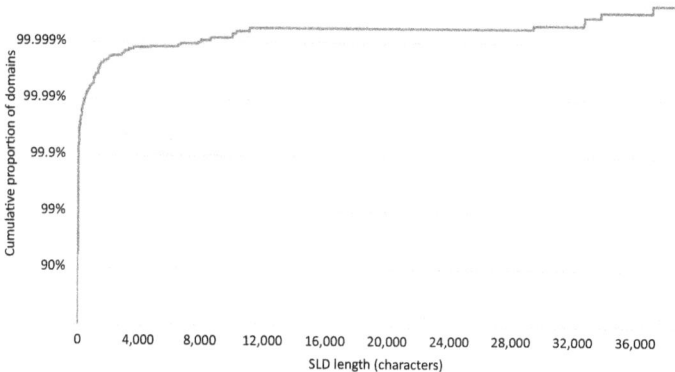

Figure 13.6 Cumulative proportion of domains with SLD length less than or equal to the value shown on the horizontal axis, for the full dataset of .eth blockchain domains

Overall, there are 14 instances of domains with a SLD length of 8,000 characters or more. These appear generally to be nonsensical, often just consisting of large numbers of repeated characters (Table 13.1).

The same conclusion can be drawn by considering the distribution of domain name entropy values (Section 5.2.2.3) as a function of length (Figure 13.7); this analysis shows that many of the longest

(Continued)

Table 13.1 First 20 characters in each of the top 14 longest blockchain domain names in the dataset

SLD length (chars)	First 20 characters
38,894	11111111111111111111
38,894	00000000000000000000
38,894	
37,058	accordingtoallknown1
33,792	⎰⎱⎰⎱⎰⎱⎰⎱⎰⎱
32,745	00000000000000000000
32,713	00000000000000000000
29,425	
11,111	11111111111111111111
10,245	55555555555555555555
10,000	
10,000	
8,613	
8,000	00000000000000000000

domain names actually have very low entropy values, a reflection of their large numbers of *repeated* characters (and small numbers of *distinct* characters).

These domain names appear to serve no meaningful purpose and may simply be a reflection of a movement away from the 'core' use cases of blockchain domain names (for decentralized website hosting and as cryptocurrency wallet addresses), toward increased interest in the collectability and trade of domain names which are interesting or unusual in themselves. The concept of domain *'clubs'*, comprising collectible groups of domains with shared characteristics (e.g., *999 Club* and *10k Club*—domains with names consisting of three and four digits, respectively), is certainly already established.[19]

---

19 https://ens.vision/market

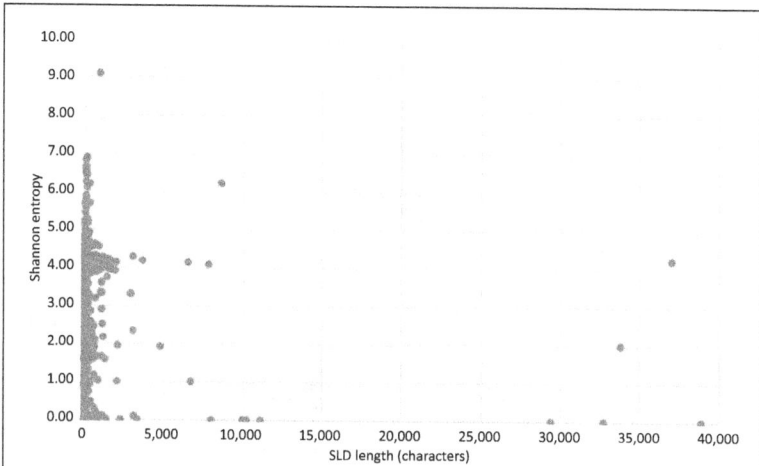

Figure 13.7 Scatter plot of SLD length against entropy, for the full dataset

Graphical 'artwork' blockchain domain names

Among the intermediate-length names is a special class of block-chain domains where the name *itself* constitutes a graphical artwork in its own right. One such example is the following 1,024-character domain name, for which, the SLD name consists entirely of col-ored-square characters:

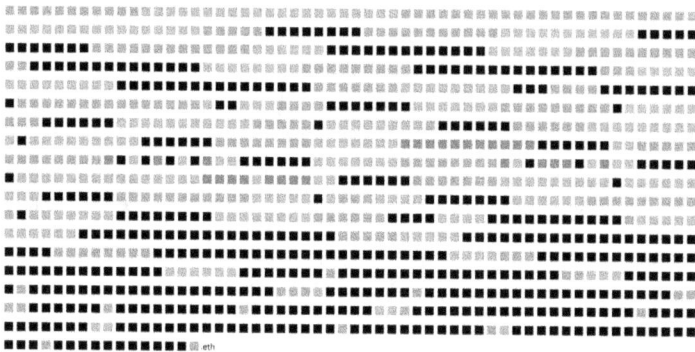

When this domain name is displayed in a 32 × 32 grid, however, it takes on the appearance of a pixelated artwork (Figure 13.8).

The blockchain domain dataset includes a number of additional similar examples, where the domain names take on an artwork

(*Continued*)

*Figure 13.8 The artwork resulting when a 1,024-character
domain name (shown above) is displayed in a grid of 32 × 32
characters*

appearance when displayed in a suitable grid (sometimes with a specific character in the name denoting the positions of the line-breaks).

Significantly, a number of the identified 'artwork' domains resemble particular characters or other imagery covered by intellectual property protection, with examples including Pokémon, Donkey Kong, Super Mario, and the CryptoPunks[20] NFT collection (Figure 13.9).

It is worth noting that the final example shown in Figure 13.9 appears to be one of a 'set' of five similar artworks (all 577

---

[20] https://www.larvalabs.com/cryptopunks

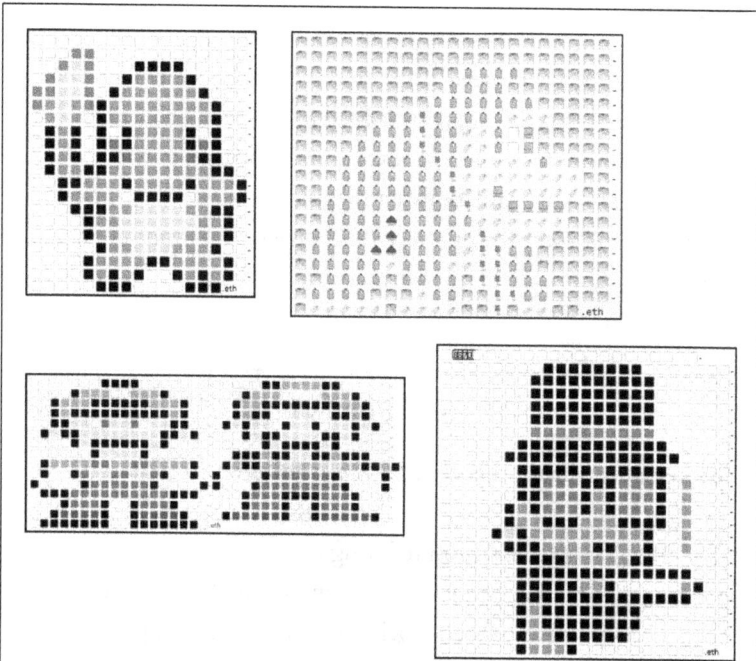

Figure 13.9 Examples of artwork blockchain domain names resembling particular characters

characters in length), which appear to contain 'numberings' (apparently as some sort of 'limited edition' indicator) within their names; the first ten characters of the domain name shown are as follows: □8870□ □□□□□

The blockchain domain dataset is showing that—even without consideration of the content of any associated *websites*—simply the names of the domains themselves are being utilized in novel ways. Alongside the 'classic' forms of domain abuse such as *cybersquatting* (where domains with names containing protected (textual) brand terms are registered by third parties), there is an emergence of a graphical style of abuse, where domain names are configured to incorporate imagery which may constitute protected intellectual property. It seems likely that this new class of 'artwork' domain names may be being created and traded in the same way as the earlier phase of NFTs.

(Continued)

(Continued)

> Brand owners will need to be mindful of this emerging trend. Brand protection technologies will need to evolve in order to be able to detect and interpret these types of domain names, and it is likely to be necessary for regulations and legislation to develop in order to allow brand owners to protect their intellectual property in this context.

Key Points

The key points from this chapter are as follows:

- Web3 is a general term referring to decentralized content on the internet and is most commonly used in relation to technologies based on blockchains (i.e., cryptographically sealed, publicly available digital ledgers that form the basis of many cryptocurrencies).
- Nonfungible tokens (NFTs) are digital files whose ownership is recorded on a blockchain. Brand owners are increasingly incorporating NFTs into their business models, through the creation and trade of virtual branded items, but are also subject to abuse through NFTs incorporating unauthorized use of branded content.
- Blockchain domains have some similarities to regular ('Web2') domains, in that they consist of a SLD name and a domain extension (TLD), but are unregulated by ICANN and are recorded on a blockchain. Most commonly, blockchain domains are used as

cryptocurrency wallet addresses, or in the creation of decentralized websites.

- Blockchain domains can be associated with brand abuse in similar ways to regular ('Web2') domains, and the range of characters permissible in blockchain domain names presents even greater potential for the construction of deceptive URLs and websites (cf. Chapter 7).

- New use cases for blockchain domains are emerging, with the appearance of very long (otherwise nonsensical) names, and of graphical 'artwork' names consisting of colored characters, which comprise an image when the domain name is displayed in a suitable grid configuration, both of which seem to be registered purely for the purposes of trading and collectability.

PART 4

Going Forward

CHAPTER 14

New Developments

Overview

This chapter will cover:

- Possible implications of increasing development of artificial intelligence technologies.
- Ways in which the Web3 environment (Chapter 13) may evolve, including consideration of NFT-related infringements, possible new use cases for blockchain domains, and increasing *crossover* (i.e., interconnection) between Web2 and Web3 content.

14.1 The Growth of Artificial Intelligence

14.1.1 AI Use in Brand Protection Technologies

It is almost inconceivable that developments in artificial intelligence (AI) tools and technologies will not have an impact on brand protection. One obvious opportunity is the increasing incorporation of AI into monitoring tools.

Many legacy brand monitoring technologies already have functionality in areas such as result prioritization (Chapter 5) and clustering (Chapter 6). Often, such systems will make use of preconfigured rules (e.g., to identify a string on the page with the format of (say) a telephone number or email address) or scrapers (e.g., to extract a piece of contact information from a specific location on a page, on sites where the page format is known in advance). While these are *technically* AI applications (in that they are automated systems making 'decisions' based on internal algorithms), they would not be classed as AI according to the most common current interpretation of the term. It is likely that the newer generations of monitoring tools will increasingly make use of *machine learning*, in areas such as automatically 'tuning' prioritization algorithms, optimizing search queries, and identifying relevant pieces of information on web pages as bases for clustering together relevant results (without the extraction criteria being 'hard coded')—with these types of system likely to be able to be 'trained' using datasets based on manual classification regarding which results are 'good' and which are not. However, the basic principles *behind* these algorithms (as discussed in this book) are likely to remain unchanged to a significant degree.

It is also worth noting that increasing use of AI (as interpreted with its current more usual meaning) is already being seen in areas such as automated image recognition and video-content analysis, which are likely to become increasingly important in the prioritization of media-rich content. Some major platforms are already making use of such technologies. One example is YouTube's Content ID system, which automatically scans uploaded content to identify matches against a library of copyright-protected content submitted by rights owners. In cases where a match is found, the infringing video may be blocked, monetized, or tracked.[1,2] In brand monitoring tools more generally, image analysis technologies are likely to be particularly useful in areas such as the identification of lookalike products, infringements of design rights, and use of copyrighted imagery, where less sophisticated technologies have tended to struggle.

AI-based improvements in other areas such as sentiment analysis (cf. Chapter 10) are also likely to feature in monitoring tools in the near future.

Going forward, AI applications are also likely to be increasingly integrated into other products and services relevant to brand protection. This might include areas such as automated detection of indicators of DNS or brand abuse (Thio, Christiawan and Wagiman, 2024),[¶¶] generation of relevant strings and brand variations to be used in monitoring applications and for domain registration recommendations, and analysis of

---

[1] https://support.google.com/youtube/answer/2797370
[2] https://support.google.com/youtube/answer/6013276

changes in the infringement and commercial landscape in response to brand protection or marketing initiatives, for example.[3]

Finally, increased automation of systems to send enforcement notices in response to identified infringements may become a more reliable option. Currently, it is advisable in many cases to incorporate a stage of manual checks before a takedown is actioned, particularly in cases where the sending of a notice may have legal, process-related or partnership implications, or where an assessment of infringement is in any way subjective. AI may be able to make some of these decisions, but it is unlikely that it will ever be possible to entirely move to fully automated systems, especially where definitive assessment is not possible from the information that is available online (e.g., where a test purchase is required in order to verify that an item is counterfeit).

The usage of standalone AI tools can also have brand protection applications in its own right. The nature of the training methodologies employed in the production of the underlying large language models (LLMs) means that the output from such systems tends to be reflective of content that features consistently and extensively in the training data. Asking an AI tool (typically trained using large volumes of online content) for an overview of a specific brand, product, or industry area can therefore provide valuable insights for brand owners into how their brand is generally perceived online, and into any specific public relations issues. This provides an opportunity for making informed decisions regarding suitable remediative actions, such as corrective marketing campaigns and customer responses (areas where generative AI can also assist with content creation).****

14.1.2 AI Use by Infringers

It is certainly already the case that AI applications are also being utilized by infringers to create more effective scams and reduce the technical entry barrier required to produce a range of types of malicious content. Numerous

---

[3] https://hub.internetx.com/en/global-domain-report-2024

cases have been reported of phishing content[4] or malware[5,6] produced using AI tools. AI may also assist with the generation of other more effective types of infringement, such as in the suggestion of typos or brand variants most likely to attract web traffic and result in customer confusion.

More generally, the methods of construction of many AI tools (i.e., the enormous datasets on which they are typically trained) means that—unless the data are screened for integrity, which is currently rare—the models will often have access to information relating to some of the most sophisticated scams on the internet. Furthermore, their intended functionality (i.e., the creation of the most convincing reconstruction of those datapoints in response to a prompt) provides—by definition—a very powerful means of creating effective infringements. Although many AI tools do incorporate features designed to prevent unethical use, in practice, these are relatively simple for determined users to circumvent.[††††]

14.1.3 Other Potential Threats Posed by AI

Overall, the evolution of AI raises a number of open questions relevant to the brand protection and cybersecurity landscapes. In this context, these considerations primarily relate to generative AI or LLMs, which are systems able to generate high-quality outputs of a range of types, including natural-language text (e.g., ChatGPT), computer code (e.g., Copilot), or images (e.g., Midjourney), based on data on which they have been trained. Some of the uncertainty relates to the *outputs* from such models, and concerns factors such as the difficulty in monitoring this content (which is generally produced dynamically, in response to user-prompts), the ownership to the rights of AI-produced content[7] (with current U.S. legislation generally assigning copyright only to works created by humans;[8] protection *was* initially granted for a comic book created

---

[4] https://securityboulevard.com/2023/01/what-does-chat-gpt-imply-for-brand-impersonation-qa-with-dr-salvatore-stolfo/

[5] https://www.digitaltrends.com/computing/chatgpt-created-malware/

[6] https://thehackernews.com/2023/07/wormgpt-new-ai-tool-allows.html

[7] https://intellectual-property-helpdesk.ec.europa.eu/news-events/news/intellectual-property-chatgpt-2023-02-20_en

[8] https://www.jdsupra.com/legalnews/u-s-copyright-law-protects-only-human-4254611/

using the Midjourney tool in September 2022,[9] but was subsequently revoked[10]), and the implications if models generate content that infringes IP, is inaccurate, or potentially defamatory. One high-profile example is the legal case brought by Getty Images against Stability AI Inc, the creator of the Stable Diffusion AI image-generation model. The lawsuit alleged that Stable Diffusion had used more than 12 million Getty photos without license as part of its training dataset, as evidenced by the presence of Getty watermarks appearing in some of the images generated by the model, and also thereby providing a potential source of customer confusion.[11,12] Other similar areas of concern are the possibilities for the generation of 'soundalikes' of music and vocals of existing artists,[‡‡‡‡] or the use of similarities to voice or physical likenesses of actors, based on the ingestion of copyrighted content.

The use of training datasets for AI tools (see Section 13.3.1) also itself raises a number of significant points, such as whether the use of these data is inherently associated with breaches of IP. Much of the early discussion has focused on the claim that the use of protected IP for model training falls under 'fair use', but the question of whether the model outputs may constitute 'derivative works' remains open. In one 2022 case, for example, a series of artworks by illustrator Hollie Mengert were apparently used, without her permission, to train a Stable Diffusion model intended to produce outputs in a similar style.[13] Currently, the availability of routes of recourse is unclear, with the legal landscape complex and rapidly evolving.[14,15,16]

---

[9] https://arstechnica.com/information-technology/2022/09/artist-receives-first-known-us-copyright-registration-for-generative-ai-art/

[10] https://arstechnica.com/information-technology/2023/02/us-copyright-office-withdraws-copyright-for-ai-generated-comic-artwork/

[11] https://www.reuters.com/legal/getty-images-lawsuit-says-stability-ai-misused-photos-train-ai-2023-02-06/

[12] https://www.forbes.com/sites/mattnovak/2023/02/06/getty-images-sues-ai-company-over-hideous-frankenphotos/

[13] https://waxy.org/2022/11/invasive-diffusion-how-one-unwilling-illustrator-found-herself-turned-into-an-ai-model/

[14] https://www.scintilla-ip.com/openai-faces-copyright-lawsuit-over-ai-model-training/

[15] https://www.theverge.com/23444685/generative-ai-copyright-infringement-legal-fair-use-training-data

[16] https://www.unite.ai/the-murky-world-of-ai-and-copyright/

Additionally, in cases where users are training their own models with potentially sensitive content (or using prompts consisting of confidential information), there remains uncertainty regarding the extent to which these datasets may be shared and incorporated into models potentially accessible by other users.[17] In response to such concerns, the use of ChatGPT was banned in Italy by the country's data protection authority in early 2023,[18] with other bans or restrictions also imposed on employees by a number of organizations, including JP Morgan Chase, Bank of America, Citigroup, and Samsung.[19] In the near future, it is also likely that there will be significant developments in the legislation surrounding the safe and responsible use of AI technologies, such as the EU AI Act.[20,21]

A possible additional issue is the risk that the internet may begin to be dominated by large volumes of (potentially low-quality) AI-generated content, which, when indexed by search engines, may start to degrade the overall quality of search results.[22,23] Conversely, the use of synthetic data in training datasets can itself degrade the quality of the resulting AI models.[24] These issues may, in turn, result in impacts on other areas, such as the ability to meaningfully calculate real consumer sentiment (Chapter 10).§§§§

---

[17] https://www.icaew.com/technical/technology/artificial-intelligence/generative-ai-guide/cyber-security

[18] https://www.bbc.co.uk/news/technology-65139406

[19] https://www.bloomberg.com/news/articles/2023-05-02/samsung-bans-chatgpt-and-other-generative-ai-use-by-staff-after-leak?embedded-checkout=true

[20] https://digital-strategy.ec.europa.eu/en/policies/regulatory-framework-ai

[21] https://www.consilium.europa.eu/en/press/press-releases/2024/05/21/artificial-intelligence-ai-act-council-gives-final-green-light-to-the-first-worldwide-rules-on-ai/

[22] https://web.archive.org/web/20240221045824/https://stolber.com/ais-ripple-effect-on-google-the-evolving-landscape-of-search-results/

[23] https://www.axios.com/2023/08/28/ai-content-flood-model-collapse

[24] https://www.linkedin.com/posts/rebecca-newman-267a7756_syntheticdata-ai-creativity-activity-7196079302742790144-3DgQ

14.1.4 Trends in the Evolution of AI Brands

Analysis of the online prominence (cf. Chapter 10) of AI brands can also provide useful insights and potentially allow trends over time to be tracked (Case Study 14.1).

Case Study 14.1: Online Prominence of the Top Generative-AI Brands

Figure 14.1 shows the prominence scores of the top 30 most prominent generative-AI brands as of January 2024.[25]

It is perhaps unsurprising that the very popular GPT/ChatGPT brand and its parent company OpenAI are the most prominent brands online by a significant margin. However, other well-known names, including Copilot, Bard, Gemini, DeepMind, and Midjourney, have significant presences, all featuring within the top 12.

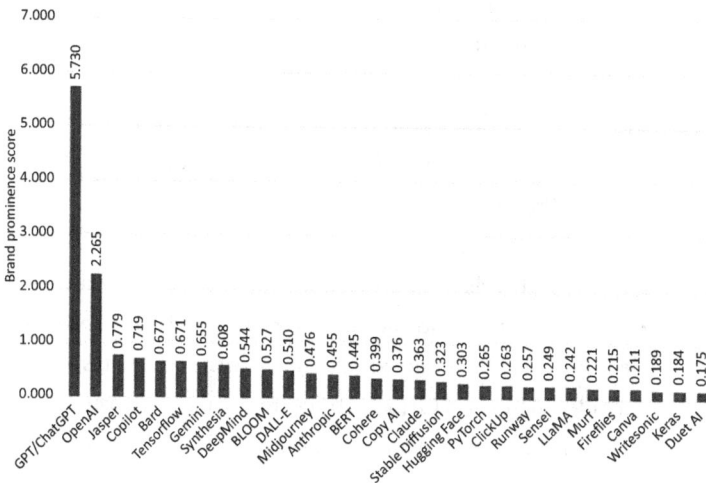

Figure 14.1 Prominence scores for the top 30 most prominent generative-AI brands

(Continued)

25 https://www.iamstobbs.com/opinion/the-top-generative-ai-brands-in-2024

(Continued)

However, the following more in-depth insights, relating to relevant trends as of the time of analysis, can also be drawn from the dataset:

- The popularity of several of the brands in the list (e.g., Jasper, Copilot, BLOOM, Cohere, Copy AI, ClickUp) is consistent with an increasing focus on the enterprise use of AI applications to drive efficiency.
- The growing recognition of open-source collaboration in AI development is reflected by the prominence of TensorFlow, HuggingFace, and PyTorch, all open-source repositories and communities for machine learning and AI.
- Increasing interest in the AI generation of new complex content types is evidenced by findings such as the presence of Synthesia (for generating video content) and Murf (a voice generator).
- The results highlight the continuation of Google as a prominent player in the AI field, with a number of Google AI products powered by the newly released Gemini LLM, including Bard, Gemini Nano, and Gemini Pro, featuring highly in the list.
- Going forward, growth in the adoption of 'small' or *lightweight* LLMs—which have smaller neural networks, fewer parameters, and can be used offline and on mobile devices—may be observed. Examples within the dataset include Microsoft's Orca 2-7b (currently only at position #156 in the rankings) and Falcon 7b (#97), and Gemini Nano (#154).

14.2 Web3 Developments

14.2.1 NFTs and the Metaverse

The engagement with NFTs by some brand owners, through the production and sale of official virtual merchandise, has been noted in Section

13.2. For example, luxury brand Gucci was one of the first players in this space, launching a series of sneakers to be worn in virtual reality chat or the online game Roblox. Other early adopters experimenting with the distribution of branded products as NFTs included Dolce & Gabbana, Rebecca Minkoff,[26] and the Coach brand.[27] Although luxury collectibles accounted for less than 1 percent of all NFT transactions in 2021, they have been projected to evolve into a $25 billion business by 2030, or 10 percent of the total luxury market.[28]

The extent to which the NFT industry continues to grow may, in part, be controlled by the extent of future adoption of the *metaverse*.[29] Some brands also began to expand into this arena from around 2022, with McDonald's and Panera Bread both filing trademarks for NFTs in the metaverse, setting the scene for virtual restaurants in online environments, tied to real-world deliveries for customers.[30] Brand owners in a range of other industries also filed trademark applications covering virtual or digital goods and services across a variety of product areas, including Nike, The Brooklyn Nets, Walmart, Crocs, Skechers, Jay-Z, and The Coachella Valley Music and Arts Festival.[31] Furthermore, the Playboy brand announced plans to offer digital subscriptions and a new virtual Playboy Mansion in the metaverse, following its prior release of a range of NFT imagery based on the 'bunny' logo.[32]

Web3 content can also be associated with infringements in the Web2 ('classic internet') ecosystem (see also Section 14.2.2). A 2022 study looking at over 34,000 domains featuring NFT-related terms found that

---

[26] https://www.businessoffashion.com/articles/technology/unpacking-fashions-latest-wave-of-nft-sales/

[27] https://elle.com.sg/2021/12/21/coach-launches-its-first-collection-of-nfts-in-time-for-christmas/

[28] https://www.thefashionlaw.com/blockchain-and-nfts-are-smart-but-can-they-revolutionize-fashion/

[29] https://www.voguebusiness.com/technology/luxury-fashion-brands-poised-to-join-the-nft-party

[30] https://www.nrn.com/technology/mcdonald-s-and-panera-bread-file-trademarks-nfts-metaverse

[31] https://www.natlawreview.com/article/trademarks-metaverse-brand-protection-virtual-goods-services

[32] https://www.cnbc.com/amp/2022/02/11/playboy-plans-to-join-the-metaverse.html

significant numbers may be associated with NFT scams, served as attack vectors for malware distribution, or comprised instances of cybersquatting.[33,34] Such scams can take a variety of forms, including phishing, advance-fee frauds (e.g., investment scams), and cryptocurrency harvesting. NFTs themselves can also have security implications, with a report in January 2022 of a type of NFT that could harvest viewers' IP addresses.[35]

The trade in NFTs can itself be subject to fraudulent activity. One such example is the practice of *wash trading*, where an individual NFT is repeatedly traded between multiple accounts owned by the same seller, as a means of artificially inflating its price.[36] In February 2022, the first associated law enforcement action in the United Kingdom was taken in response to a VAT (tax) repayment fraud involving 250 fake companies.[37]

NFTs also raise questions regarding intellectual property rights, with NFT ownership not necessarily granting ownership of copyright for the *content*, for example. In November 2021, production company Miramax sued writer and director Quentin Tarantino over his sale of a collection of NFTs related to the movie Pulp Fiction. Although Tarantino had retained limited contractual rights for the film, Miramax alleged that his sale of the NFTs violated the company's copyright and trademark rights.[38,39] Cases become more complicated when content is moved from one blockchain to another, as occurred in a case involving an NFT named *Quantum*.[40]

---

[33] https://cybersecurityventures.com/as-nfts-popularity-grows-so-does-cyber-squatting/

[34] https://circleid.com/posts/20220128-65000-nft-related-domains-and-subdo-mains-possible-vehicles-for-nft-scams

[35] https://www.vice.com/en/article/xgdvaz/nft-steal-ip-address-opensea

[36] https://news.sky.com/story/nft-fraudsters-making-millions-by-wash-trading-new-study-finds-12531135

[37] https://news.sky.com/story/hmrc-officials-seize-nft-crypto-assets-as-three-arrested-on-suspicion-fraud-12541831

[38] https://www.theverge.com/2021/11/17/22787216/miramax-pulp-fiction-quentin-tarantino-nft-lawsuit

[39] https://torrentfreak.com/tarantinos-nft-auction-goes-ahead-despite-miramax-copyright-lawsuit-220105/

[40] https://www.ledgerinsights.com/sothebys-sued-over-quantum-nft-auction/

14.2.2 Web2/Web3 'Crossover'

Interaction (sometimes referred to as *crossover*) between the previously disparate areas of Web2 and Web3 content is (as mentioned in the previous section) increasingly becoming a significant consideration. Two of the earliest manifestations[41] included:

- **Development of the .box new-gTLD**—the .box extension initially launched in August 2023, followed by an early announcement that the TLD would be associated with an innovative Web2/Web3 offering. By February 2024, .box was fully live, and domains were generally available for registration. At this time, a payment of $120 in cryptocurrency granted the user a 'classic' (Web2) domain (including options for website and email functionality), an identically named Web3 domain (including the associated potential functionality of being able to create a decentralized website and accept transfers of cryptocurrency and other blockchain assets), and access to the .box app (used to access and make changes to the domain properties).[42] As an ICANN-regulated TLD, the registrar/registry operator offers an abuse policy and a registration agreement prohibiting trademark infringement, making it possible to file UDRP/URS disputes against bad-faith registrations. Following a successful dispute, the Web2 domain can be transferred to the brand owner, and the Web3 domain canceled and reissued to the brand owner, on request.
- **GoDaddy's partnership with Ethereum Name Service (ENS)**—on February 5, 2024, domain name registrar GoDaddy announced that it would be partnering with Web3 provider ENS offering naming services for assets on the

---

[41] https://www.iamstobbs.com/opinion/the-crossover-two-recent-developments-in-web2/web3-interaction
[42] https://www.my.box/

Ethereum blockchain.[43,44] The partnership allows owners of Web2 domains registered through GoDaddy to link their domain with an Ethereum address (registered through a Web3 provider), allowing access to a range of Web3 services, and offering the option for the domain name to be used as a human-readable address to be used for sending and receiving assets such as cryptocurrency and NFTs. Users who do not require this functionality retain the option to keep their domain name unintegrated.

More generally, Web2/Web3 crossover can take a variety of forms, including instances where specific domain names resolve to content in *both* environments (e.g., cases where providers offer domains on extensions with dual Web2 and Web3 functionality, such as .box and .shib[45]), instances where Web2 URLs 'map' to Web3 content (as for the eth.link service referenced in Section 14.2.3), and promotion of Web3 services and offerings within the Web2 landscape—or a combination of all of these. One increasingly common example is the promotion of (potentially fraudulent) cryptocurrencies (or related services such as exchanges) claiming to be associated with, or endorsed by, well-known and trusted brands, or making unauthorized use of branded imagery (Case Study 14.2).

Case Study 14.2: Brand-Related Cryptocurrency Infringements[46]

The use of trusted brand names in conjunction with the promotion of cryptocurrencies is one relatively common example of a Web2/Web3 *crossover* infringement type. In many cases, this type of infringement occurs in conjunction with the use of a branded domain registration, typically featuring the brand name in conjunction with a relevant keyword such as *coin*, *token*, or *deployer*. As of February 2024, there

---

[43] https://uk.godaddy.com/help/what-is-ens-41952

[44] https://blog.ens.domains/post/godaddy-partners-with-ens

[45] https://coinpedia.org/news/shiba-inu-announces-launch-of-shib-domain-for-shib-holders-bridging-web2-and-web3/

[46] https://www.iamstobbs.com/opinion/web2/web3-crossover-brand-related-crypto-infringements

were over 154,000 registered gTLD domains with names ending with *coin*, *token*, or *deployer*, of which over 500 also included the name of any of the top 12 technology brands[47] (including organizations such as Apple, Google, Microsoft, Facebook, and Amazon). This type of infringement is sufficiently popular that many of these registrations had been monetized through the inclusion of pay-per-click links or offers to sell the domain names (in some cases for prices of $1 million+) shown on the associated web pages, and many others were inactive, suggesting that they had been registered speculatively, or with the intention of subsequent use or sale.

Within the dataset, numerous examples were identified of domains resolving to live sites using brand references to promote cryptocurrency-related content (Figure 14.2).

Beyond this list of companies, numerous other high-profile brands were also found to be targeted in similar ways, as were prominent figures such as technology leaders (particularly Elon Musk, Mark Zuckerberg, and Jeff Bezos).

It is also informative to consider similar trends of activity across the blockchain domain landscape, since (by the very nature of Web2/Web3 crossover) these types of scams might be expected to be associated with analogous registrations in the Web3 environment.

A dataset from Dune Analytics was used to consider one year's worth of .eth blockchain domain registrations through the ENS provider, showing that 7,266 names containing *coin*, *token*, or *deployer* were registered between February 22, 2023 and February 22, 2024, of which 37 also contained the names of any of the top 12 technology brands considered previously. As of the time of analysis, none resolved to any live content, although the popularity of this type of infringement indicates that the space is worthy of monitoring for developments.

A final note is that there is no clear long-term trend over the one-year analysis period, although there were two notable spikes in activity on December 10 and 12, 2023 (Figure 14.3). Many of the

(Continued)

---

[47] https://www.top10-websitehosting.co.uk/biggest-brands/

(Continued)

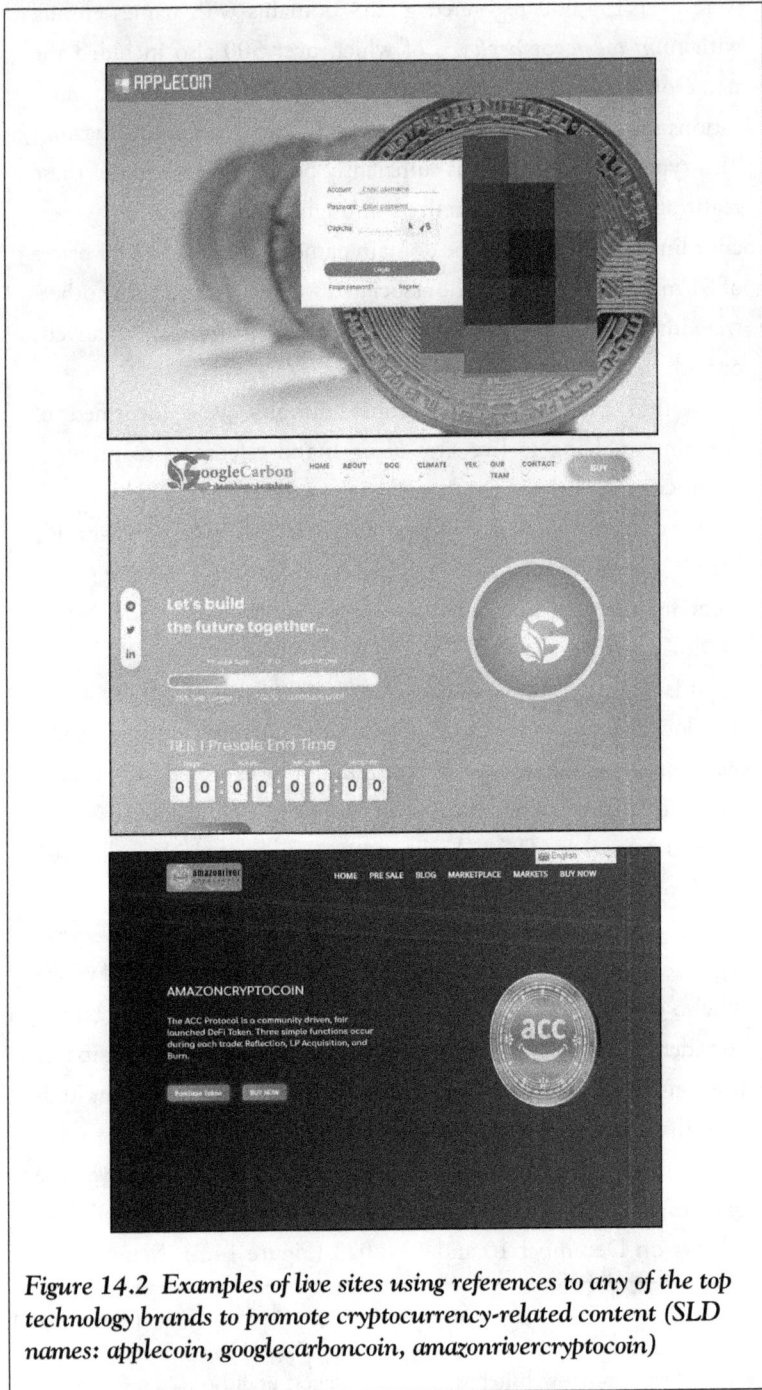

Figure 14.2 Examples of live sites using references to any of the top
technology brands to promote cryptocurrency-related content (SLD
names: applecoin, googlecarboncoin, amazonrivercryptocoin)

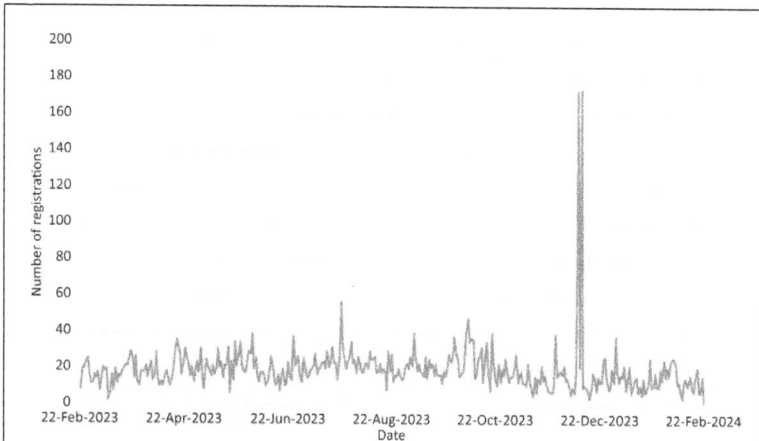

Figure 14.3 Daily numbers of registrations of ENS.eth blockchain domains with names containing coin, token, or deployer

associated domains appear to constitute *clusters* of similar names targeting prominent celebrities, with multiple examples of domains of the form *[name]deployer.eth* all registered at the same time, presumably by one or more related entities. For example, a batch of 45 celebrity infringements was recorded at 10:45 on December 12, 2023, with examples including *jeffbezosdeployer.eth*, *andrewtatedeployer.eth*, *johnnydeppdeployer.eth*, *arnoldschwarzeneggerdeployer.eth*, *angelinajoliedeployer.eth*, *scarlettjohanssondeployer.eth*, *edwardsnowdendeployer.eth*, *mileycyrusdeployer.eth*, and *dollypartondeployer.eth*.

14.2.3 Evolution of Blockchain Domains

Currently, mainstream use of blockchain domains is relatively limited, but future development of native support of blockchain domains by mainstream web browsers may drive increased adoption by users. Already, blockchain domain operators are seeking technical workarounds to drive the interoperability of blockchain domains with regular browsers. One example is *eth.link*,[48] a service allowing .eth blockchain domains to be accessed via DNS (i.e., through the 'classic' Web2 environment), by appending *.link* to the blockchain domain name. Additionally, a move

---

[48] https://eth.link/

toward Web3 may result from the increased lack of availability in the Web2 domain name space (Section 9.3).

The issue of Web2/Web3 interaction (Section 14.2.2) also raises the possibility of domain name '*collisions*', where the same name can occur on an unrelated basis in both the Web2 and Web3 environments (or even wholly within Web3, on different blockchains). This issue is largely the result of the lack of centralization, governance, and regulation in the Web3 space and will need to be addressed if browsers are to be able to resolve content in both environments. Cases where this question has been raised have already been observed, such as with the announcement in July 2023 by IoT-technology provider IoTeX of their plans to offer .io Web3 domains[49] (already an existing Web2 TLD).[50] Their proposal is one example of a decision approved through the use of a *decentralized autonomous organization* (DAO),[51] an entity managed by a decentralized computer program handled through a blockchain.[52] Increased use of DAOs may become another significant trend as Web3 evolves but also raises its own questions, such as the implications regarding the liability of voters when company decisions are made.

An additional development in the case of the IoTeX Name Service is the option to offer *name wrappers*, a type of smart contract (i.e., a self-executing program on a blockchain, which can be configured to run when certain predefined conditions are met) granting the owner the ability to create subdomains of domains under their ownership and trade them as NFTs in their own right. This functionality has the issue to become a significant area of potential infringements for brands.

Questions over the control of new Web3 extensions have also arisen in disputes. One example is the case in October 2022 where provider Unstoppable Domains ceased selling .coin blockchain domains, apparently to boost its argument—as used in a disagreement with competitor

---

[49] https://iotex.io/blog/iip-22-proposes-to-simplify-iotex-domain-names/
[50] https://www.iamstobbs.com/opinion/the-iotex-case-domain-naming-collisions-and-other-emerging-risks-in-the-blockchain-ecosystem
[51] https://cryptodaily.co.uk/2023/07/iotex-blockchain-dao-votes-94-in-favor-of-simplifying-iotex-domain-names
[52] https://en.wikipedia.org/wiki/Decentralized_autonomous_organization

provider Handshake over the .wallet extension—that the first provider to achieve market penetration should receive exclusive rights.[53]

The existence of the Web3 Domain Alliance[54] is also noteworthy. It features many of the major Web3 service providers as members and is intended to drive *"consumer protection, preventing naming collisions, fair and open use of intellectual property in the industry, and interoperability of blockchain naming systems"*.[55]

The emergence of a new class of graphical *'artwork'* blockchain domain names has already also been noted (Case Study 13.1), and it is likely that continuing trends along similar lines will be observed. Groups of associated blockchain domain names—similar to collections of NFTs seen previously—are already being observed, with one example including a set of names ending with the string *ensart.eth* (presumably a reference to ENS), registered in the third quarter of 2023. This collection may be associated with a specific user on the cryptocurrency-trading website

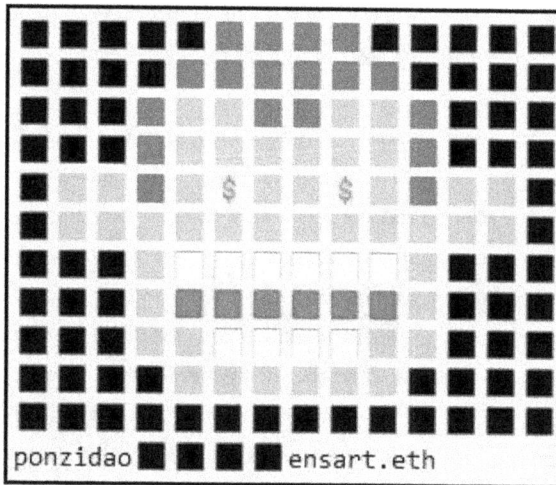

Figure 14.4 *Artwork username for a profile on Coinbase which may be associated with the ensart.eth collection of artwork blockchain domain names*

[53] https://domainnamewire.com/2022/10/18/unstoppable-domains-kills-coin-in-the-name-of-wallet/

[54] https://www.web3domainalliance.com/

[55] https://cointelegraph.com/news/web3-domain-alliance-expands-with-51-new-members

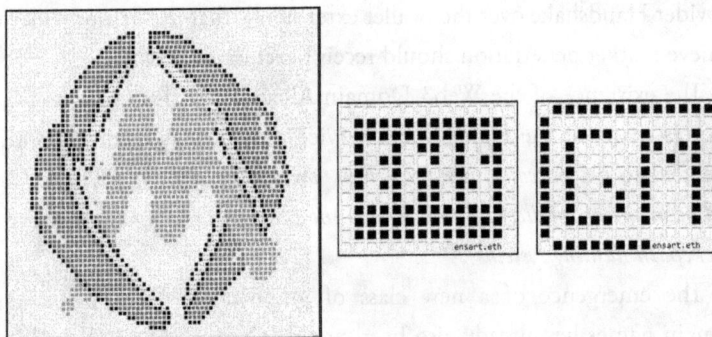

Figure 14.5 Examples of artwork blockchain domain names constituting 'pseudo-logos' (including two ensart.eth domains)

Coinbase, whose username also constitutes an 'artwork' string terminating with the same set of characters, and displaying a 'portrait' when displayed in an appropriate grid (Figure 14.4).

Among the examples of 'artwork' blockchain domain names already registered is a specific 'subclass', where the graphical content constitutes particular designs and/or lettering (which might be termed *'pseudo-logos'*) (Figure 14.5).

It does not seem unrealistic that a natural evolution of this trend might be a move toward the use of 'artwork' blockchain domain names incorporating trademarked content, such as company logos—either by brand owners or by infringers. Exactly how these names (and the associated infringements) may be utilized in practice is likely to be determined by the ways in which the domain names and associated website content are displayed and interpreted by the next generation of Web3-compatible browsers. One possibility might be that, rather than simply displaying the domain names in *plain text* in an address bar, the browsers may interpret and display these graphical domain names in their meaningful grid-based format, similar to the favicons in classic (Web2) websites. If so, the construction of blockchain domain names comprising company logos may turn out to be a key element of the creation of deceptive websites in the emerging Web3 ecosystem.[56]

As discussed in Chapter 6, the practices of clustering and investigation encompass a range of analysis techniques that can be used to establish

---

[56] https://www.iamstobbs.com/trends-in-web3-part-3

links between infringements and build a fuller picture of activity by a particular entity. One of the principal appeals of the Web3 environment is the opportunity for high levels of anonymity (associated with lower levels of restriction and regulation), and a lack of ties to 'real-world' contact details. However, many of the characteristics associated with Web3 content—such as cryptocurrency wallet addresses—are unique and distinctive, and can still be used as the basis of open-source (*OSINT*)-style investigations, to build insights on links and associations between content across both Web3 and Web2. Case Study 14.3 presents two (anonymized) 'mini-investigations' illustrating how these types of techniques can be applied. Key to this process is the existence of publicly available databases (*ledgers*) of information relating to Web3 content, which can be accessed through Web2 infrastructure. One such example is the *etherscan.io* website.

Case Study 14.3: Two 'Mini-Investigations' Relating to Web2/Web3 Crossover Content[57]

The two cases presented in this study concern instances where bad actors were infringing particular marks (referred to in this overview as *BrandA* and *BrandB*), to promote cryptocurrencies (similar to the examples presented in Case Study 14.2).

Case 1: 'BrandAdeployer.eth'

The first case made use of an associated infringing blockchain domain (*BrandAdeployer.eth*) for which details were available on the *etherscan.io* public ledger. The ledger provides information on a number of unique strings ('hashes') relating to the domain and its registrant. Of these, the 'resolved address' string can be queried to given information on transactions made to and from the domain (Figure 14.6).

In this case, the fourth row from the bottom is the most significant; the content of the 'To' column reads '*Create: BrandA.*'

(Continued)

---

[57] https://www.iamstobbs.com/opinion/web2/web3-crossover-investigations-and-clustering

(*Continued*)

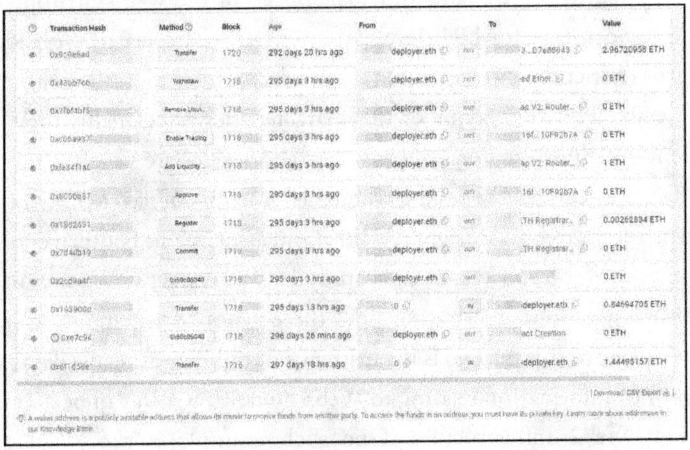

Figure 14.6 *Extracts from the etherscan.io page giving details of transactions associated with BrandAdeployer.eth*

indicating that this transaction is associated with creation of the '*BrandA*'-infringing smart contract (a blockchain program set to run when certain conditions are met, and typically used to execute the terms of an agreement). This field can be used as the basis of a further 'deep-dive', giving information pertaining to the particular smart contract specifically, including details pertaining to users who have purchased the currency and the associated transactions.

Similarly, *etherscan.io* includes datasets giving details and connections associated with the domain registrant, and so on, which can serve as a basis for building further links.

Case 2: 'BrandB Coin'

This case involved the cryptocurrency '*BrandB Coin*' or '*$BrandB*', which was available to be viewed and purchased through reputable decentralised exchanges (DEXs) such as UniSwap, and was also involved in the sale of NFTs via the OpenSea marketplace. The case also utilised a blockchain domain name (*BrandBdeployer.eth*), but was additionally promoted across Web2 content. In this instance,

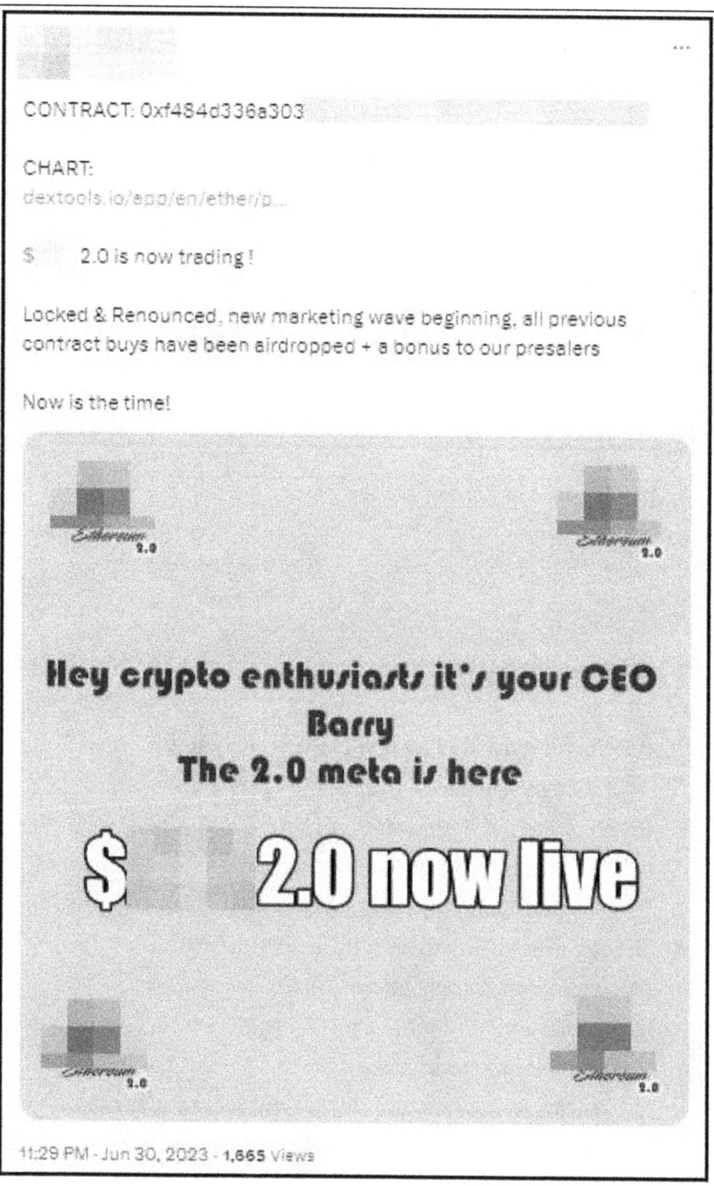

Figure 14.7 An X (Twitter) post advertising the 'BrandB Coin 2.0' infringing cryptocurrency

(*Continued*)

(Continued)

an associated X (Twitter) account ('*@BrandB2Coin*') was set up and used to promote the infringing currency, with the smart contract hash (the string beginning '0xf484...') also explicitly given in some postings (Figure 14.7).

The X profile also gave the address of an associated Web2 website (*BrandBcoin.xyz*) and a Telegram link (*t.me/BrandBcoinportal*). Using a similar approach to that shown in Case 1, it is possible to search for the smart contract string on the *etherscan.io* public ledger to reveal associated details, such as information relating to the contract creator ('*BrandBdeployer.eth*').

Key Points

The key points from this chapter are as follows:

- Going forward, AI technologies are likely to become increasingly integrated into brand protection tools, in areas such as optimization of search and result prioritization techniques, identification of links between related findings ('clustering'), image-and video-content recognition and analysis, and sentiment analysis.
- AI is also increasingly being utilized by infringers, in the construction of more effective scams with a lower requirement for technical expertise.
- AI-generated content also raises a number of questions relating to IP protection, such as the difficulty in monitoring dynamically produced content, the implications of the use of IP in AI model training, and the risks associated with the use of sensitive data in training bespoke models.
- Interconnection ('crossover') between Web2 and Web3 content is becoming increasingly common and can be

manifested in a number of ways, including instances where individual domain names resolve to content in both environments and the promotion of Web3 content on Web2 channels. An increasingly common example is the existence of scams involving the promotion of fraudulent cryptocurrency schemes. OSINT-style investigations, making use of unique and distinctive identifiers such as cryptocurrency wallet addresses, are also possible across Web2/Web3 environments.

- The possibility of name 'collisions' (i.e., the same domain name existing in unrelated contexts in both Web2 and Web3 environments, or on distinct blockchains within Web3) is also likely to need to be addressed as mainstream adoption of Web3 technologies becomes more common.

- Use cases of blockchain domain names may also continue to evolve, with the possibility for graphical domain names comprising company logos or other protected IP, for example. Monitoring technologies and legislation are likely to need to develop in order to tackle these risks.

PART 5

Discussion

CHAPTER 15

Links to Offline Data

Overview

This chapter will cover:

- Ways in which analysis techniques can also be applied to offline data, such as information on the physical supply chain of counterfeit goods, derived from partnerships with customs and law enforcement.

The previous discussion has focused almost entirely on the analysis of online data, which—of course—is key to gaining insights into trends and patterns in infringements in the vast internet landscape and identifying priority targets for takedown. However, online insights do overlap with 'real-world' data, a consideration which is particularly relevant when considering clustering analysis and OSINT investigations. An overview of the scale of infringement activity by a specific entity, and insights into associated physical contact details, can be key when considering enforcement actions, particularly those such as on-the-ground investigations, raids and goods seizures, and litigation activities.

More generally, a significant proportion of online infringements are really just a newer manifestation of many types of abuse familiar from the earlier, pre-internet world, such as counterfeiting, fraud, brand abuse, and false claims of affiliation. Offline activity also remains a significant contributor to online infringement, in areas such as the physical supply chain for goods to be sold online.

Many brand protection service providers will include offline offerings as part of their overall suite of services, including aspects such as test purchasing (often necessary for demonstrating proof of counterfeiting in e-commerce activity), on-the-ground investigations, and partnerships with customs and law enforcement (aimed to disrupt the infringement supply chain). As part of this work, it can be informative to track and map 'hotspots' of activity, for geographical locations identified as being associated with the distribution of infringing goods. These might be *goods out* (sender or consigner) or *goods in* (recipient or consignee) locations; the former will potentially be associated with the *origin* of goods (manufacturing centers, shipping points or onward distribution hubs, or points of direct sale), which can form focuses for further on-the-ground investigation work, while the latter will typically include locations through which goods *arrive* at the country or area of distribution by various different methods of transportation, and can help inform policies on where, for example, customs training initiatives should be focused.[1]

Figure 15.1 is an example of a series of activity *'heat maps'*, showing the locations of interception in the United Kingdom of incoming goods from three countries identified as the top points of origin, based on a case study of partnerships with customs and law enforcement put in place by a brand protection service provider for three key clients in different industry areas (clothing, food, and physical goods manufacturing).[2] These types of insights are key to building a picture of where future efforts should be focused, with a view to providing intelligence and evidence of the source of goods, carrying out further on-the-ground action, and ultimately disrupting the overall supply chain for infringing items.

---

[1] https//www.iamstobbs.com/opinion/tracking-the-uk-trade-in-fakes-counterfeit-hotspots

[2] https//www.iamstobbs.com/opinion/tracking-the-uk-trade-in-fakes-ins-and-outs

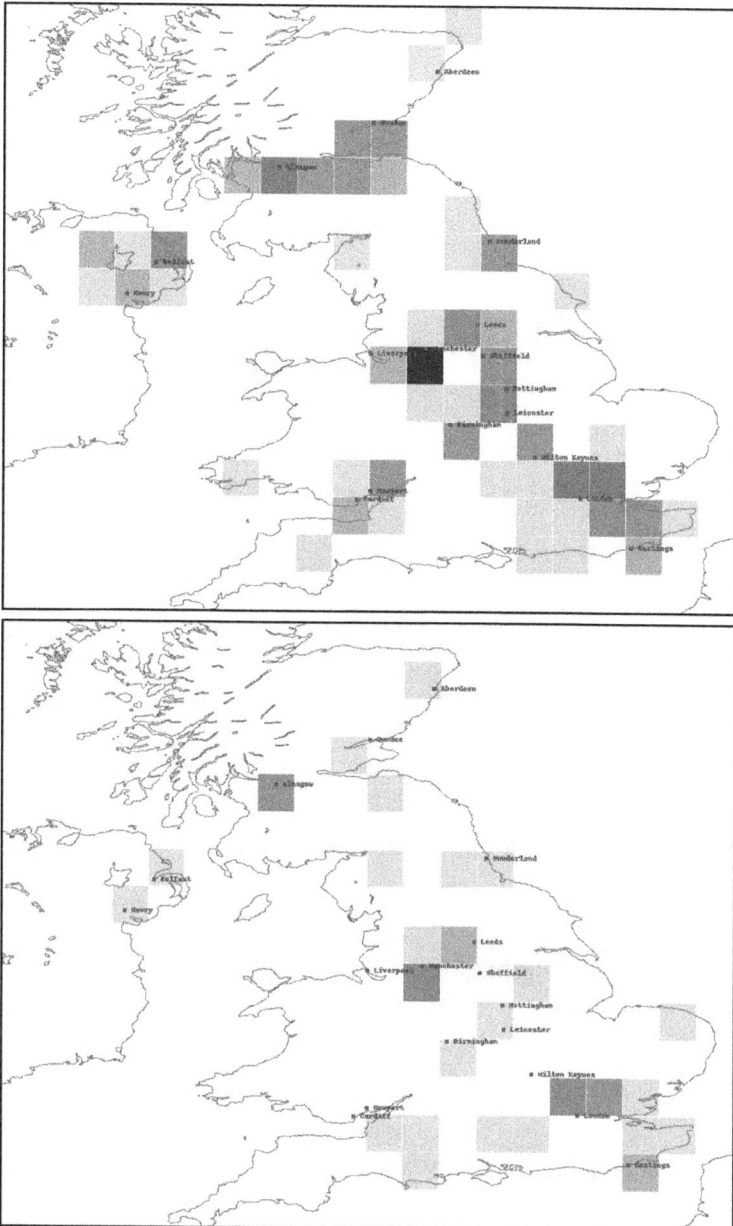

Figure 15.1 Heat maps showing the frequency with which locations in the United Kingdom have been associated with the physical interception of infringing goods originating from Turkey (top), China (middle), and Hong Kong (bottom), based on a case study of partnerships with customs and law enforcement, for brands in the clothing, food, and physical goods manufacturing industries (data from January 2020 to February 2024)

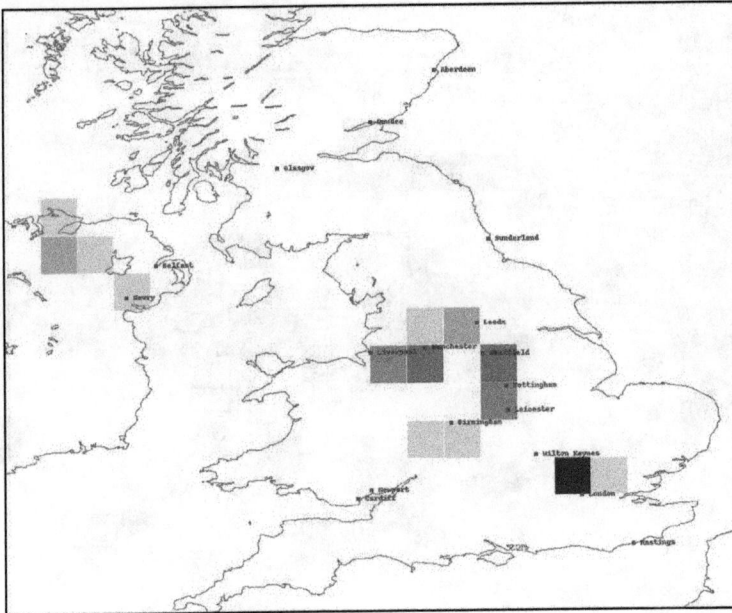

Figure 15.1 (Continued)

Key Points

The key points from this chapter are as follows:

- Disruption of the offline physical supply chain for counterfeit goods is a key element of addressing the online infringement landscape.
- Analysis of insights gained from on-the-ground partnerships with customs and law enforcement authorities can be used to guide further real-world actions, including the identification of key targets for further investigations, raids and seizures, and areas where additional focus should be applied (e.g., for customs training initiatives).

CHAPTER 16

Final Thoughts

The online environment is continually changing, and brand protection tools, products, services, and analysis techniques must similarly evolve continuously in order to be able to continue to address the issues at hand. On a most basic level, many previously disparate different areas ('channels') of the internet have become increasingly interlinked (see Section 1.3), and a 'siloed' approach to brand protection (considering just (say) domain name monitoring or e-commerce marketplace monitoring) is ever more inappropriate. These types of consideration will become more relevant as new channels emerge (as has been discussed in, e.g., the context of Web2/Web3 'crossover'; Section 14.2.2), and the interconnection between online and offline activity (Chapter 15) is increasingly recognized.

Brand owners will continue to expect brand protection service providers to be able to monitor and enforce within the increasingly rich areas of content in which infringements can be manifested. These have moved beyond just the areas in which monitoring has traditionally been difficult—such as dynamically generated (e.g., by scripting languages) website content, material requiring image and video analysis or optical character recognition, geo-restricted content, and other parts of the internet with specific access requirements or limitations (social media, domain names not covered by public zone files, dark web, mobile-based platforms, etc.[1])—and now incorporate whole new ecosystems such as blockchain-based technologies (Chapter 13 and Section 14.2.3), the metaverse (Section 14.2.1), and the outputs from generative AI applications (Sections 14.1.2 and 14.1.3). The industry will also need to be able to move

---

[1] https://circleid.com/posts/20230525-the-millennium-problems-in-brand-protection

quickly, to keep pace with the next phases of—as yet unknown—new relevant channels and technologies as they emerge.

The demands for analysis capabilities are also likely to continue to extend, with an inevitable growth in expectations regarding the ability to cluster and draw insights from rich datasets (Chapters 3 to 6), carry out analysis of sentiment (Chapter 10), and quantify the value of brand protection initiatives (Chapters 11 and 12). Many of these requirements are likely to involve applications of artificial intelligence and machine learning approaches, and the developments of new methodologies and algorithms.

Initiatives such as the new phase of the ongoing new-gTLD program, combined with factors such as the emergence and growth of blockchain domains, and the decreasing lack of availability of attractive domain names across the set of popular legacy extensions (Chapter 9), may also drive changes in behavior of the ways in which brands are presented and marketed, perhaps with increased moves toward the use of dot-brand extensions and Web3 content.

It is also likely that significant developments will be required in relevant regulations and legislation, allowing brand owners to protect their intellectual property—and providing a safe environment for internet users generally (see Section 1.3)—in the evolving landscape. Relevant areas for consideration are likely to include the development of AI tools (and their use of training data and outputs), the ability to balance privacy against protection, and the new ways in which brand infringements can be manifested in the context of emerging technologies (such as the use of imagery in graphical blockchain domain names). Some initiatives (such as the Registration Data Request Service (RDRS) scheme for requesting nonpublic domain registration information) are steps in the right direction for addressing brand abuse but frequently do not go far enough (e.g., in the case of RDRS, allowing participation to be voluntary, and leaving the final decision on information disclosure in the hands of individual registrars). Frequently, the introduction of new legal and regulatory frameworks has been found to be many steps behind the emergence of relevant technologies—particularly as the speed of change continues to increase—and will likely require a transformation to a much more proactive approach.

Glossary

A (address) record	A domain configuration setting providing the IP address associated with a domain name
AI	Artificial intelligence (*see also* Generative AI)
Blockchain	A publicly accessible digital ledger on which transactions are recorded, and the basis for blockchain domains and many cryptocurrencies
Blockchain domain	A domain name recorded on a blockchain, typically used as a cryptocurrency wallet address or the basis for the construction of a decentralized website
ccTLD	A country-specific TLD, such as .co.uk (UK), .fr (France), or .de (Germany)
Conversion rate (*see also* Substitution rate)	The proportion of visitors to a transactional website who make a purchase
Cryptocurrency	A digital currency (such as Bitcoin), usually based on blockchain technology
Delegation (of a TLD)	The process of a TLD being added to the internet root zone
DNS	Domain name system; the naming and communications system for resources connected to the internet
Dot-brand	A brand-specific TLD, for which the brand owner acts as registry (e.g., .barclays and .bmw)
DRS	Dispute resolution service; a dispute policy for .uk domain names
Entropy (e.g. of a SLD name)	*See* Shannon entropy
Favicon	A small graphical feature of a website, usually displayed as an icon alongside the address bar in a web browser
GDPR	General Data Protection Regulation; a European Union policy relating to information privacy
Generative AI (*see also* AI)	A class of artificial intelligence applications able to produce high-quality complex outputs
gTLD	A generic TLD, such as .com, .net, or .org (also including new-gTLDs delegated in the period since 2012, such as .top, .xyz, or .online)
Homoglyph (domain name)	A domain name in which one or more characters have been replaced by another appearing visibly similar

(Continued)

(*Continued*)

ICANN	The Internet Corporation for Assigned Names and Numbers; the organization responsible for overseeing and coordinating much of the infrastructure of the internet
IDN (*see also* Punycode)	Internationalized domain name; a domain name incorporating characters in non-Latin scripts
IP (Internet Protocol) address	A numerical label indicating a specific networked device such as a web server
Malware	Malicious software, such as keyloggers (which record a user's keyboard strokes) or ransomware (which encrypts files and demands a ransom in order for access to be regranted)
Metaverse	A generalized term for a connected environment of 3D virtual worlds
MX (mail exchange) record	A domain configuration setting indicating that the domain has the capability to send and receive emails
Netblock	A continuous range of IP addresses sharing initial elements in common
NFT	Nonfungible token; a collectible digital item for which ownership is recorded on a blockchain
Phishing	The fraudulent practice of attempting to acquire confidential information such as log in details
PPC	Pay-per-click; sponsored advertisements displayed on a website, which generate revenue for the site owner when visitors click on the links
Punycode (*see also* IDN)	A way of representing IDNs in an encoded format using only Latin characters
RDRS	Registration Data Request Service; a scheme for requesting nonpublic domain registration information from registrars
Registrant	The owner of a domain name
Registrar	The organization through which a domain name is registered/purchased
Registry	The organization responsible for overseeing the infrastructure of a TLD
Root zone	The highest level of DNS and the basis for domain infrastructure
Scraper (website scraper)	An automated script or tool for extracting key pieces of information from locations on a web page whose format is known in advance

SEO (search engine optimization)	The configuration of the content of a website (or other piece of online content) with the aim of ensuring that it is as highly ranked as possible in response to searches for relevant terms
Shannon entropy	A mathematical construct providing a measure of the amount of information stored in a string of characters
SLD (second-level domain)	The part of a domain name to the left of the dot
Subdomain	The part of a URL to the left of the domain name (and separated from it by a dot)
Substitution rate (see also Conversion rate)	The proportion of customers who will purchase a legitimate item once an alternative infringing version has been made unavailable
Sunrise period	The initial period of launch of a new TLD, in which brand owners are able to apply for domain names
TLD (top-level domain)	The part of a domain name to the right of the dot; a domain name extension
UDRP	Uniform Domain Name Dispute Resolution Policy; a domain dispute policy that can result in the cancellation, suspension, or transfer (of ownership) of a domain name
URL	Uniform resource locator; the address of a unique resource (such as a web page) on the internet
URS	Uniform Rapid Suspension; a rights-protection mechanism for suspension of domain names, offering a low-cost, rapid resolution in cases of clear-cut infringement
Web2	The phase of internet development characterized by user-generated content (such as social media); now more usually taken to mean 'classic', DNS-based internet content
Web3	A general term referring to decentralized internet content, usually taken to refer to blockchain-based technologies
Web traffic	The number of visitors (in a given time period) to a website
Whois	A look-up for identifying ownership details and other configuration information for a domain
Zone file	A data file maintained by a registry, containing configuration information for all domains registered across a particular TLD

References

* López García, M.A. "IPRs On-line." Personal communication, May 18, 2024.

† Williams, J. "XConnect." Personal communication, April 02, 2024.

‡ Vajapeyam, S. "Understanding Shannon's entropy metric for information." 2014. https://arxiv.org/ftp/arxiv/papers/1405/1405.2061.pdf.

§ Agten, P et al., "Seven months' Worth of Mistakes: A Longitudinal Study of Typosquatting Abuse." *NDSS Symposium. San Diego, CA, USA.* 2015 https://www.ndss-symposium.org/wp-content/uploads/2017/09/01_3_1.pdf.

¶ Quinkert et al. "It's Not What it Looks Like: Measuring Attacks and Defensive Registrations of Homograph Domains." *IEEE Conference on Communications and Network Security (CNS).* Washington, DC, USA. 2019. https://ieeexplore.ieee.org/document/8802671.

** Fuller, S. "Com Laude" Personal communication, April 28, 2024.

†† Hu, M and B. Liu. "Mining and Summarizing Customer Reviews." *Proceedings of the ACM SIGKDD International Conference on Knowledge Discovery and Data Mining (KDD-2004).* Seattle: Washington, USA., 2004.

‡‡ Ustel, S. *Digital Brand Protection: Investigating Brand Piracy and Intellectual Property Abuse.* Amazon, UK, 2019. Chapter 17: "Accounting and Accountability."

§§ Rob, R and J. Waldfogel. "Piracy on the High Cs: Music Downloading, Sales Displacement, and Social Welfare in a Sample of College Students." *Journal of Law and Economics* 49 (2009), reported by WIPO.

¶¶ Ipsos MediaCT and Oxford Economics, "Economic Consequences of Movie Piracy in Australia," report on behalf of AFACT, 2011.

*** IPI. 2007. https://www.acte.be/wp-content/uploads/2020/07/Measuring-IPR-infringements-in-the-internal-market.-Development-of-a-new-approach-to-estimating-the-impact-of-infringements-on-sales.pdf.

††† G. Tom, et al. "Consumer Demand for Counterfeit Goods." *Psychology & Marketing* 15, no. 5 (1998): 405–421.

‡‡‡ Huang, J. "A Review of Brand Valuation Method." *Journal of Service Science and Management* 8, no. 1 (2015). article ID 53780. https://www.scirp.org/html/8-9201743_53780.htm.

§§§   O. Oriekhoe *et al.* "Blockchain Technology in Supply Chain Management: A Comprehensive Review." *International Journal of Management & Entrepreneurship Research* 6, no. 1 (2024). https://fepbl.com/index.php/ijmer/article/view/714.

¶¶¶   Thio, R., R. Christiawan and W. Wagiman. "Trademark Law in the Digital Age: Challenges and Solutions for Online Brand Protection." *Global International Journal of Innovative Research* 2, no. 4 (2024): 710–721. https://global-us.mellbaou.com/index.php/global/article/view/125/219.

**** Newman, R. "Trademarks 2024: The Reputation Edit." Stobbs webinar. https://www.youtube.com/watch?v=rD0IjY5ZmMI.

†††† Newman, R. "Stobbs" Personal communication, April 05, 2024.

‡‡‡‡ Price, D. "IFPI" Personal communication, May 20, 2024.

§§§§ Ibid.

About the Author

David N. Barnett is an expert online brand protection consultant and analyst.

He was born in London in 1976 and is a graduate of the University of Cambridge, completing an MA in Natural Sciences and a PhD in Planetary Geophysics (2001), followed by two years' experience in climate change research.

He has 20 years' experience in the online brand protection industry, serving clients across a range of sectors and industries. He started his career at Envisional in 2004, subsequently moving (via company acquisitions) to NetNames (2007) and CSC (2016), where he worked as Head of Consultancy, Brand Monitoring, and served as a key member of the Product and Analyst leadership team. Since 2023 he has been working as Brand Protection Strategist at Stobbs, a brand advisory consultancy and legal service provider.

Key areas of work have included analysis and open-source investigation (OSINT) investigations for clients, and the delivery of expert consultancy to product, sales, commercial, account management, and analyst teams, from presales through to quality assurance. He has also driven R&D programs for brand protection projects, and has particular interests in domain-name monitoring and analysis, threat-level quantification for brand infringements, calculation of ROI for brand protection programs, and Web3 technologies.

David is an experienced thought leader, with an extensive portfolio of articles and experience of speaking at industry events, and is also author of *Brand Protection in the Online World* (Kogan Page, 2016).

Index

www.ingramcontent.com/pod-product-compliance
Lightning Source LLC
Chambersburg PA
CBHW061137220326
41599CB00025B/4264